MULTIMEDIA ILLUSTRATED

Written by
Nat Gertler

Designed by
Amy Peppler-Adams
and
Sandra Stevenson

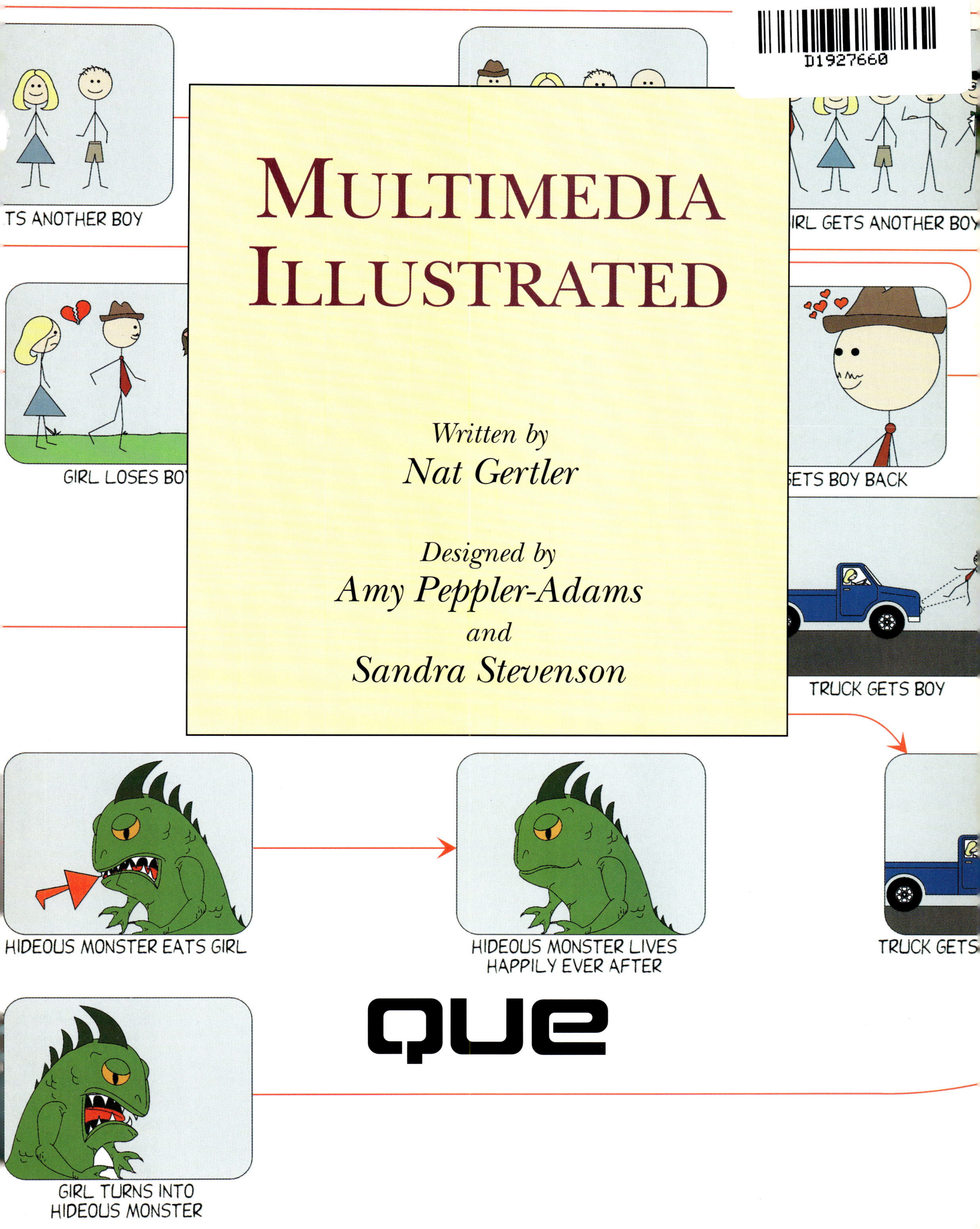

que

Multimedia Illustrated

Library of Congress Catalog No.: 94-68832

ISBN: 1-56529-936-1

97 96 95 94 4 3 2 1

Interpretation of the printing code: the rightmost double-digit number is the year of the book's printing; the rightmost single-digit number is the number of the book's printing. For example, a printing code of 94-1 shows that the first printing of the book occurred in 1994.

Publisher: David P. Ewing

Associate Publisher: Don Roche, Jr.

Managing Editor: Michael Cunningham

Marketing Manager: Greg Wiegand

Associate Product Marketing Manager: Stacy Collins

Composed in *New Baskerville* and *FranklinGothic* by Que Corporation.

Credits

Title Manager
Kathie-Jo Arnoff

Acquisitions Editor
Jenny Watson

Production Editor
Thomas F. Hayes

Copy Editors
Lisa Gebken
Julie A. McNamee
Jeff Riley
Nicole Rodandello

Technical Editor
Michael Watson

Acquisitions Coordinator
Jill L. Stanley

Book Designers
Amy Peppler-Adams
Sandra Stevenson

Cover Designer
Dan Armstrong

Production Team
Jeff Baker
Claudia Bell
Cameron Booker
Anne Dickerson
Karen Dodson
Terri Edwards
DiMonique Ford
Aren Howell
Michael Hughes
Debbie Kincaid
Erika Millen
Wendy Ott
Dennis Sheehan
Kristine Simmons

About the Author

"**Nat Gertler** is the best-selling author of *Computers Illustrated*" is, according to the biography in his last book, how he hoped the biography in the next book would start—so here it is. It is certainly the best-selling book that he has ever written.

The son of two programmers, he pursued a programming career himself until led astray by his senseless need to be a writer. Nat has written professionally for television, books, magazines, and even buttons. He is best known in the field of comic books, where he has written stories about such diverse characters as Fred Flintstone, Richard Petty, Blood Syndicate, and Santa Claus. A former actor and occasional troupe comedian, his only real joy is writing about himself in the third person. This New Jersey native recently transplanted to Pasadena, California, where he dwells with his lovely friend Anita (who is giving him nasty looks for not being considered a "real joy") and far too many boxes of unsorted stuff, some of which might be important.

Dedication

This book is dedicated to the first girl that I ever kissed. After well over a decade, she is now a larger part of my life than ever. Anita, I love you.

Acknowledgments

Writing a book is a difficult and often trying task. It was only once I realized that the world actually had formed a Vast International Conspiracy Against Nat (that's me) that I was able to make some headway. Luckily, I was aided by the very able forces in favor of Nat, rebellious individuals who bucked the general plan and instead put extraordinary effort toward easing my burden and making this book possible.

The most conspicuous rebel stronghold is that upstanding company known as Que Corporation. Kathie-Jo Arnoff spearheaded this production, and put up with out-of-order pages, strange marginalia, and the other eccentricities that allow me to pretend to be an *artisté* instead of just another tech writer. Brad Koch was fool enough to enlist me on this project after seeing the havoc I wrought with my previous book (*Computers Illustrated,* still available and heavily recommended to anyone who still has money in his pocket!). Jenny Watson helped arrange deadlines that I could make, and leaned on me to make sure that I made those deadlines. Tom Hayes made sure that I didn't make any mistakes. I owe all of you donuts.

Thanks to pro-Nat crusader Amy Peppler-Adams for bringing her design vision to this book. Double thanks, in fact, since I somehow failed to thank her in the last book.

Thanks to Rich Whitney and his loyal army at Accent Technical Communications, for taking some of the bizarre diagram requests that I had and turning them into the bizarre but lush and beautiful original drawings that you see inside here. Don't blame them for the space bunny shot, though; that one was mine.

The illustrations, color renderings, and 3D modeling in this book were produced by Craig Thurmond, Anthony StuART, Michael Steiner, Shelley Norris, and Dennis Ladigo, of Accent Technical Communications, an Indianapolis-based company.

Accent's staff of 53 professionals includes designers, illustrators, writers, page composers, programmers, and engineers who use powerful computers and software to produce high-quality text and graphics for printed publications. Other communication services offered by Accent include computer animation, interactive multimedia presentations, database publishing of industrial catalogs, and CD-ROM production.

Big thanks to the Nat Defense League: Michelle Wortman at Microsoft, Peter Murray at ABC, Larry Dale at Ford Motor Company, and the fine folks at Paramount Interactive, Optical Media International, Broderbund, Animotion Development, and ID Software who provided software and assistance that made many of the illustrated examples in the book possible. (I thought about getting into rock'n'roll for all the fans, but instead I got into computer book writing for the *free software*!)

No thanks to the company that made the monitor that blew out on me, slowing down the project. They are clearly part of the Vast International Conspiracy. The forces of good and Nat shall not allow them to flourish.

A warm thanks to the top-notch Nat co-conspirators at Milestone Comics, Entity Comics, Marks Comics, and Malibu/Ultraverse Comics for their patience during the period of deadline insanity that this book caused.

Finally, thanks to the pro-Nat development crew: all of the software and hardware designers and engineers out there who created all the wonderful technology that made this book necessary, and who are now working hard on amazing new things which will soon make this book, if not obsolete, then in need of a major revision.

Trademark Acknowledgments

Contents at a Glance

Part III: How Multimedia Is Created

PART IV: MULTIMEDIA OF THE FUTURE

Table of Contents

Introduction

Welcome to *Multimedia Illustrated.* This book should give you a good background in the growing world of multimedia computing, whether you're new to computers and fascinated by their sound and graphics capabilities, or whether you're a long-time computer user trying to understand what all this fuss about "multimedia" is really all about.

The book is designed to be easy (even fun!) to read without talking down to you. Every page has illustrated explanations and examples that should make the topic even clearer.

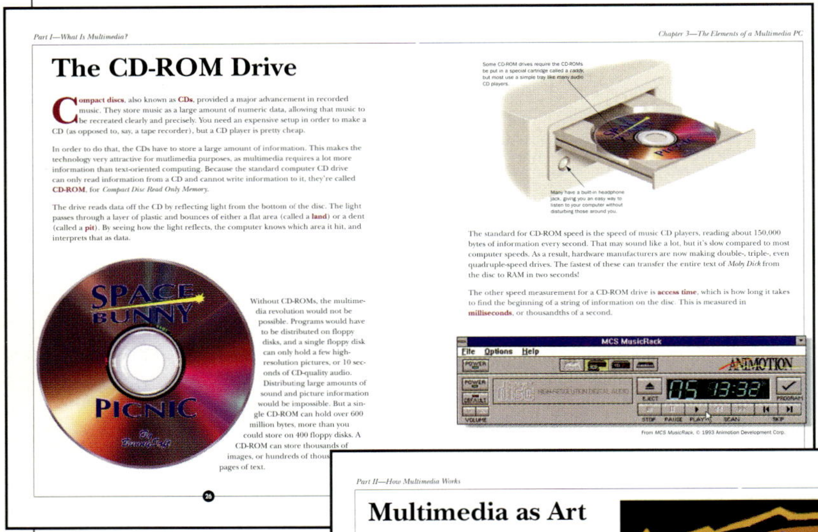

Part I—What Is Multimedia?

The CD-ROM Drive

Compact discs, also known as **CDs**, provided a major advancement in recorded music. They store music as a large amount of numeric data, allowing that music to be recreated clearly and precisely. You need an expensive setup in order to make a CD (as opposed to, say, a tape recorder), but a CD player is pretty cheap.

In order to do that, the CDs have to store a large amount of information. This makes the technology very attractive for mutlimedia purposes, as multimedia requires a lot more information than text-oriented computing. Because the standard computer CD drive can only read information from a CD and cannot write information to it, they're called **CD-ROM**, for *Compact Disc Read Only Memory*.

The drive reads data off the CD by reflecting light from the bottom of the disc. The light passes through a layer of plastic and bounces of either a flat area (called a **land**) or a dent (called a **pit**). By seeing how the light reflects, the computer knows which area it hit, and interprets that as data.

Without CD-ROMs, the multimedia revolution would not be possible. Programs would have to be distributed on floppy disks, and a single floppy disk can only hold a few high-resolution pictures, or 10 seconds of CD-quality audio. Distributing large amounts of sound and picture information would be impossible. But a single CD-ROM can hold over 600 million bytes, more than you could store on 400 floppy disks. A CD-ROM can store thousands of images, or hundreds of thous pages of text.

26

Chapter 3—The Elements of a Multimedia PC

The standard for CD-ROM speed is the speed of music CD players, reading about 150,000 bytes of information every second. That may sound like a lot, but it's slow compared to most computer speeds. As a result, hardware manufacturers are now making double-, triple-, even quadruple-speed drives. The fastest of these can transfer the entire text of *Moby Dick* from the disc to RAM in two seconds!

The other speed measurement for a CD-ROM drive is **access time**, which is how long it takes to find the beginning of a string of information on the disc. This is measured in **milliseconds**, or thousandths of a second.

From *MCS MusicRack*, © 1993 Animotion Development Corp.

The book is made up of four parts, each with its own focus.

- Part I, "What Is Multimedia?" tells you what multimedia computing is and what elements make it up. Part I also covers what equipment is needed to run multimedia software.

Part II—How Multimedia Works

Multimedia as Art

Multimedia is an art form and an art tool. You can do video, text, and sound in any combination, and with the unique addition of active user involvement, this surely qualifies it as a separate art form. Or, you can have a multimedia-based program allowing you to edit sound or pictures on your computer, giving you expert assistance and power.

Different multimedia artworks take advantage of the art form in different ways. Some are basically works taken from some other form, with multimedia features added. Take, for example, this multimedia adaptation (right) of the comic book *Freex*. It still presents the material as a comic book, but with some minor animation added, as well as dialogue and sound.

In contrast (below) is *Myriam*, an original multimedia work. John W. Ratcliff and Rob Wallace created *John & Rob's Multimedia Kaleidoscope*, a tool which displays computer images with music and a viewer-controllable set of special effects, adding a level of interactivity to any piece of art. John (a computer game designer) put a digitized picture of an old friend (Myriam Levinson) into this display engine and released it on the computer networks. His hope is that someone will recognize Myriam and help him get back in contact with her. (If you have any information on her whereabouts, please drop him a note at his Internet address, 70253.3237@compuserve.com, and tell him we sent you!)

Chapter 8—Multimedia Entertainment

From *CD-ROMIX: Freex #1*, © 1993 Malibu Comics Entertainment.

64 65

- Part II, "How Multimedia Works," shows you how multimedia is used. This section explains how the user interacts with the computer, and shows many examples of innovative multimedia programs used for education, entertainment, business, and the arts.

- Part III, "How Multimedia Is Created," gets into the nitty-gritty of how sound, pictures, and moving video are processed for inclusion in multimedia packages. Even if you never want to make your own multimedia projects, this will help you understand how your computer works—but if you do want to make your own projects, this section provides a guide for how to go about it, including sections on good multimedia design and how to make your own CD-ROMs!

- Part IV, "Multimedia of the Future," takes a look into the multimedia crystal ball and sees what multimedia computing may bring us in the years to come.

Computer terms that you may be unfamiliar with are defined where we first use them. In addition, we have a handy **Glossary** in the back of the book, so you can double-check terms that you may have forgotten. These terms appear in **color** throughout the book.

So settle back in a comfortable chair, put your feet up, make sure you have some good light to read by, and be prepared to discover the latest trend in computing!

Part I

What Is Multimedia?

chapter

Welcome to the World of Multimedia

In the old days (and in computing, the *old days* are less than 20 years ago), computers displayed everything as text. This was fine for some things (such as word processing), but for other things it just would not do. If a picture is worth a thousand words, then early days of computing left you worlds behind because instead of a picture, you got a thousand words. Imagine how cumbersome that was.

Take, for example, an educational program that needs to explain the human heart. In the old days, it might go on and on explaining the shape of the heart, how it breaks down into different ventricles, how the blood flows in through one part and out through another, how the whole thing is a muscle that pulses at regular intervals, and things like that. And even after wading through all that explanation, the user had a very limited sense of what a heart is like.

With a multimedia approach to computing, though, you can do things differently. Instead of using words, you use diagrams, photos, and even moving video images to show something much more effectively! Imagine how much clearer it is to see a diagram of a human heart—even a moving, pulsing animation of a heart—than to look at all those words. While words are great for some things, a picture like that can be understood almost instantly.

Wait a minute! We're doing this all wrong. We're espousing theory without following it ourselves. Let's give this another try…

The multimedia revolution has changed forever what computers can do for us by giving them new ways to present information.

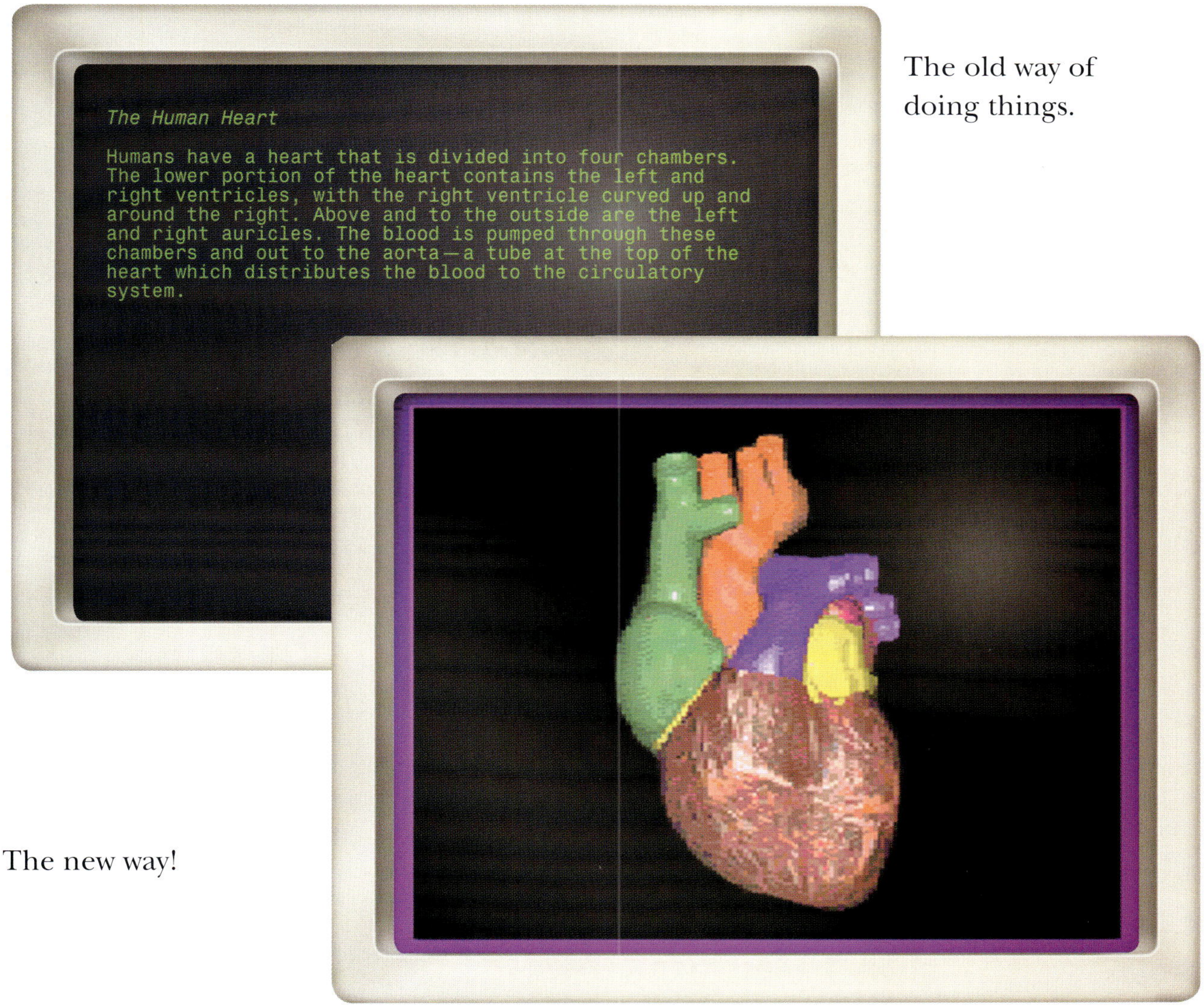

The old way of doing things.

The new way!

From *3-D Body Adventure*, © 1993 Knowledge Adventure.

This book will give you more than a description of what multimedia is and how it works—it will bring you the *feel* of multimedia as well!

Defining Multimedia

You can't deal with computers these days without seeing the term **multimedia computing**. Most computer products have **multimedia** on them somewhere, as if it were something wonderfully new that the computer is able to bring us.

Actually, working with multimedia is nothing new. Any time you use more than one method of communicating information, you are using multimedia. A **medium** (the singular of **media**) is just a way of communicating information.

A movie is a perfect example of multimedia.

What makes a movie a movie is the moving picture. The earliest movies were nothing but the picture.

Adding a second medium—sound—added a lot to movies. Not only could you hear the actors talk, but also the cars crashing, the kisses smooching, and the hideous slavering beasts slavering. Plus, background music helped create a mood.

Before the "talkies," movies used the text medium to convey dialog. Films from other languages still do (as subtitles), but most popular films now use text only for credits and titles.

So the real advancement is the mixture of computers and multimedia. Computers have long been able to do some mixing of media—video games, for example, have always mixed a moving image with sound effects—but new computers can do much more. Modern personal computer programs use all of the elements of a movie—moving pictures, sound effects, voices, text, music, animation, and still shots.

Multimedia Makes Everything Better

This book says a lot about presenting information. With all that information being talked about, though, don't assume that multimedia is good for only "informational" programs—reference works, educational programs, and things like that. While multimedia is excellent for these programs, everything the computer does is informational. If you're looking at a beautiful flower, the look of that flower is information that your brain is receiving. If you're playing a video game, the direction of the fireball the Evil Space Bunny Lord just fired at you is a piece of information. If you're eating ice cream, the taste of that ice cream is information (although not a type of information that a computer can adequately convey—yet).

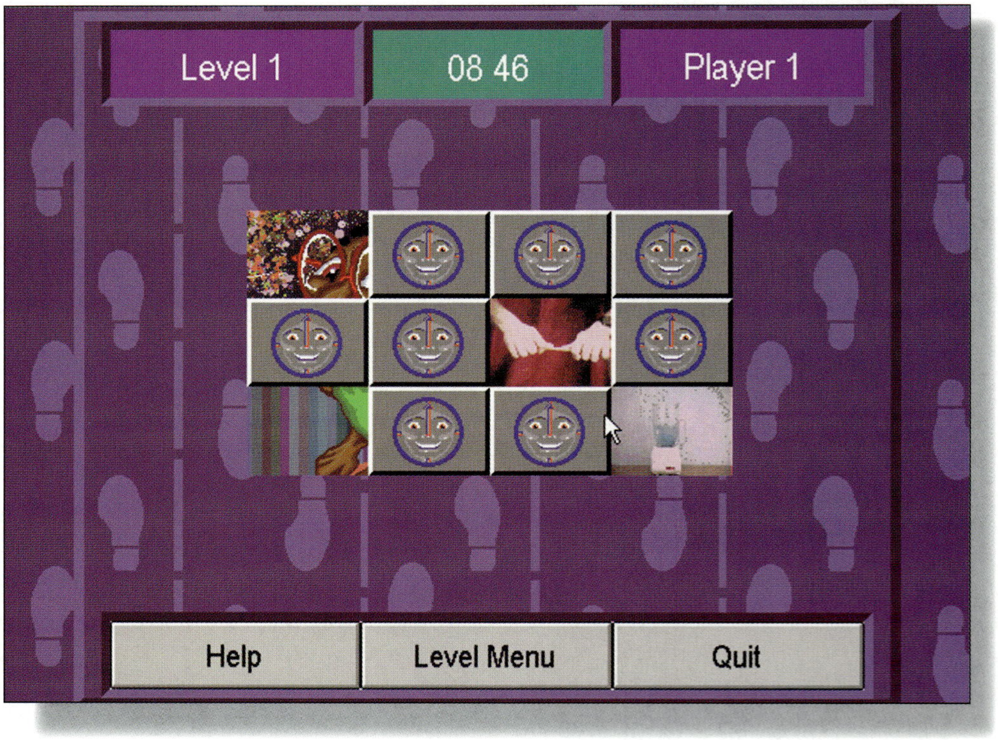

From *Race The Clock*, © 1993 Mindplay, Methods, & Solutions, Inc.

Multimedia puts a sharper edge on things you are already doing. This version of the classic kids game of Concentration gains from having moving video added to the mix.

From *Maxiplan 500*, © 1986, 1987 Maxisoft and Intuitive Technologies

It would be easy to assume that such a functional, basic, established computer task like a spreadsheet isn't going to gain much from multimedia. After all, you don't want a lot of fancy frills and distractions when your business or personal finances are at stake.

But if you've ever had to double-check a column of figures you typed into a spreadsheet and spend a long time bouncing your eyes between the screen and a sheet of paper, you know it's an inefficient process. How much easier it is to stare at the paper while the computer reads the screen to you!

Multimedia is a set of tools, and it's rare that all of the tools are ever needed for a single task. Each program uses whatever tools are best to present information in an interesting, efficient manner.

What Is Hypermedia?

Multimedia is a great way of displaying information, but it doesn't address how you find the information you want displayed. The power of multimedia makes possible an information access system called **hypermedia.**

With hypermedia, you can look at a screen of information, and if there is a topic or word that you want more information about, simply click it, and that information comes up!

When this concept is applied to text, it's called **hypertext.** In a hypertext display, certain words or phrases are highlighted. This lets you know that more information is available about those items.

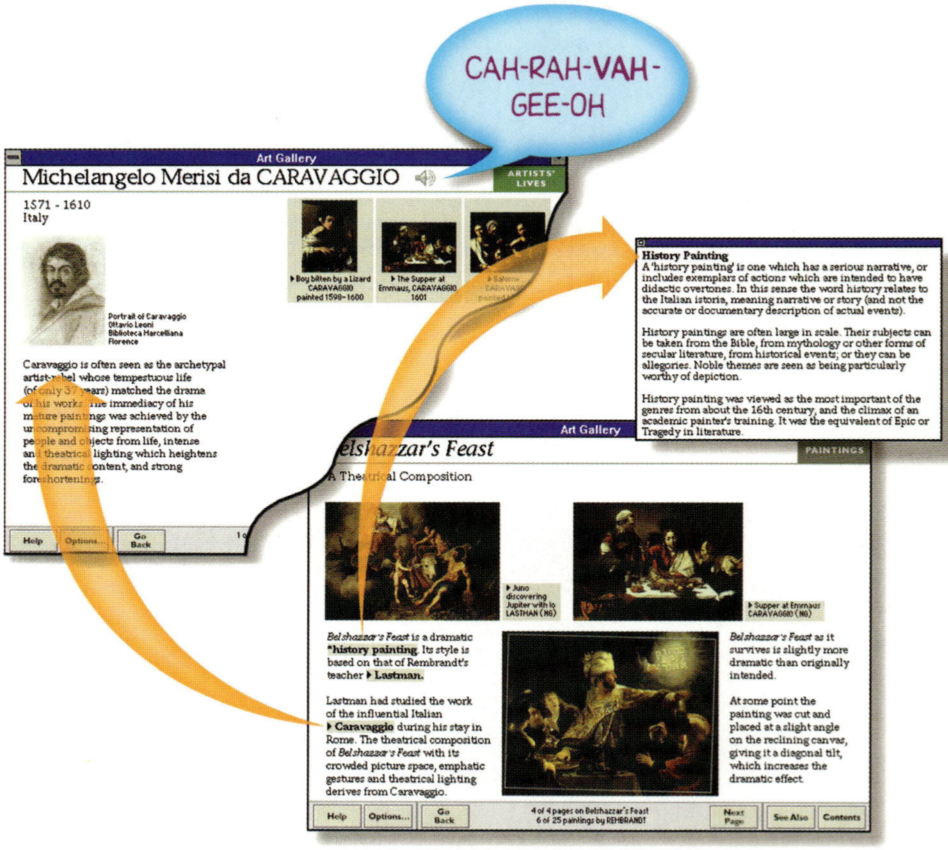

From *Microsoft Art Gallery*, © 1993 Microsoft Corp.

On this screen, you see the highlighted art terms and artist names. Clicking these, you get a definition of the term or a screen of text about the artist and examples of his work. Or, click the name at the top of the next page and you hear how it's pronounced.

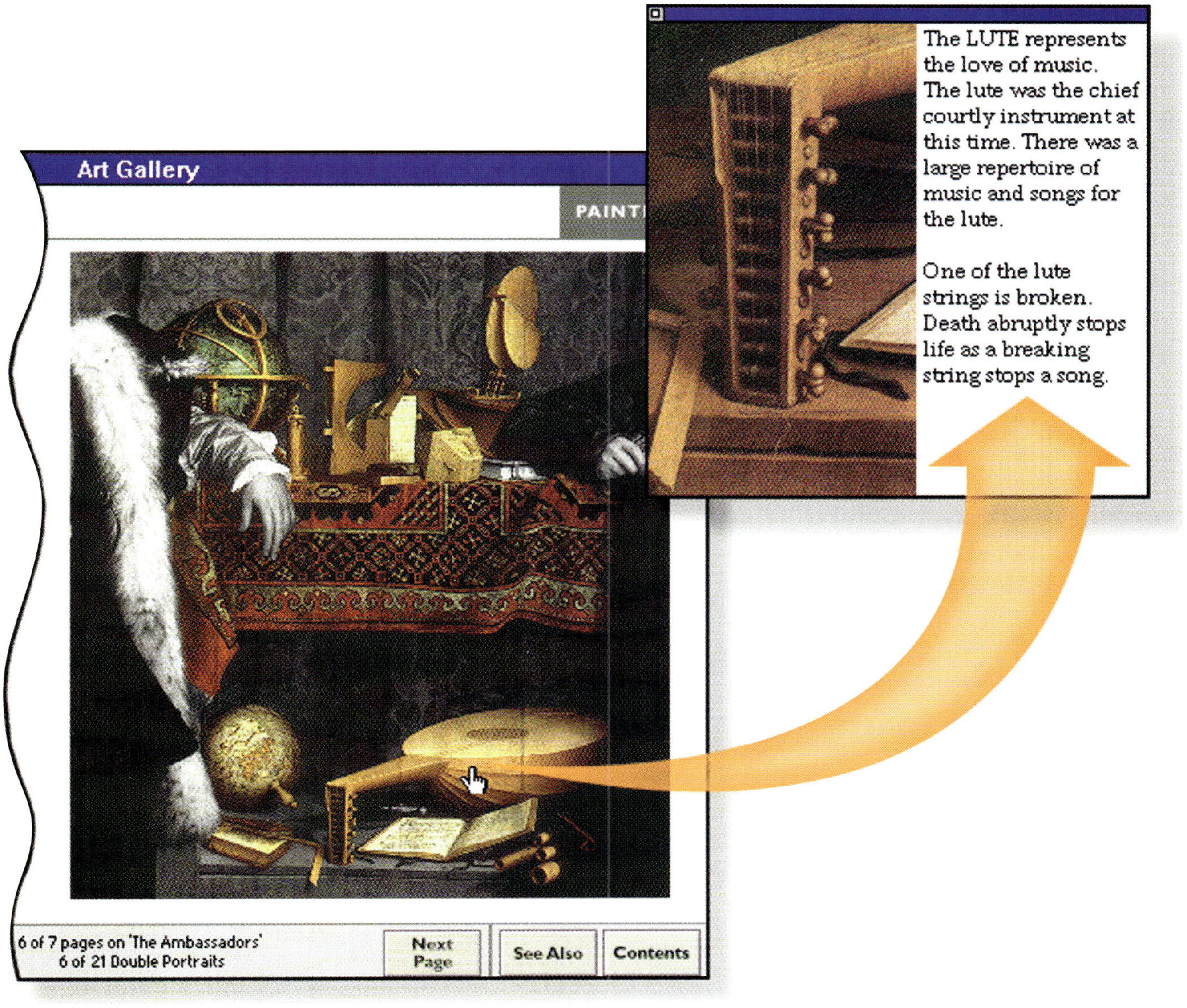

From *Microsoft Art Gallery*, © 1993 Microsoft Corp.

Full hypermedia takes cues from more than just text. On this screen, click an object in the picture, and you find out more about that object.

Not every multimedia title uses hypermedia. It's used mainly in reference works (and not even all of those). Where it's used, hypermedia makes cruising through a vast amount of data a snap.

Passive vs. Interactive Multimedia

When you say "multimedia," you are talking about how the computer gives you information. Whether you are giving information to the computer is a different question, one that draws the line between **passive multimedia** and **interactive multimedia**.

When you watch a tennis match on TV, you're an **observer**—you aren't involved in the game. Nothing you do will effect the outcome of the game. This is an example of passive multimedia.

From *Tennis*, © 1985 Imagic, Inc.

When you play a tennis video game, you are a participant in the game. You use the controller to move your player, and the computer takes that information and uses it to decide what happens in the game. Because you are interacting with the computer, this is considered interactive multimedia.

Passive Multimedia

Many multimedia computer packages are passive, treating the computer as little more than a glorified VCR, merely spewing forward images with no user interaction. These include traditional movies (which are frequently packaged with additional material, such as scripts and commentary that often has interactive material, but the core movie is still not interactive), as well as product demonstrations and sales pitches. In a passive multimedia presentation, there is only a single path for the presentation to follow. The viewer may be able to speed, back-up, or pause on that path, but it is still on the same path.

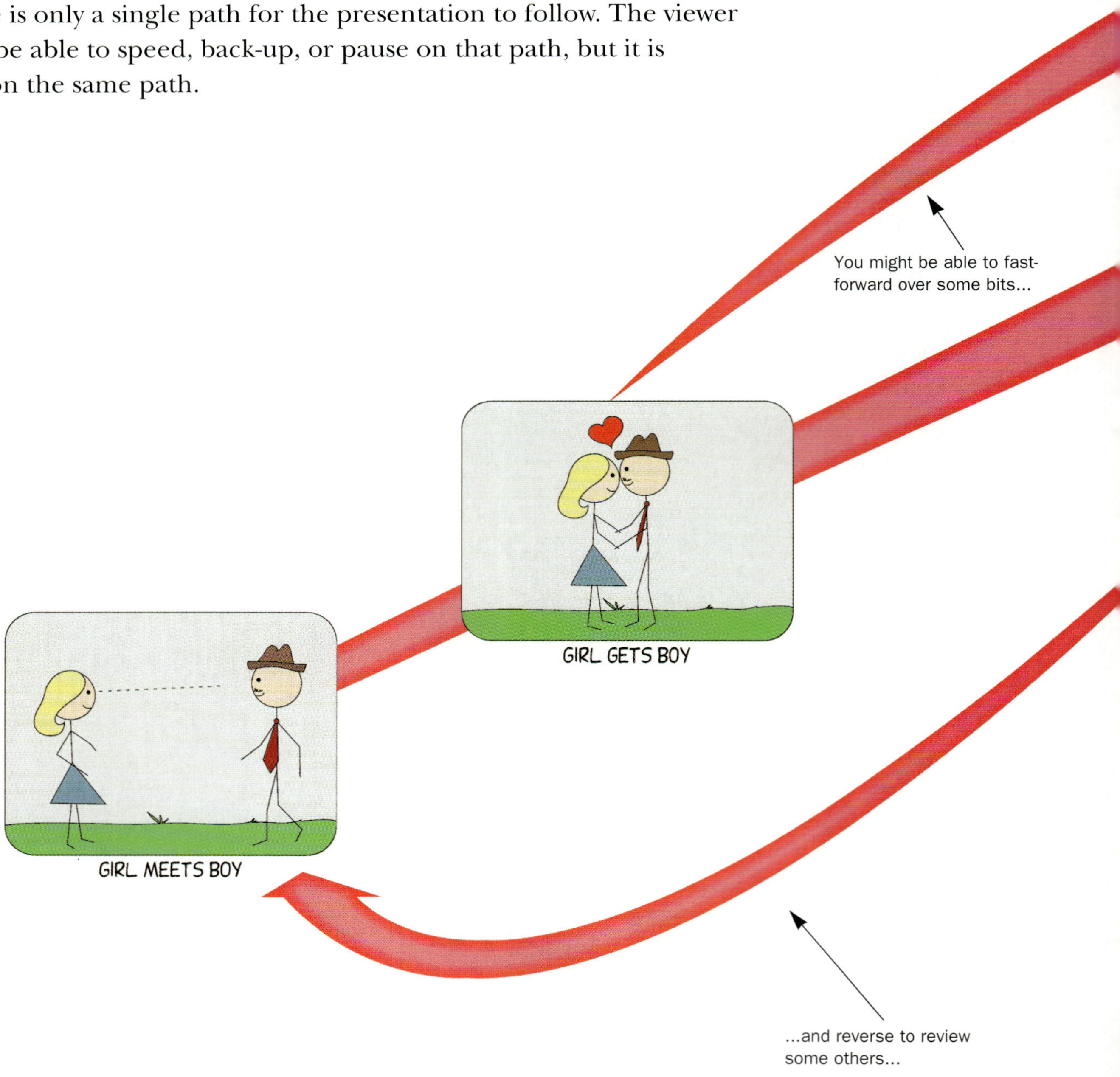

Many uses of passive multimedia are suited to VCRs, which can easily handle the large amount of video. More people use VCR tapes than personal computers, because more people have VCRs than computers. However, there are some specific advantages to computer-based passive multimedia:

- **A presentation can easily be created with a standard multimedia computer, without the need of fancy video editing machinery.**
- **The presentation can be distributed via modem, getting it to the intended recipient quickly and efficiently.**
- **If your presentation is a demonstration of a computer product, you are aiming at people who have computers, whether or not they have VCRs. As such, you know they will be able to view something released on disk, while they may not be able to view something released on video tape.**
- **For store displays, a computer presentation can automatically repeat on an endless cycle, without loss of quality, as opposed to a videotape display, which will start to show tape wear after prolonged use.**

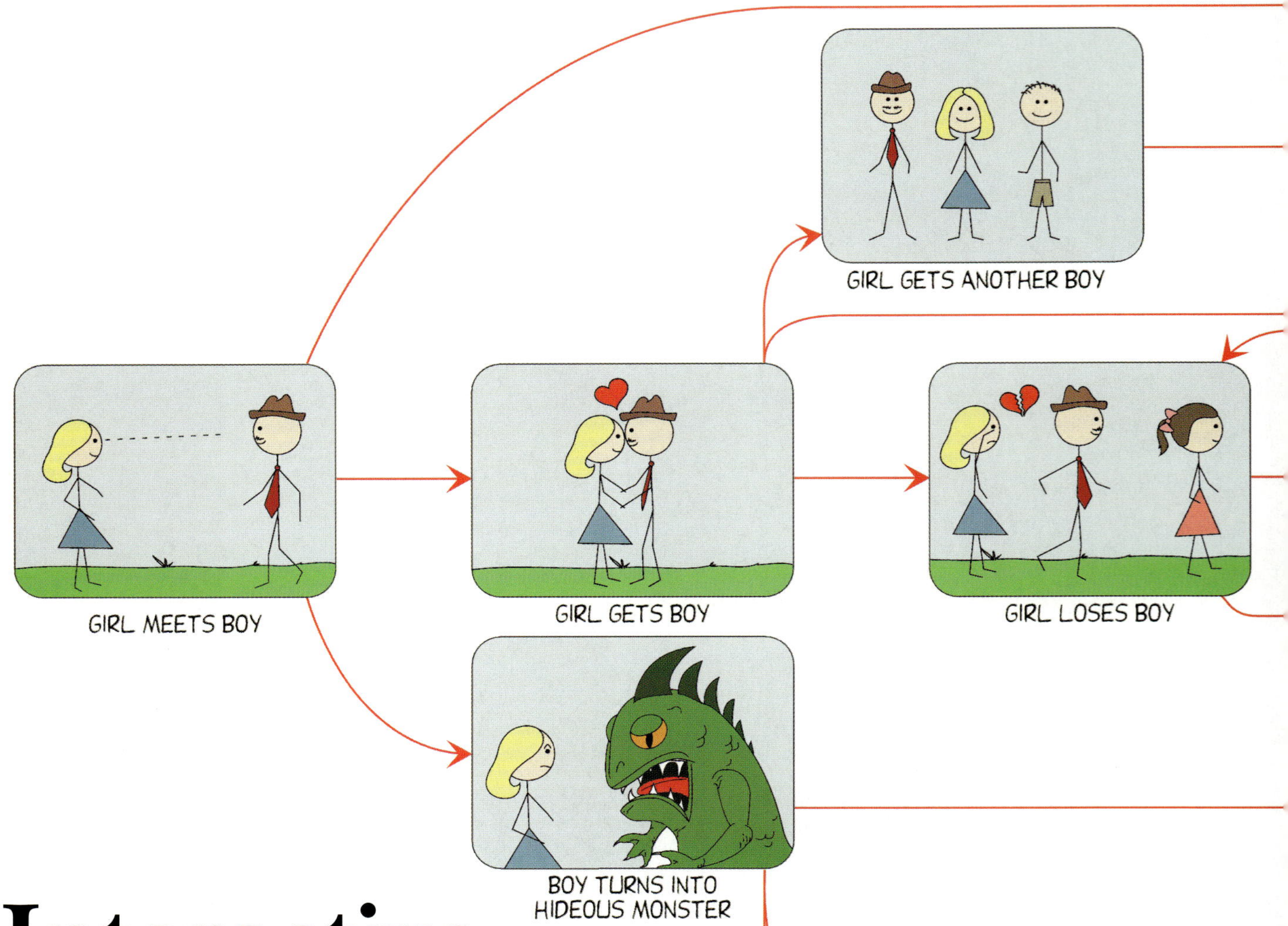

Interactive Multimedia

Interactive multimedia takes a different approach as compared to its passive cousin. The presentation can take a number of different paths, depending on what the computer user does along the way. You can still do demonstrations and stories, but the demonstration now shows the user what he wants to see, and gets the user interacting with it. And the stories—just about anything can happen with the stories.

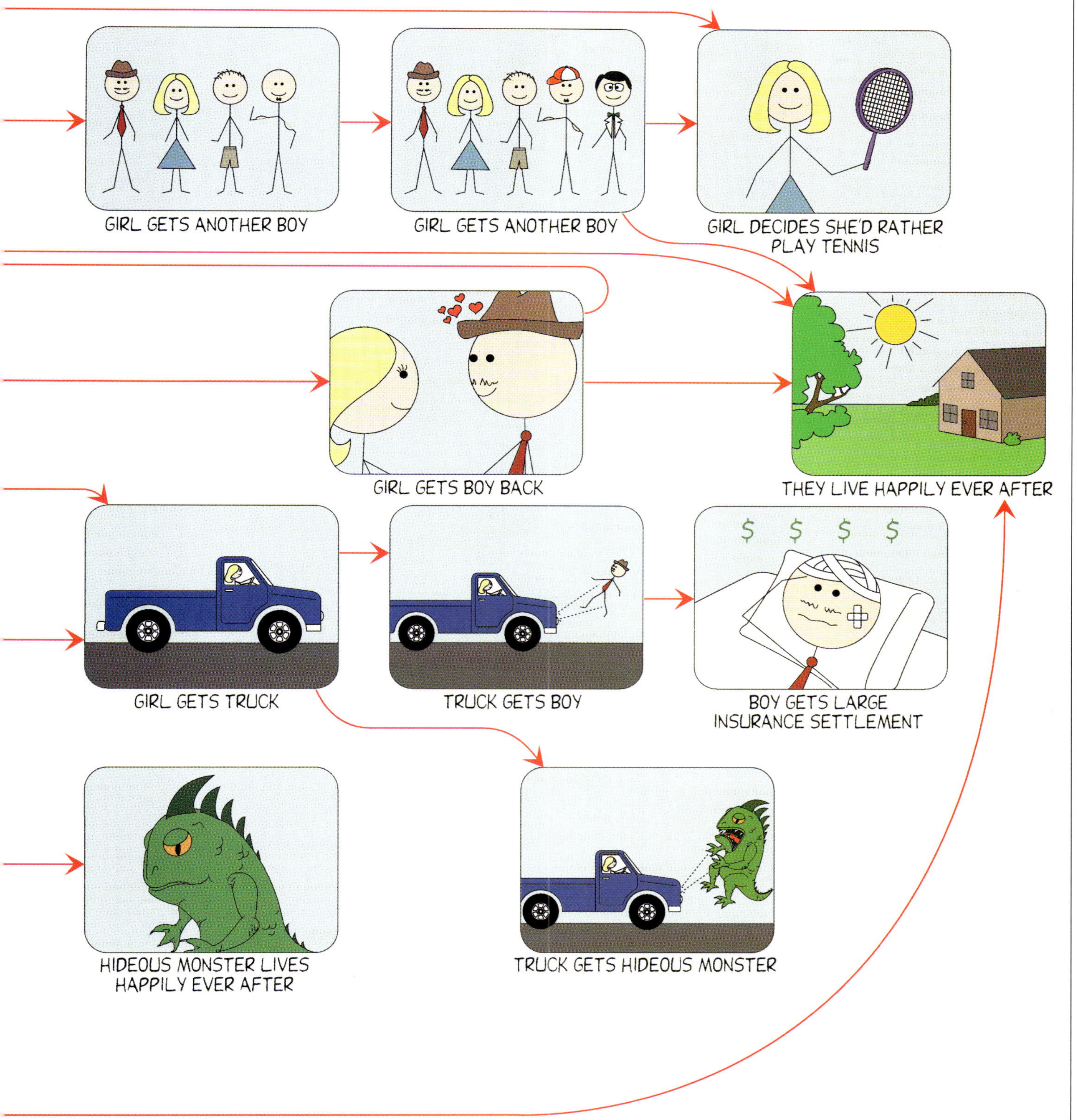

Of course, interactive multimedia is used for things other than telling stories. When the people developing the interactive multimedia project plot out what each user choice will lead to, they call it a **storyboard**.

Levels of Interactivity

Not all interactive multimedia is equally interactive. A simple product demonstration, for example, may allow you to select what you want demonstrated from a handful of options, with each of those options being a passive multimedia experience.

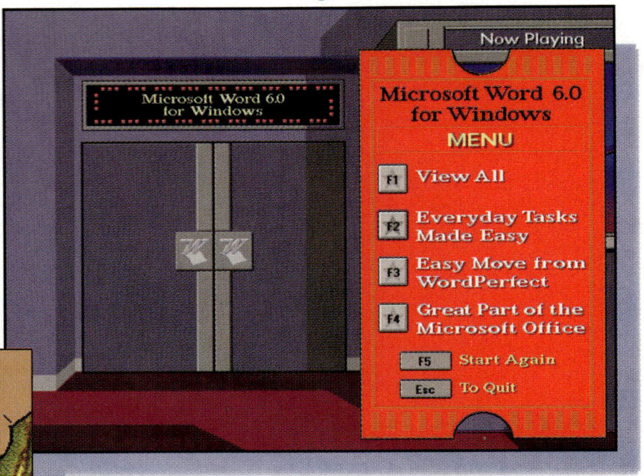

A *Microsoft Word for Windows* word processor demonstration program, © 1994 Microsoft.

Other programs allow you to interact in different ways with each screen, while still leading you through the screens in a fixed order. In this multimedia version of *The Ugly Duckling*, for example, you can click any of the creatures on-screen to see their animated reaction to this most unlikely duck, but the following screens will still lead him to find that he is not so ugly after all.

From Morgan Interactive's *The Ugly Duckling*, based on a story by Hans Christian Anderson. © 1993 Morgan Interactive, Inc.

Other interactive software puts you in the driver's seat. With a complex game or a good hypermedia reference work, you can go to many different screens from any one screen. The storyboard is not so much a set of fixed paths as it is a vast maze of possible routes.

Using these buttons, you can search in various ways for whichever movie review or actor's biography you want.

Using these controls, you can go to other reviews or different information about this movie.

Using the hypermedia functions of this program, you can go directly to the biographies of the actors or director of this movie, or to the reviews of any movie referenced in this review.

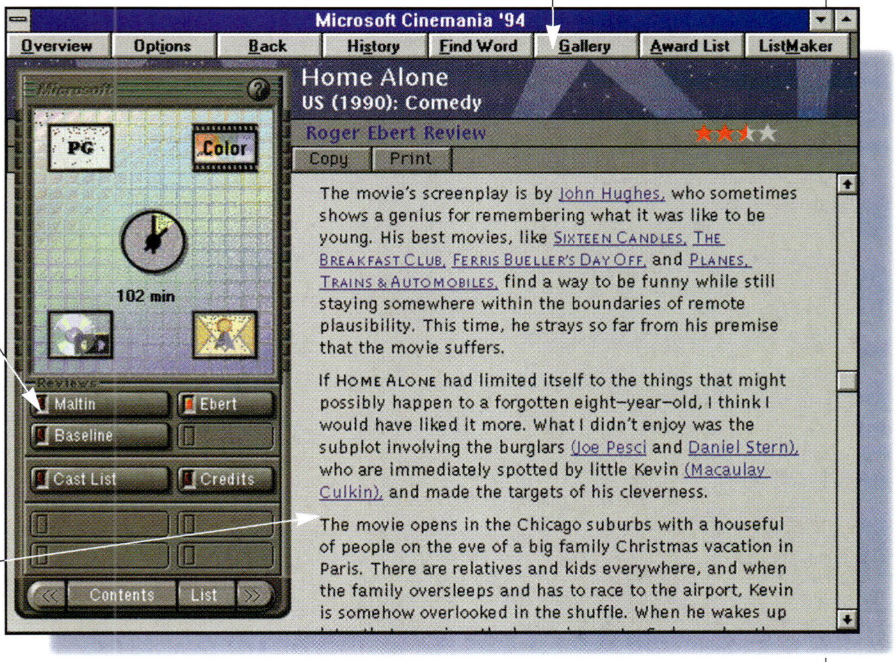

From *Microsoft Cinemania '94*, © 1993 Microsoft.

The Elements of a Multimedia PC

To use multimedia software on your computer, you need a system that is capable of displaying the high-quality pictures and playing the high fidelity sound that multimedia depends on. If you already have a computer but the sound or graphics are not up to multimedia standards, you can probably add on or improve these features.

What might not be so clear is that you also need a powerful computer, one that is capable of processing and storing a large amount of data. Pictures and sound take up *lots* of data. One second of CD-quality stereo sound, for example, takes up 150,000 bytes of memory—as much space as a 50-page word processor document! And a single full-screen picture can take up to hundreds of thousands of bytes, so when you start dealing with the series of pictures that full-motion video takes up, you are talking about quite a large amount of data. That data has to be moved very quickly through the various components of the computer, hence the need for a fast and powerful processor.

A well-equipped multimedia personal computer will have all of these things. A number of manufacturers are now offering **multimedia upgrade packages** to help you get your existing computer up to this point. These packages generally include a CD-ROM drive, a sound card, a set of speakers, and a starter set of software.

In addition to all this high-end hardware, you'll want to have a very recent version of the System (for Macintoshes), Windows (for IBM compatibles) or Amiga-DOS (for Amigas). The most recent versions are designed with multimedia in mind and are better able to support the multimedia hardware.

Stereo speakers.

High-resolution monitor.
CD-ROM drive.
Lots of software.
Multi
Large hard disk.
Mouse.
Headphones.
Several megabytes of RAM.
A powerful processor.

Sound and Video Systems

The sound system built into IBM-compatible computers is only a tiny speaker, which is hard-pressed to create much more than the basic video game beeps and bloops. Luckily, it is fairly easy to add a **sound card**, an expansion board that lets the computer process sound and attach external speakers or headphones.

These boards come with different capabilities and features. Computers handle sound by breaking it into little slices a thousandth of a second long. Some boards only support **8-bit sound** (each little slice can have one of 256 different values), but if you can, you should get a board with **16-bit sound** (each slice has one of 65,536 different values). CDs use 16-bit sound to get their clear, crisp reproduction. The difference in sound quality between the two types of boards is vast.

The standard sound card that new software is designed around is Creative Technology's *SoundBlaster.* Most other boards available today, such as the one pictured, are designed to be compatible with SoundBlaster (so that all the software will work with them) while competing in terms of price or features.

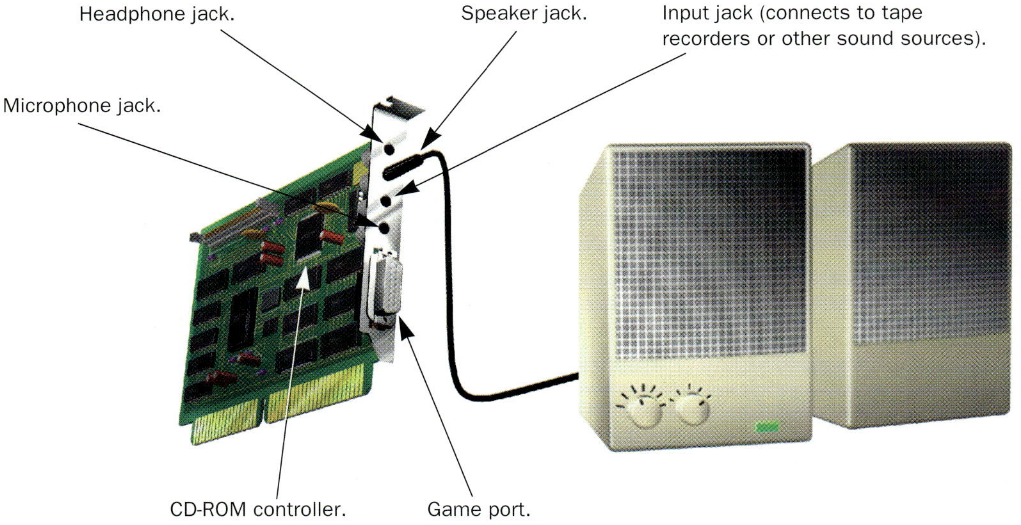

Most sound cards provide a **game port**, which allows you to plug a joystick into your computer. Many of them also include a **CD-ROM controller**, the interface which allows your computer to access a CD-ROM drive.

Another feature to look for is **Wavetables**. These are prerecorded instrument sounds stored on the sound card, allowing the system to better play stored musical scores. (See Chapter 10, "Creating Sounds," for more information on how the system stores and recreates sounds.)

For sharp reproduction of pictures and video, you should have a graphics system that supports at least 256 colors on a screen at least 600 dots (or **pixels**) across and 400 dots up and down.

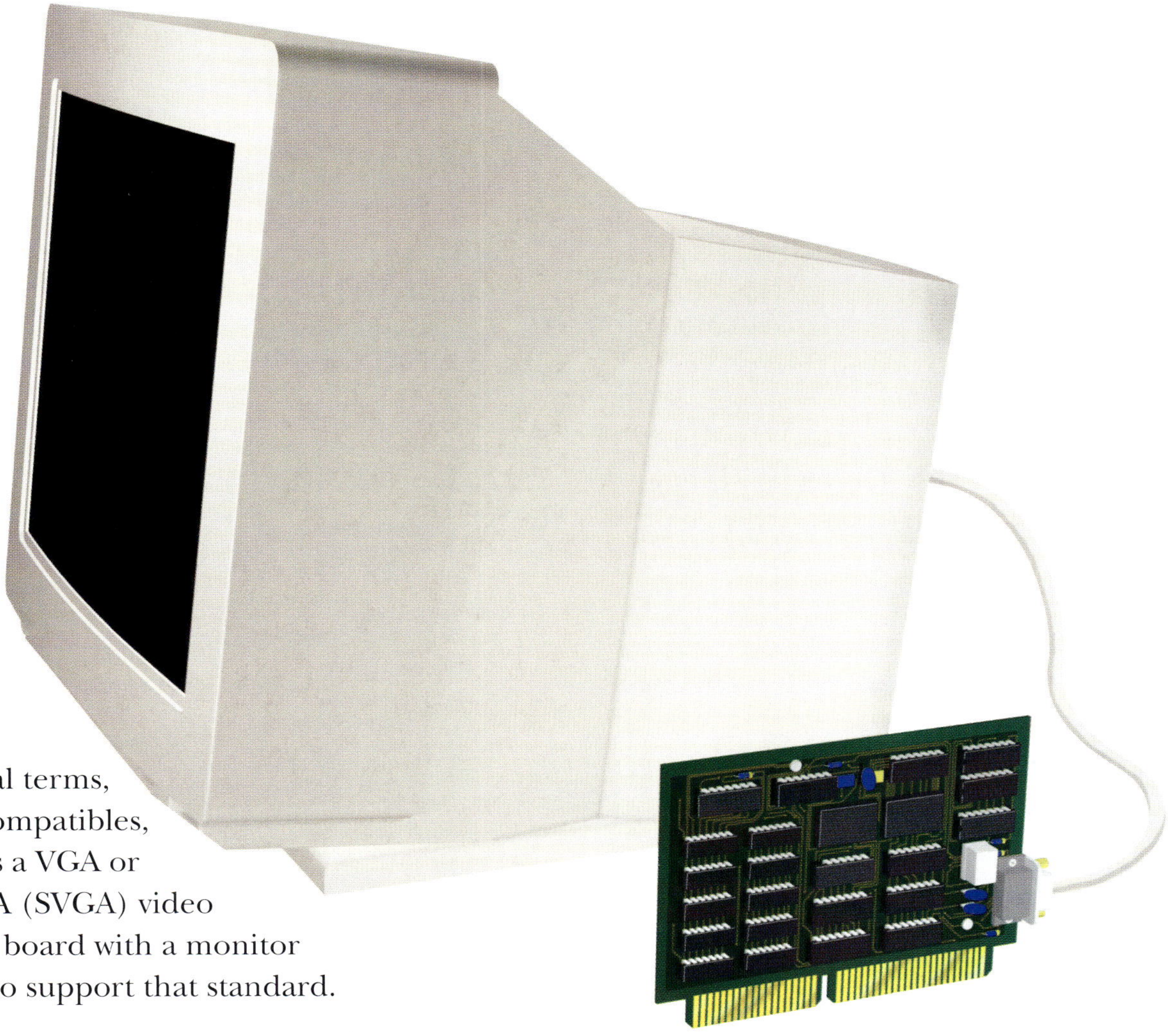

In practical terms, for IBM compatibles, this means a VGA or Super VGA (SVGA) video controller board with a monitor designed to support that standard.

Many new systems support **local bus video**. This creates a shortcut path between the computer's processor and the video board, allowing for new screens to update more quickly and moving images to move more smoothly. However, you need both a computer and a video board that supports the local bus.

Boards that attach to your video controller and provide it with additional power and features are available. Some of these, such as the ReelMagic board, will allow you to view full-screen, full-motion video, which is beyond the power of most boards. Make sure that your video adapter is **VESA** (Video Electronics Standards Association) compliant, so that you know you can connect these add-on boards.

The CD-ROM Drive

Compact discs, also known as **CDs**, provided a major advancement in recorded music. They store music as a large amount of numeric data, allowing that music to be recreated clearly and precisely. You need an expensive setup in order to make a CD (as opposed to, say, a tape recorder), but a CD player is pretty cheap.

In order to do that, the CDs have to store a large amount of information. This makes the technology very attractive for mutlimedia purposes, as multimedia requires a lot more information than text-oriented computing. Because the standard computer CD drive can only read information from a CD and cannot write information to it, they're called **CD-ROM**, for *Compact Disc Read Only Memory.*

The drive reads data off the CD by reflecting light from the bottom of the disc. The light passes through a layer of plastic and bounces of either a flat area (called a **land**) or a dent (called a **pit**). By seeing how the light reflects, the computer knows which area it hit, and interprets that as data.

Without CD-ROMs, the multimedia revolution would not be possible. Programs would have to be distributed on floppy disks, and a single floppy disk can only hold a few high-resolution pictures, or 10 seconds of CD-quality audio. Distributing large amounts of sound and picture information would be impossible. But a single CD-ROM can hold over 600 million bytes, more than you could store on 400 floppy disks. A CD-ROM can store thousands of images, or hundreds of thousands of pages of text.

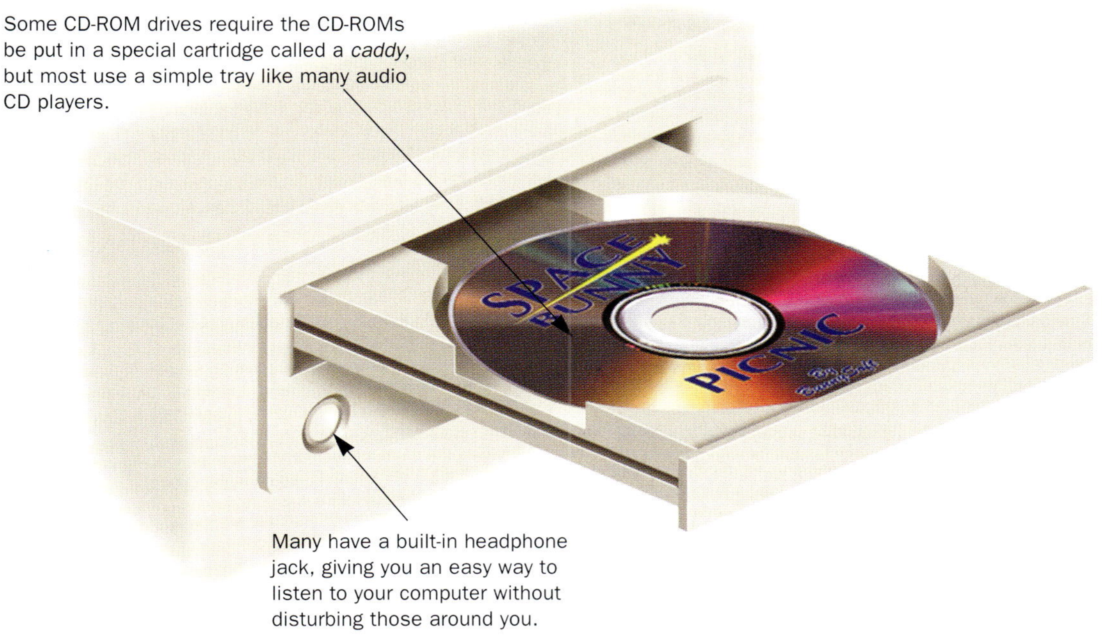

The standard for CD-ROM speed is the speed of music CD players, reading about 150,000 bytes of information every second. That may sound like a lot, but it's slow compared to most computer speeds. As a result, hardware manufacturers are now making double-, triple-, even quadruple-speed drives. The fastest of these can transfer the entire text of *Moby Dick* from the disc to RAM in two seconds!

The other speed measurement for a CD-ROM drive is **access time**, which is how long it takes to find the beginning of a string of information on the disc. This is measured in **milliseconds**, or thousandths of a second.

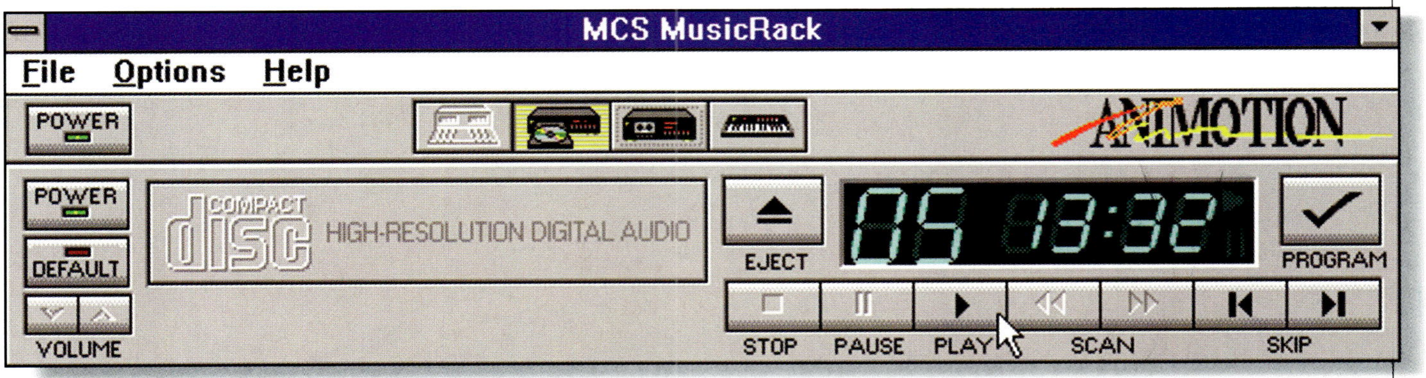

From *MCS MusicRack*, © 1993 Animotion Development Corp.

Some external CD-ROM drives also double as portable music CD players. You also can use your CD-ROM drive, the computer's speakers, and a software driver to use your computer as an audio CD player, playing music in the background while you work on other things.

The MPC Standards

There are so many different possible IBM-compatible computer configurations that it's difficult to know if your system is in every way powerful enough to run a given piece of software. In order to make it easier for you to tell if your hardware meets the requirements to complete a given task, the industry formed an organization which has set two standards for multimedia machines: **MPC** (for *multimedia personal computer*) and **MPC2**.

If you have a computer that meets all of the MPC standards and recommendations, you can be pretty sure that it will run any software with the MPC logo. Similarly, if you own a computer that meets all of the MPC2 standards and recommendations, you can count on running software that bears either the MPC or MPC2 logo.

With the large variety of computers, sound cards, and graphic cards that are on the market, compatibility problems abound. While software manufacturers try hard to get their software to work on as many systems as possible, they cannot anticipate every combination of hardware and existing software that they might face. As such, you should realize that the MPC standards indicate only that your machine is powerful enough to handle the software, and cannot guarantee that the software actually *will* work.

Hardware and Software Requirements for Multimedia PCs

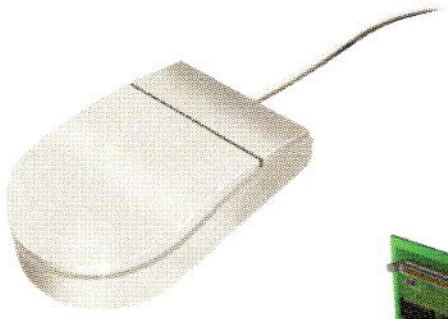

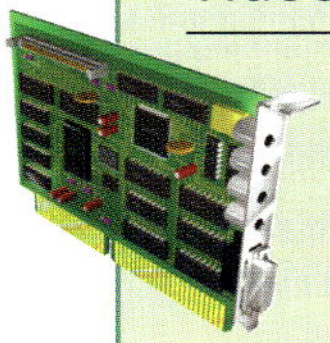

	MPC	**MPC2**
DOS version	3.1	3.1
Windows version	3.1	3.1
Memory	4M	8M
Hard disk	30M	160M
Processor	386SX	486SX
System speed	16 MHz	25 MHz
CD-ROM data speed	single	double
CD-ROM access time	1000 ms or less	400 ms or less
CD-ROM buffer	none	64K
Mouse	Yes	Yes
Video display	640 × 480	640 × 480
Palette	256 color	65,536 colors
Sound card	8 bit	16 bit
MIDI support	Yes	Yes
Microphone	Yes	Yes
Speakers	Yes	Yes

Trademarks of The Multimedia PC Marketing Council, Inc.

chapt

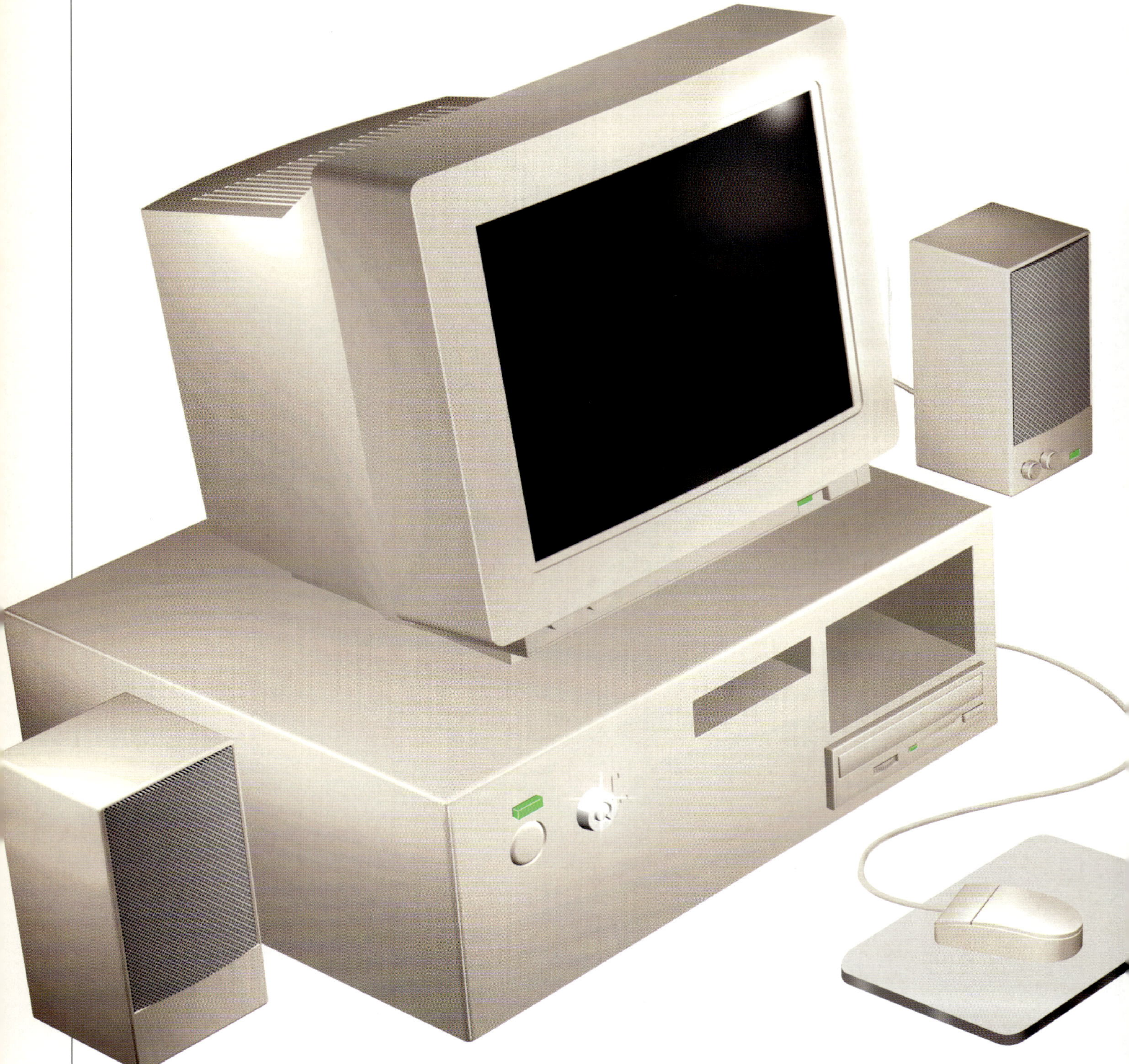

Non-PC Multimedia Systems

Talking about *multimedia computing* makes it easy to assume that you need a special desktop computer to take advantage of multimedia's benefits. However, there are computers in all sorts of products these days—your digital watch has a computer in it, as does your microwave oven, VCR, and even your car.

All that's really needed is a system with a display screen, speakers, some method for user interaction, access to some form of stored data, and the ability to process it. Many of the elements of a standard PC simply aren't needed for basic multimedia use.

Among other alternatives to PC multimedia platforms is cable TV-based multimedia, discussed in Part IV, "Multimedia of the Future."

Multimedia-Capable Video Game Consoles

The current generation of home video game machines seems like a likely route for multimedia. After all, systems like the **Super Nintendo Entertainment System** (**SNES**) or Sega's **Genesis** have pad controllers for user interaction and are capable of putting out colorful high-speed graphics and stereo sound. They also have the advantage of already being in a large number of homes, which would seem to make them an attractive platform for multimedia products.

Certainly, the games that they include do qualify as multimedia. They use sound and graphics capabilities, including more and more use of modeled graphics (such as these characters from Accolade's *Cybernauts* for Sega Genesis).

Other than games, however, there hasn't been much software released for these machines. One of the problems is that the base systems accept programs only in the form of cartridges. These plastic boxes are filled with **ROM** (**Read Only Memory**) chips, which are expensive when measured in cost per megabyte (at least when compared to floppy disk or CD-ROM based storage). As such, even the cartridge for a complex video game will store only about 1/100th as much information as a CD-ROM disk. This prohibits them from having anything more than brief moments of moving video, and limits just how much they can do with graphics and sound.

From *Cybernauts*, © 1994 Accolade.

Sega addressed this problem by releasing the **Sega CD**, an add-on for the Genesis system which allows it to use CD-ROM software. Different programs take advantage of the extra stored memory in different ways—some have larger play fields, others have better sound and graphics, and many of the games are based around video segments (although the system cannot handle full-speed, full-screen videos).

Unfortunately, all of the software released for the Sega CD are still entertainment packages. While the market for the Genesis systems is clearly the home user—and therefore business software would not be appropriate—there would still seem to be a large potential market for home reference programs (multimedia encyclopedias, cookbooks, and so on). After all, many households do not have a home computer but do have a Genesis console in the living room. However, due to lack of this reference software, the Genesis may be a reasonably powerful multimedia machine, but it's not nearly as useful as a multimedia desktop computer.

More recently, Sega has released the CDX, a complete Genesis-compatible system that can use cartridges or CDs in a single unit small enough to be used as a portable audio CD player.

Multimedia Consoles

Bridging the gap between video game machines and full personal computers are the **multimedia consoles**. These machines are built around CD-ROM drives (rather than having them available as an add-on, as with the video games) and do not require keyboards, floppy disk drives, or printer ports that are now part of the standard personal computer. They can be attached to a TV like a video game machine, thus saving the cost of a separate monitor.

A number of companies have released console systems, although generally with less success than they had anticipated. Phillips' **CD-I** and Commodore's **CDTV** and **CD-32** had trouble getting a large customer base, in part because they weren't much cheaper than a full computer system, and in part because there were not enough programs available to convince people that they needed these machines.

Still, a console system has some advantages. Its simplicity makes it easy to use without complex software installation procedures. Also, the system's complete, ready-to-use, all-from-one-manufacturer nature means that you don't run into the compatibility problems that plague some personal computer platforms.

The latest foray in this market takes things a bit differently. The 3DO Company designed the technology behind the **3DO interactive multiplayer** console unit. Instead of manufacturing 3DO systems themselves, they license the technology to manufacturers with absolutely no royalty cost. This way, they hope to have a number of manufacturers distributing competing, compatible machines, and thus keep the price down. The first manufacturer to release a 3DO console was Panasonic with their **REAL 3DO** console.

As with the other consoles, a 3DO system can be used not only to play 3DO discs, but also to play standard audio CDs and to view Kodak photo-CDs (a standard for still pictures stored on CD-ROM). An add-on cartridge will soon be available, allowing the 3DO systems to play movies stored on disk in the industry-standard MPEG format. (Such a cartridge is already available for the CD-I system.)

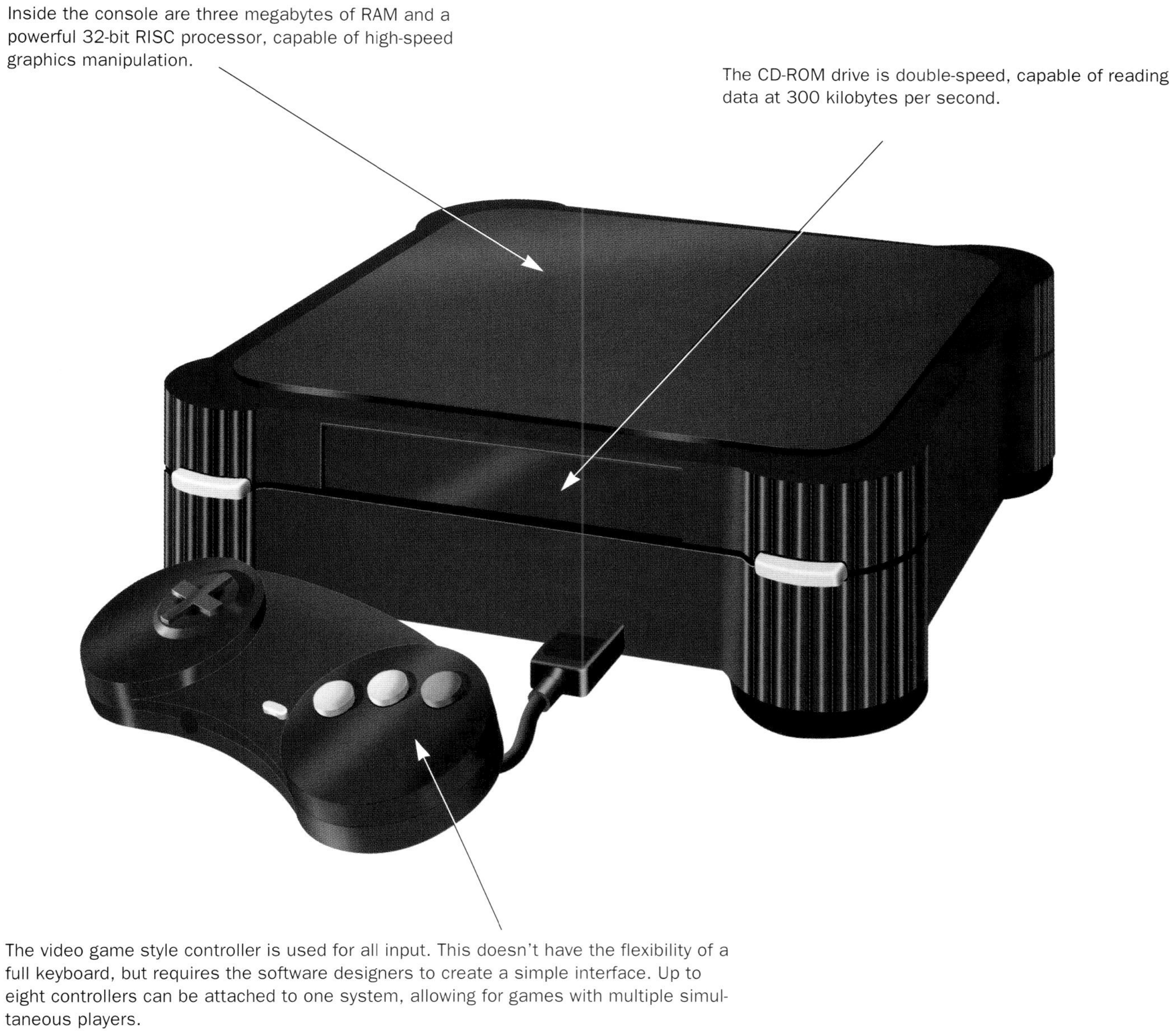

If The 3DO Company isn't charging the manufacturers for each console they make, how do they expect to make money? They're charging the software manufacturers a certain amount for every piece of 3DO software they sell. With individual titles in the video game market selling millions, it's easy to see how making a little money from each copy sold could add up to a lot of money. However, the charge is small enough that it won't scare manufacturers away from making software, particularly given that the cost of actually making the CD is far less than the cost of making a standard video game cartridge.

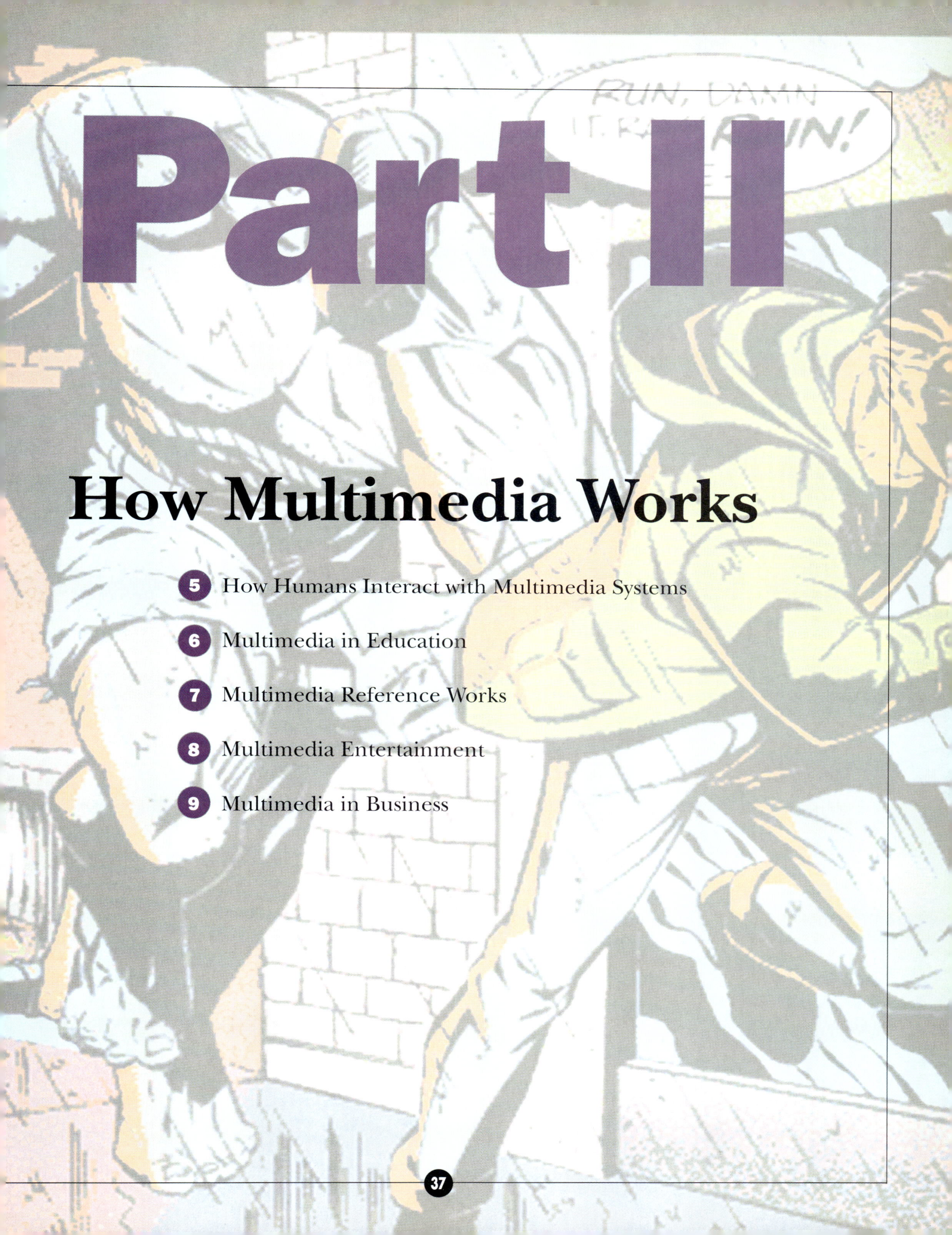

Part II

How Multimedia Works

How Humans Interact with Multimedia Systems

The goal of multimedia is to allow you and the computer to communicate in a variety of ways. In an ideal world, this communication would be as simple as a spoken command or a gesture. You would be able to point at the screen and say, "Print *that* picture." You could just walk up to an automated teller machine and say, "Give me fifty dollars," and it would recognize you and automatically take the money from your account. You'd play *Battleworld* by punching an empty space in front of you, and the computer would have the player on-screen execute the same moves.

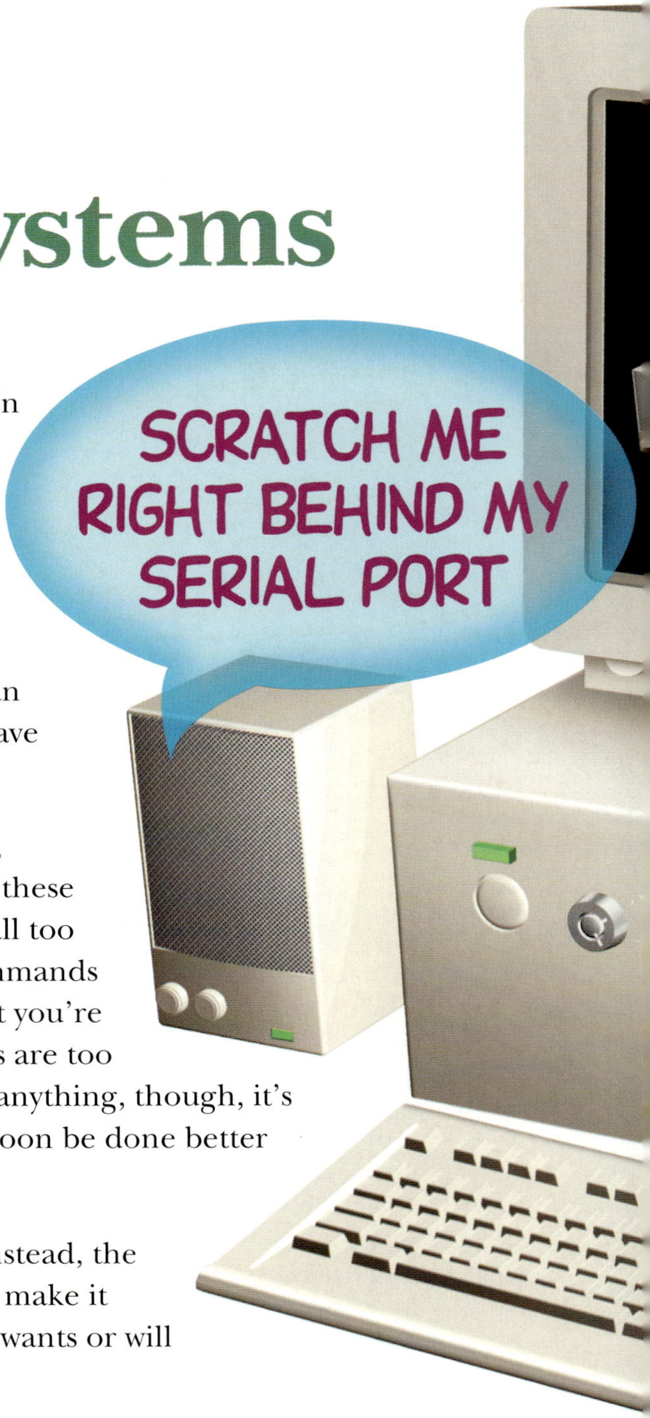

None of this is quite possible—yet. Most of these things, however, are on the drawing board. Limited versions of these features are in use in special applications, but they are all too limited. They can only recognize a limited range of commands or movements, and their guesses of who you are or what you're saying aren't very good. In addition, most of the systems are too expensive. If the history of computing has shown users anything, though, it's that what can be done poorly and expensive today will soon be done better and, eventually, cheaper.

So computers can't really understand people just yet. Instead, the multimedia capabilities of the computer can be used to make it easier for the person to understand what the computer wants or will allow you to do.

MMMMMMM MMMM!!
OH, THANK YOU!

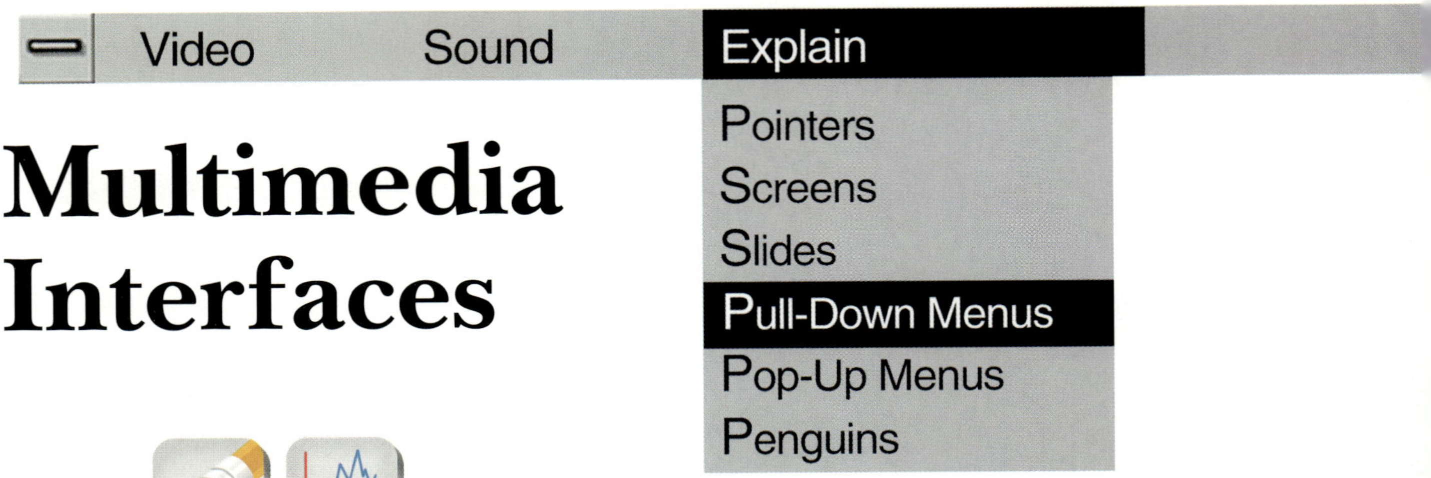

Multimedia Interfaces

Icons are pictures that represent computer commands. Instead of the word "graph" for the graphing command button, for example, a picture of a graph is shown. It takes up less space and is supposed to be more intuitive—but only if the picture is well-chosen.

Pull-down menus are an easy way to have several commands sorted into categories without using a lot of screen space. Point to the category of commands you want, and a box appears with commands for you to choose from.

Most programs use a **pointer**, a little picture of an arrow, pointing finger, or some other pointing object that you move around the screen. When you have the pointer pointing to what you want, you click the mouse to indicate that this is your selection.

Scroll bars (also known as **elevator bars**) use a box or bar (a **slider**) which can be dragged along a shaft. The shaft represents the whole document; the slider shows where you are in the document. To move further down the document, drag the slider down, click below the slider, or click the arrow at the end of the slider.

VCR controls are a very common group of buttons, particularly for controlling audio and video. Most people are familiar with their simple icons for *play, stop, pause, fast forward,* and *reverse.*

Buttons let you just click a selection. Some buttons stay "stuck in" until you click them again, so you can use them to turn features on and off.

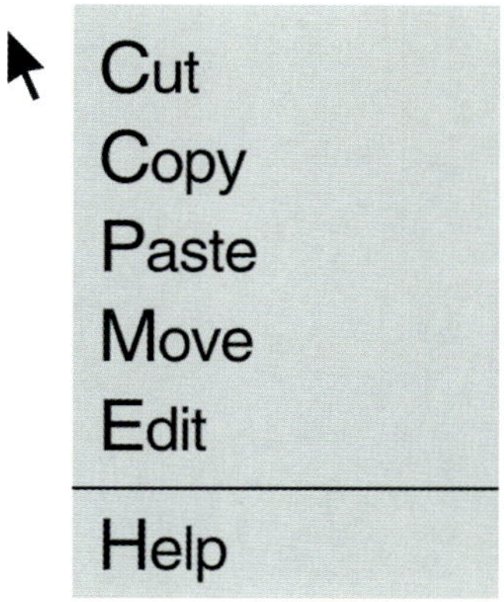

A **pop-up menu** is a box full of commands that appears anywhere other than the standard menu bar location.

Hypermedia is a system where you can use a pointer to select highlighted words or visual information within one display to get to another display about that highlighted topic.

The use of pointers and icons means that multimedia uses **graphic user interfaces** (or **GUIs** for short). As explained in Chapter 1, "Welcome to the World of Multimedia," many of the programs also take advantage of the pointer to create a **hypermedia** environment.

Joypads, Mice, and Trackballs

There are a large number of different devices used to control the on-screen pointer, but the three most common are the mouse, the trackball, and the joypad (which has been taking over the popularity of the joystick, although it's still sometimes used).

If you have special needs (such as physical disabilities) or just like to play around on the cutting edge of technology, you should take a look at some of the alternate input methods that use mouth movement or even eyeball movement.

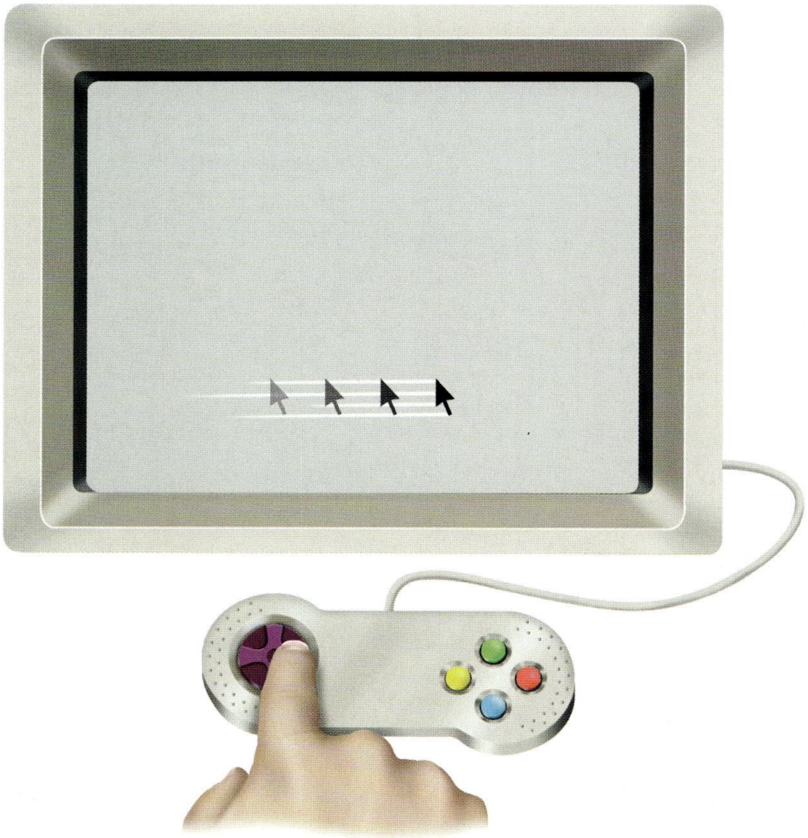

Many console units and their video game cousins use a **joypad**. Pushing down on the edge of the pad causes the pointer to move in that direction.

Sliding a **mouse** across a pad or the top of a desk causes the pointer to move in the same direction on-screen. This way, by positioning the mouse, you are positioning the pointer, which is quicker and more intuitive than steering the pointer as the joypad does.

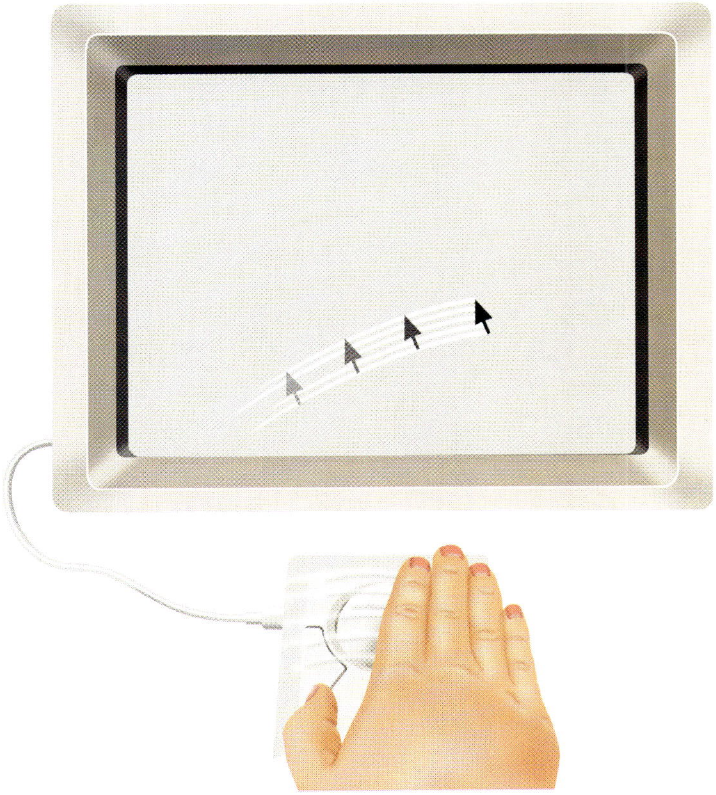

Using a **trackball** is a lot like using a mouse, only you're sliding your hand across a rolling surface rather than sliding a rolling object over a still surface. Since a trackball unit stays in place, it takes up less desk space than the mouse, which needs room to roam.

Advanced Input Systems

Touch screens detect taps right on screen, so that your finger becomes the pointer. Some detect the touch with touch sensors on the screen. Others have beams of light passing in front of the screen and can tell when your finger passes through the beam of light. In either case, they are not very precise.

Because pointing to what you want is such an easy thing to understand, touch screens are very helpful for information kiosks in malls and other places where you cannot count on the user being experienced with computers. Since the touch capability is built into the computer monitor, these also serve well where space is a consideration.

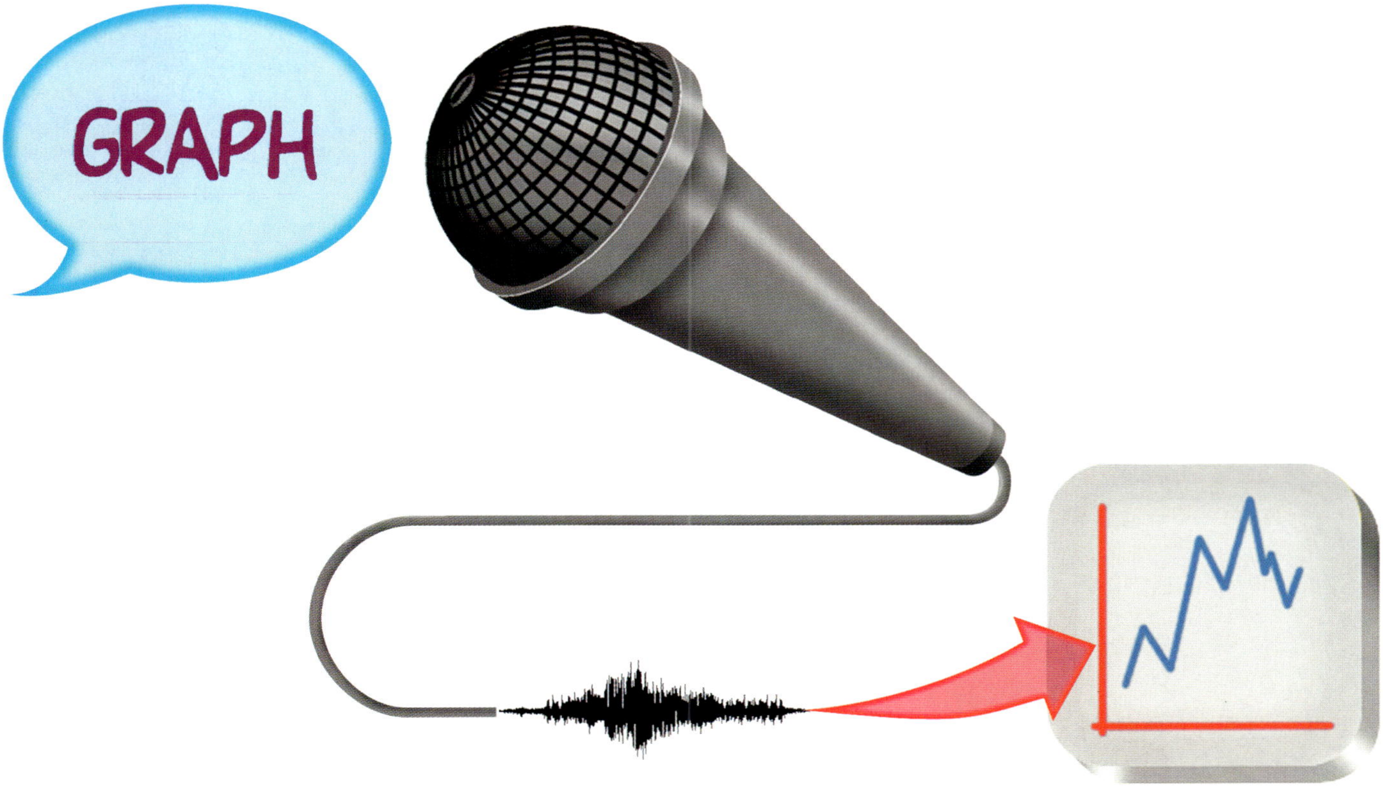

Voice recognition is a growing technology. As the name suggests, the computer doesn't actually understand what you are saying; it merely compares the vibrations of a word that you say to a group of previously recorded words, to see which (if any) it sounds like. Because everybody speaks differently, systems that accept more than a small number of commands have to be trained to recognize each separate user. Even when trained, they will have trouble telling the difference between *graph*, *graft*, and *carafe*, for example.

Despite these limitations, voice recognition is useful in situations when a computer needs the user to select from a limited set of responses, or in situations where the user is going to have his or her hands otherwise occupied.

Multimedia in Education

Educating students requires the following tasks:

1. Get their attention.
2. Provide them with information.
3. Test their understanding to make sure they understood the information.
4. Represent and support the information in ways that reinforce concepts that students might not have grasped.

Fascinate. With sounds, music, pictures, and animation, a multimedia program can firmly grab and hold someone's attention. A good multimedia program isn't so attractive that it distracts from what you're trying to communicate.

Inform. With the vast space of a CD-ROM, there can be information to spare. The same piece of information can be stored in a number of different manners. This way, if students don't seem to understand a concept presented in a certain manner, it can be presented in another.

Test. Computers are very good at giving tests, able to wait silently for the student to answer, or offer some assistance if the answer seems to be taking too long to come. Even more important, they can track right and wrong answers, looking for strong and weak spots.

Support. With all the information that has been learned through rechecking, the computer can go back into the teaching mode, shoring up specific weak spots, through repetition and different approaches.

Adapting to Kids

Computers can't replace classrooms. A lot of what you learn in school involves interaction with other people and computers aren't capable of replacing that interaction. Computers also can't check the quality of effort in your drawings and, at this point, they can't even check penmanship quality.

However, multimedia-based education greatly enhances traditional education. Although many of the possible tools don't exist yet, many are on their way. With improved programs and sagging computer prices, it's ever more likely that students will spend a sizable portion of their days in computer-aided study.

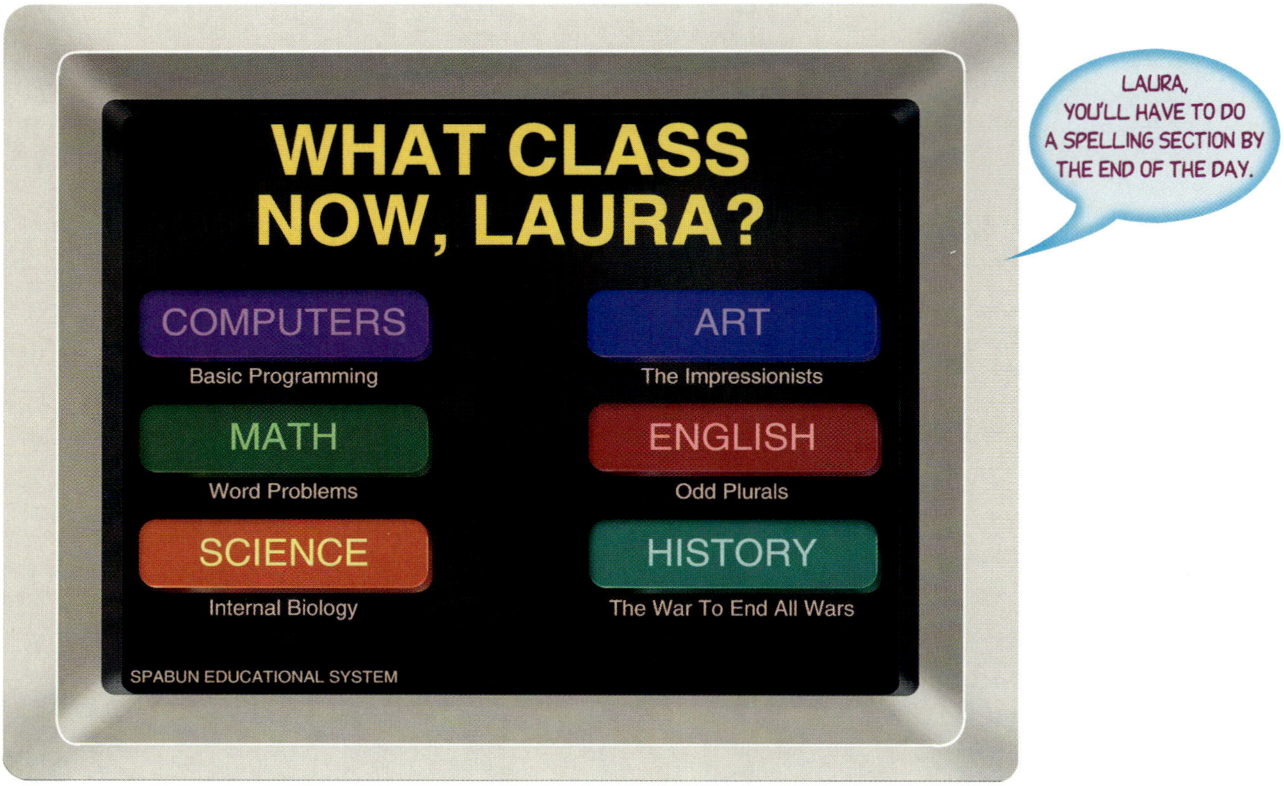

A computer is a one-on-one tutor that doesn't need to limit a student to doing the same thing, at the same speed, and at the same time as other students. If, for example, Laura can learn a day's math lesson in 15 minutes instead of the 40 minutes of her average classmate, then she might be able to learn two days worth of math in a day and still have a few extra minutes to devote to her difficulties with social studies.

If she just doesn't feel like doing math Wednesday and she's caught up in her work, then it seems logical to allow her to spend extra time on social studies.

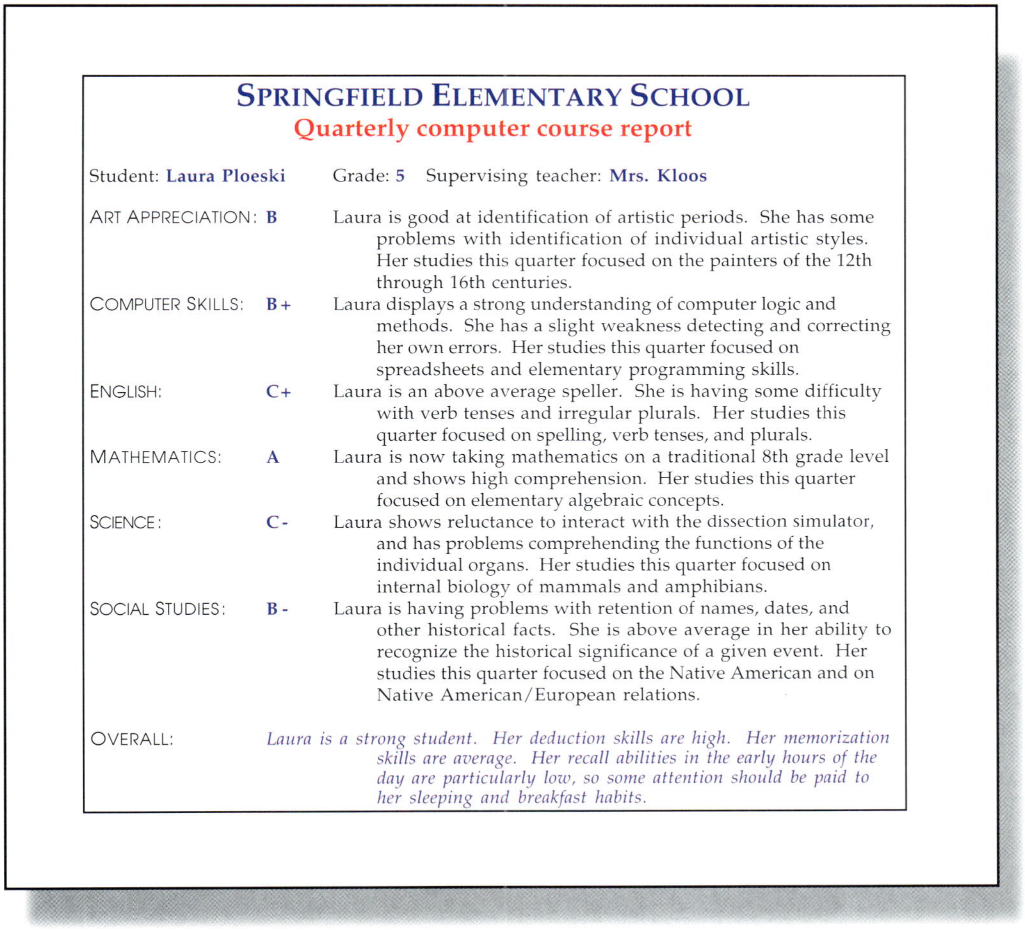

SPRINGFIELD ELEMENTARY SCHOOL
Quarterly computer course report

Student: **Laura Ploeski** Grade: **5** Supervising teacher: **Mrs. Kloos**

ART APPRECIATION:	**B**	Laura is good at identification of artistic periods. She has some problems with identification of individual artistic styles. Her studies this quarter focused on the painters of the 12th through 16th centuries.
COMPUTER SKILLS:	**B+**	Laura displays a strong understanding of computer logic and methods. She has a slight weakness detecting and correcting her own errors. Her studies this quarter focused on spreadsheets and elementary programming skills.
ENGLISH:	**C+**	Laura is an above average speller. She is having some difficulty with verb tenses and irregular plurals. Her studies this quarter focused on spelling, verb tenses, and plurals.
MATHEMATICS:	**A**	Laura is now taking mathematics on a traditional 8th grade level and shows high comprehension. Her studies this quarter focused on elementary algebraic concepts.
SCIENCE:	**C-**	Laura shows reluctance to interact with the dissection simulator, and has problems comprehending the functions of the individual organs. Her studies this quarter focused on internal biology of mammals and amphibians.
SOCIAL STUDIES:	**B-**	Laura is having problems with retention of names, dates, and other historical facts. She is above average in her ability to recognize the historical significance of a given event. Her studies this quarter focused on the Native American and on Native American/European relations.
OVERALL:		*Laura is a strong student. Her deduction skills are high. Her memorization skills are average. Her recall abilities in the early hours of the day are particularly low, so some attention should be paid to her sleeping and breakfast habits.*

By providing Laura some control over her education, you will make her feel like she's more involved and her performance will likely improve.

No, we really haven't reached this point yet, but it's coming sooner than you think.

Consider, for example, a fascinating test involving autistic children and microcomputers. These children were put in front of a computer with a word processor, without any screen savers or other time-sensitive tasks. This way, the machines had a level of patience that not even the best-intentioned human could match. The kids might hit a key and spin around in their chair or stare off into space for several minutes, absorbed in whatever world exists within the autistic brain. Then they would hit another key or two, then drift away again. Eventually they were typing stories. Because of their peculiar patience, computers allowed the autistic children to build communication during their brief moments of awareness.

Yet not all multimedia is for kids. Certain universities have begun experimenting with providing courses on CD-ROM. This creates more interactivity than courses that are released on videotape, and course software and quiz programs can be included on the disc. Students can submit their homework via modem, and never need to be anywhere near the campus.

Educational Games

From the beginning of your life, you learned through the games you played. Whether you developed the concept of gravity by dropping a ball out of the crib or you learned about the persistence of reality through a mind-bending round of peek-a-boo, you discovered things while doing what you enjoyed. There aren't any reasons why this has to stop once you move from the high chair to the computer chair.

Where in the World is Carmen Sandiego? is an example of a game that grabs a kid's attention. Getting kids to pretend to be international detectives distracts them long enough to slip both geographical knowledge and research skills past their anti-school defense screens.

This game has been popular for years on a wide variety of systems, spawning a whole series of *Where in [whatever] is Carmen Sandiego?* games, as well as two distinct TV series. With a multimedia DOS or Macintosh, you can use the CD-ROM deluxe edition, which has full speech output, more scenes, more facts, and more mystery.

The plot is this: You are an entry-level agent for Acme CrimeStoppers, dedicated to ridding the world of Carmen Sandiego and her vile crime organization, V.I.L.E. They've been creating a crime wave, stealing everything from royal cats to national monuments.

All screens from *Where in the World is Carmen Sandiego? Deluxe Edition*, © 1992, 1993 Broderbund Software, Inc.

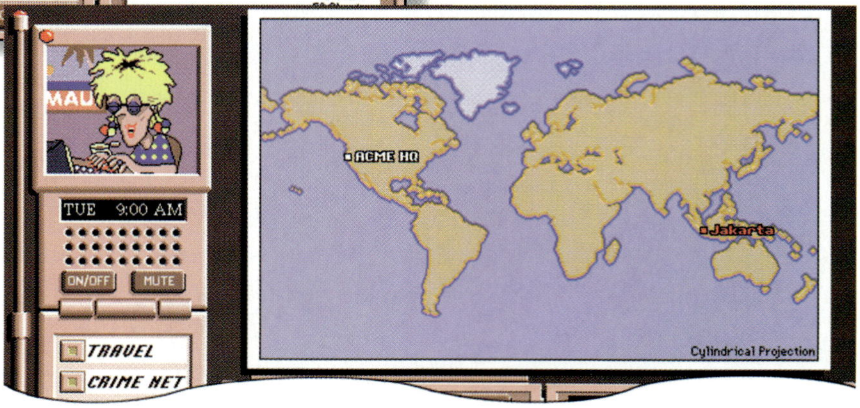

V.I.L.E. agents have a peculiar habit of globe-hopping after every heist. With the help of Acme's nasal travel agent, you globe-hop after them. The trick is knowing where to go.

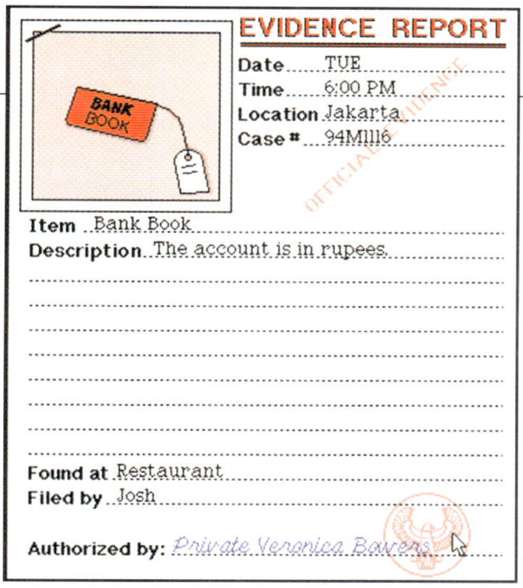

Fortunately, the V.I.L.E. agents leave clues behind, little bits of information indicating things like what currency they next expect to use, or what activities they think they will be performing at the next location.

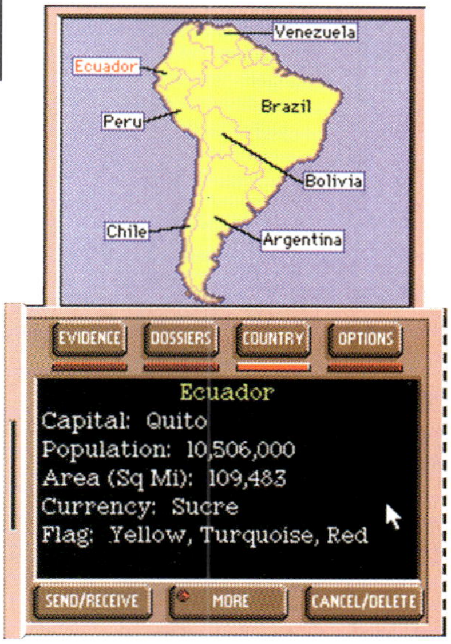

Knowledgeable detectives may figure out the country based on the clues, but others will rely on the built-in mini international reference or, better yet, a handy almanac. Navigating the almanac to find what you want is a valuable learning experience.

Along the way, you pick up little clues about the thief's identity—his or her description, hobby, favorite food, or other such tidbits. With the help of this evidence, you can obtain a warrant for the arrest of the international criminal.

Once you both identify and locate the criminal, you're rewarded with seeing the criminal in the hands of the justice system, and you're promoted to the next rank. That's just another step in your effort to ultimately arrest the ringleader herself—Carmen Sandiego.

The game is full of photographs of a wide array of countries and also includes native folk music and descriptions of the land. All this adds to the richness of the game experience and its educational value, but occasionally it can irritate the player who just wants to forget the learning experience and barrel ahead with the true goal—tossing Carmen behind bars.

Tutorial Systems

Of course, students must choose to play educational games in their spare time. There are systems for more controlled educational purposes, in which education comes first and the play, if any, is secondary.

Interactive Chinese from Powersource, Inc., is an example of one such application. Designed to teach reading skills to those with a working knowledge of spoken Chinese (like grade-school English teaches reading to kids who already know how to speak), this Windows package takes advantage of multimedia PC capabilities to make a high-tech reading primer.

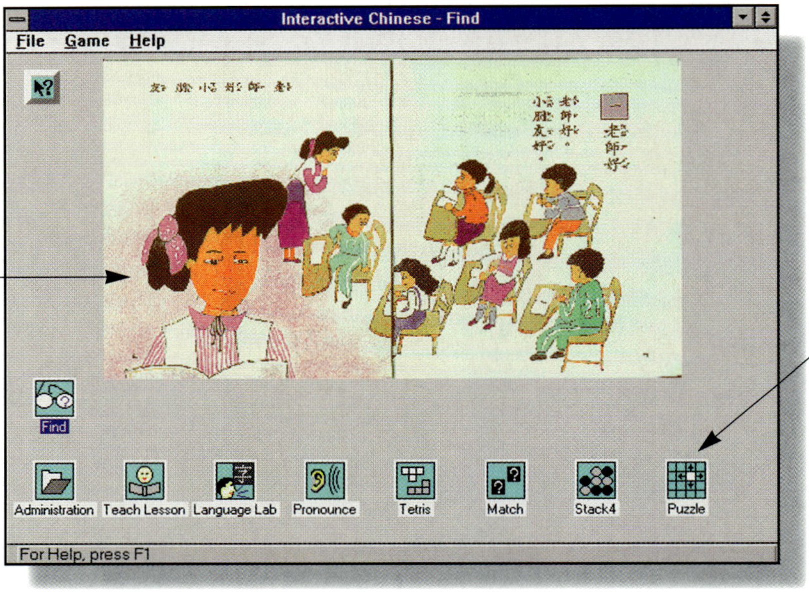

All screens from *Interactive Chinese*, © 1994 Edugames and Powersource, Inc.

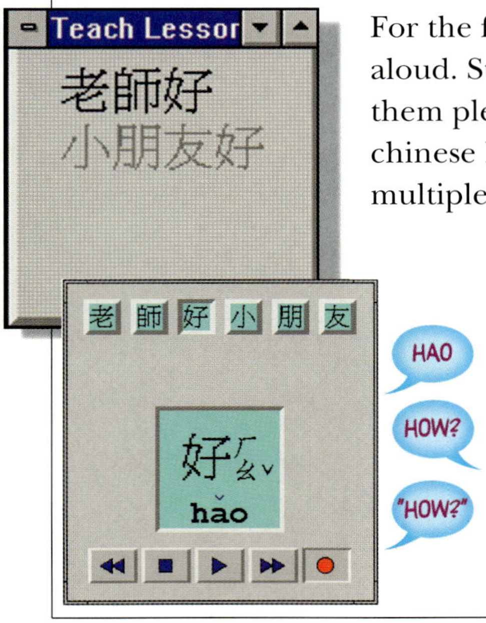

For the first part of the lesson, the computer reads the text of the page aloud. Students can select any single word or sentence to be repeated, giving them plenty of opportunities to familiarize themselves with the words. (The chinese language uses a single symbol for each word, rather than the multiple-letter symbols that comprise English words.)

If students want to check their pronunciations of the words, they can pull up the handy pronunciation checker. The computer pronounces the word and students are expected to pronounce the word into the microphone. This software isn't capable of recognizing correct pronunciation, but the users are. The computer repeats students' pronunciations so they can compare them to the stored pronunciations.

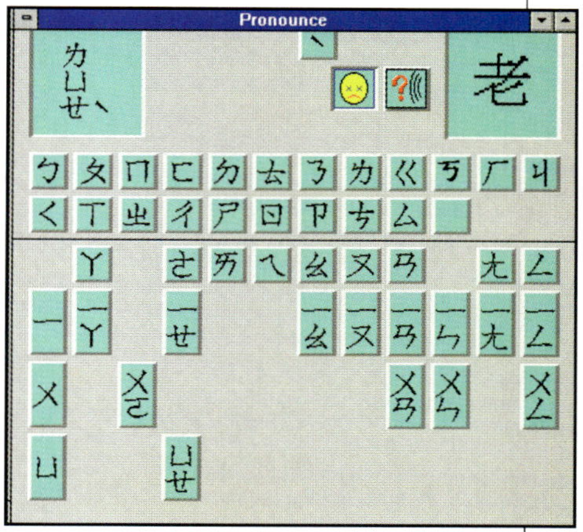

Pronunciation also includes breaking each word into the Chinese phonic characters of which it's comprised. The students construct words that the computer pronounces, presenting a happy face if the constructed word is the correct one and a sad face if it is incorrect.

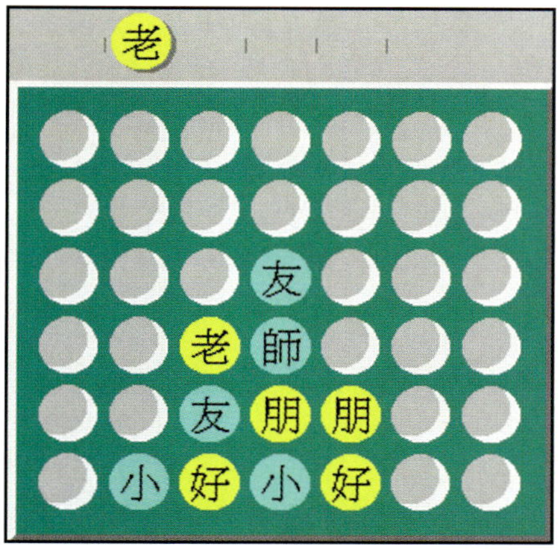

Of course, even a tutorial program offers plenty of fun. The teaching content of the games is simple word recognition—click as quick as you can on whatever word the computer pronounces. This can be played as its own game or as an intermission between rounds of versions of Tetris and Stack 4 (which also include repetition of the words from that lesson).

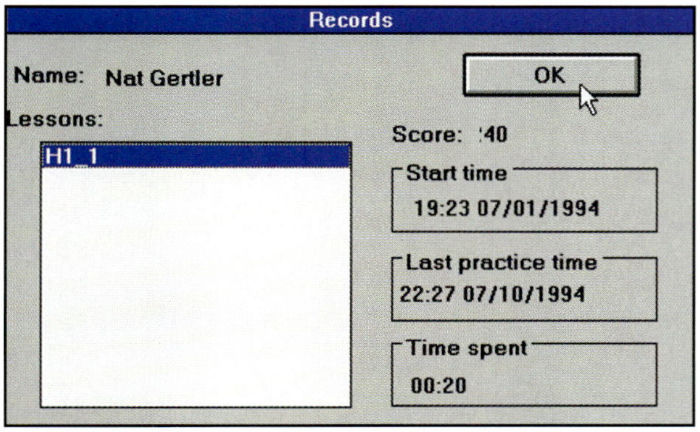

However, life can't be all fun and games. Someone has to make sure the work is completed. The administrative screen allows teachers, parents, or other supervisors to track the following information:

- How much time students spend on lessons
- How often students work on the lessons
- How much work students have completed

This information is extremely valuable to complete the learning process.

Multimedia Reference Works

Software manufacturers have been putting out many reference works on CD-ROM. Here's a small example of these reference materials:

- Encyclopedias
- References on the assassination of John F. Kennedy
- Lists of CD-ROM software

CD-ROM is popular because it's capable of holding the contents of hundreds of books and it can quickly locate the information you want.

It takes more than one CD-ROM, however, to create a multimedia product. The sound and video capabilities of a multimedia system can be used to turn out a reference work superior to many others. Here are some examples:

- The obscure pronunciation guides of dictionaries can be replaced by a human voice actually pronouncing the word.
- Drawings can be replaced by rotating 3-D models.
- Descriptions of a moving play can be replaced by the play itself.

The following pages describe a couple of examples of multimedia reference works. Other titles available include the following:

- **Atlases**
- **Phone books (and reverse phone books, which allow you to look up addresses when you know the phone number)**
- **Almanacs**
- **Prescription and non-prescription drug guides**
- **Cookbooks**
- **Astronomy guides**
- **Dictionaries**
- **Bible guides**
- **Crime histories**
- **World record lists**
- **Law guides**
- **Histories**
- **Anatomy guides**
- **Computer references**
- **Health guides**

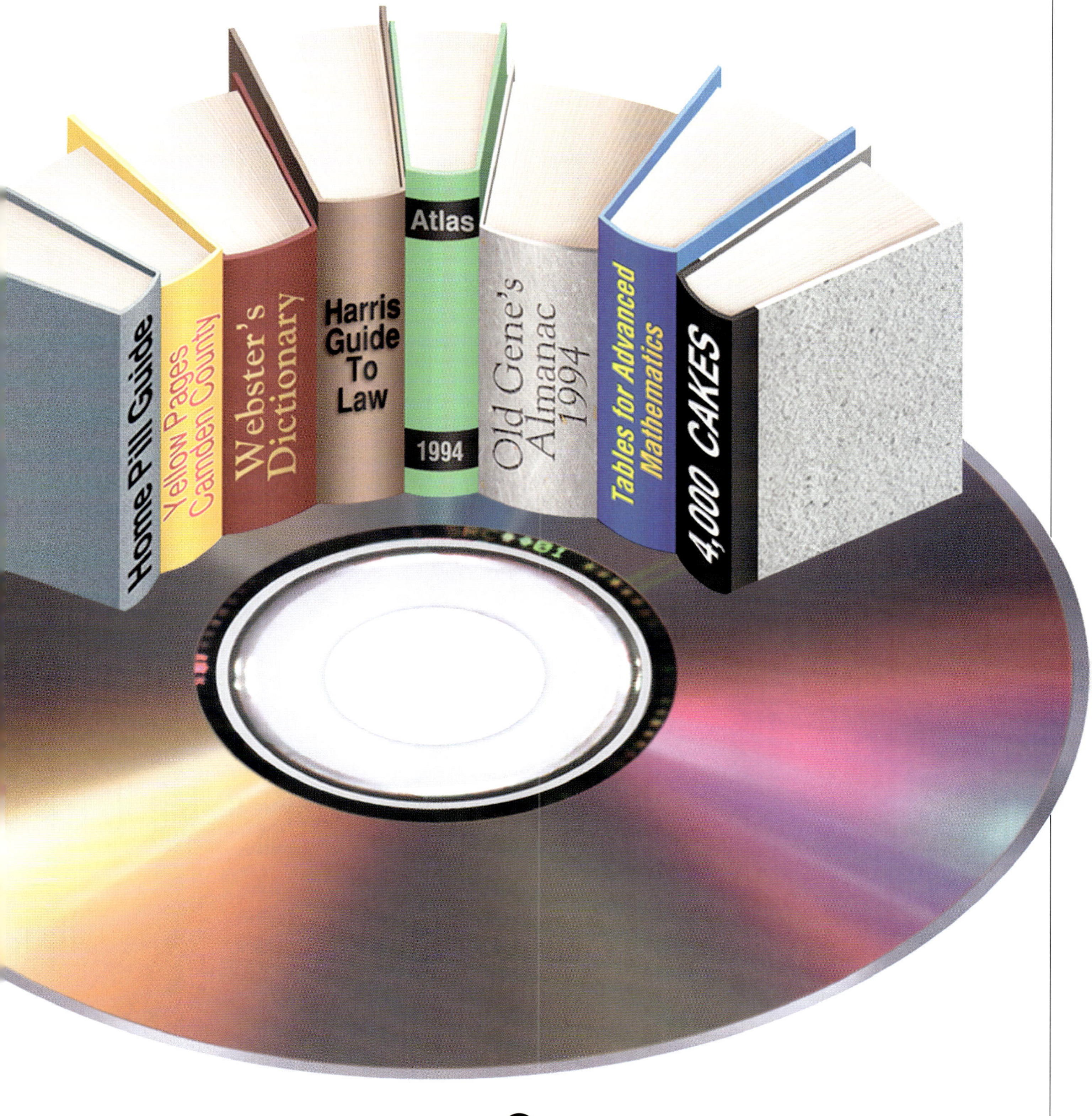
Home Pill Guide
Yellow Pages
Camden County
Webster's
Dictionary
Harris
Guide
To
Law
Atlas
1994
Old Gene's
Almanac
1994
Tables for Advanced
Mathematics
4,000 CAKES

A Multimedia Encyclopedia

Microsoft Encarta is a good example of a multimedia encyclopedia. With literally thousands of topics, it's a quality replacement for the traditional encyclopedia. It offers several advantages, including the ability to cut Encarta's pictures and text and paste them into your word-processor documents. (Don't try using that to cheat on your reports, kids; the teachers will catch you at that one almost every time!) There are many different ways to move through the encyclopedia.

These controls let you move alphabetically through different sports entries.

In this area, different pictures appear as you scroll through the text on basketball.

Clicking on symbols brings up a specific picture, animation, recording, or video.

This scroll bar lets you move up and down through the whole article.

From Microsoft Encarta, © 1994 Microsoft Corp.

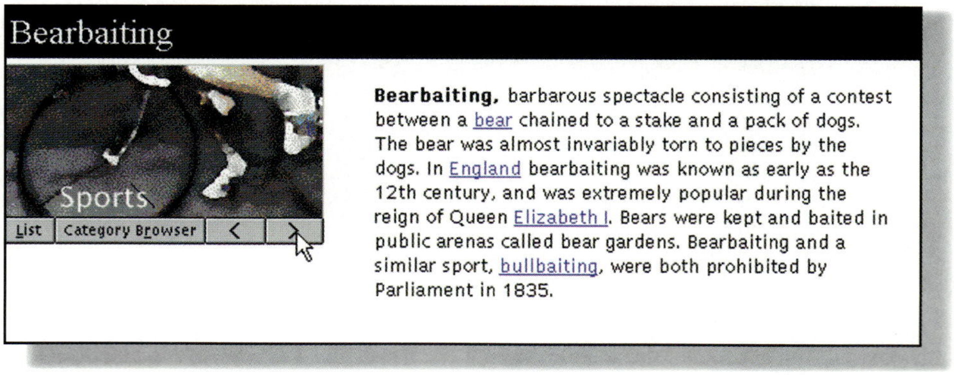

Not all entries are as full and as illustrated as the basketball entry. The next sports entry, Bearbaiting, for example, is very short.

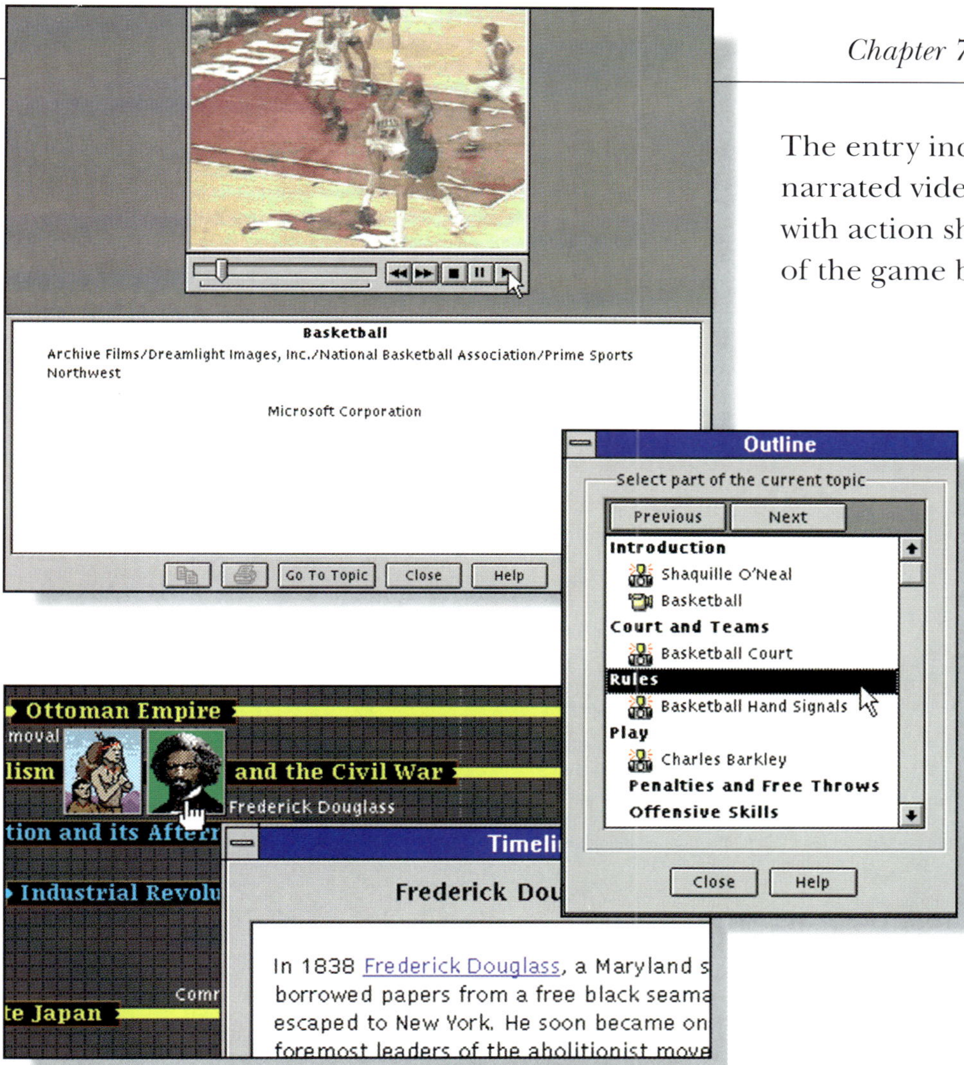

The entry includes a minute-long narrated video about basketball, with action shots that carry the feel of the game better than words.

Calling up the outline lets you jump ahead to the various subtopics and special presentations that make up the basketball article.

Encarta includes a history timeline with hypermedia capabilities.

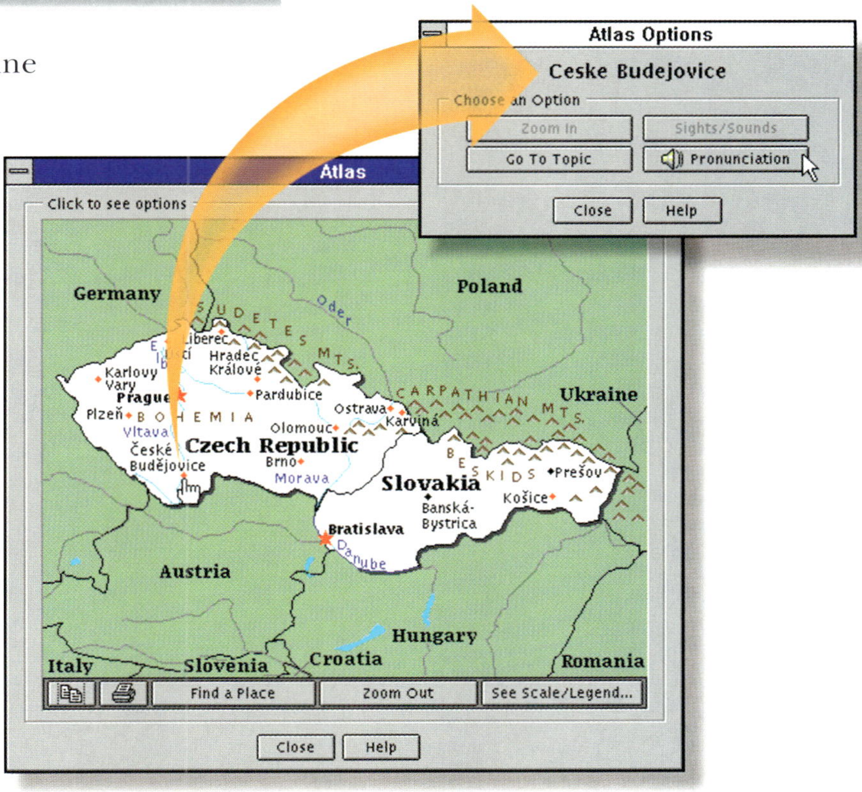

The atlas feature makes it easy to navigate the world, and recorded pronunciations help you understand just where you are!

A Multimedia Film Reference

Whether you're a reporter looking for background about an actor or just a proud couch potato looking for the next video to rent, *Microsoft Cinemania* provides easy access to about 20,000 film reviews and also provides information on about 4,000 movie stars. Some of the reviews include movie stills, recorded dialogue, and even short video sequences from some of the best movies. Because video takes up a lot of CD-ROM space, only a few films have video clips.

The remote control lets you get different information about the film.

The help button, which gives you help information on using the product, is hard to find.

See the opinions of different reviewers.

From *Microsoft Cinemania '94*, © Microsoft Corp.

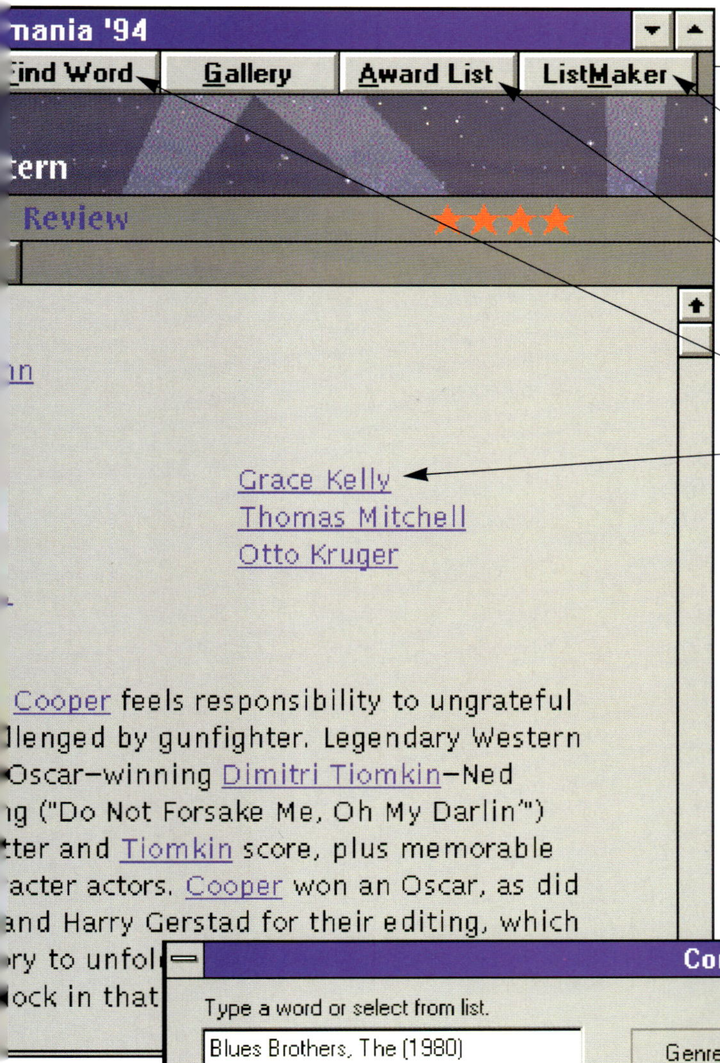

ListMaker keeps a list of movies that are of interest to you.

Award List provides easy access to a list of Oscar winners.

Find Word searches the reviews for any word.

The highlighted words are hypermedia links that make it easy to move between movie reviews and facts on the stars.

History enables you to return easily to screens you've already looked at.

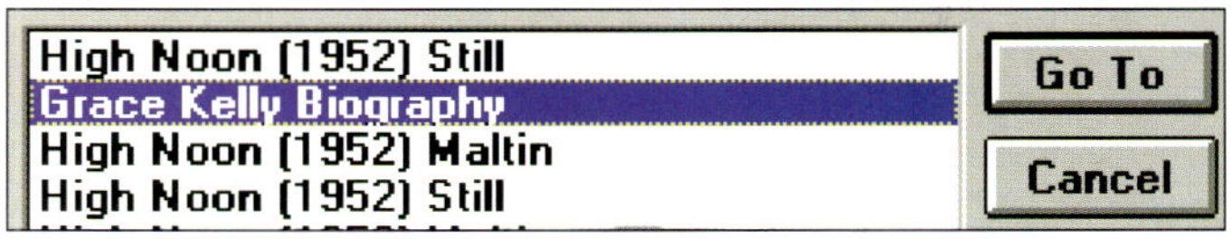

The Contents feature enables you to search for films based on your own criteria.

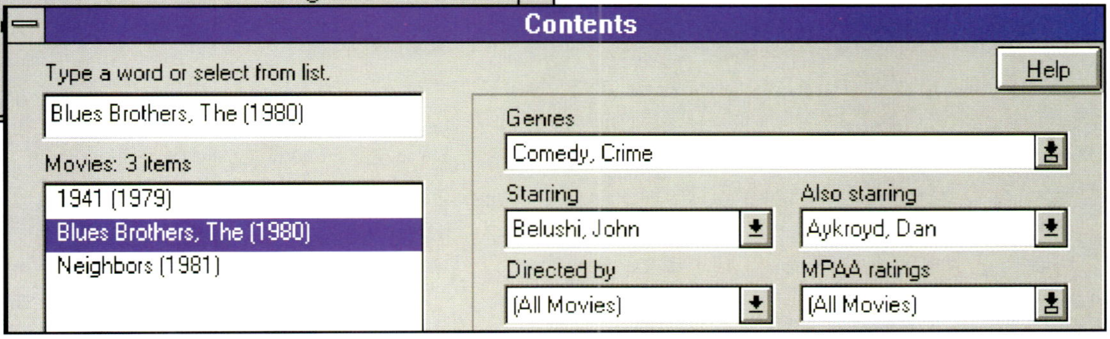

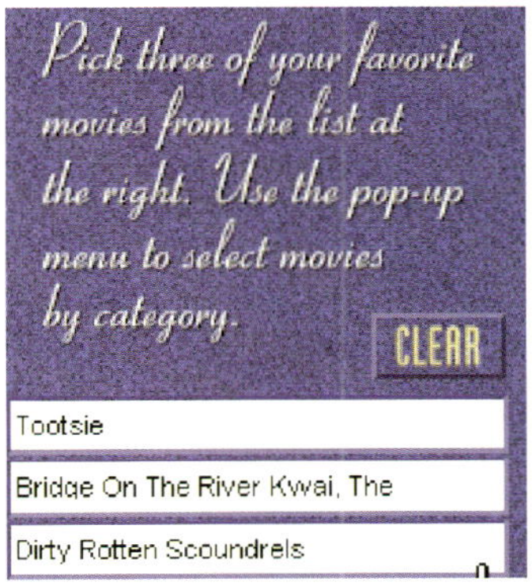

From *MovieSelect*, © Medior Incorporated

MovieSelect, a competing product, analyzes a list of movies you like to suggest to other movies you may enjoy. The analysis logic is so complex, it comes close to mimicking the human thought processes.

Multimedia Entertainment

It should come as no surprise that multimedia's power is used for new ways of having fun. After all, it's always easier to find a way to have fun with new technology than it is to get some use out of it. Technology that involves sound and moving pictures is a clear source of fun, because it is related to music, movies, video games, and other things we already have fun with.

The computer may have been intended as a tool, but it has always been used as a toy. Indeed, there probably has not been so significant an addition to games since the invention of the ball. The computer can act as both referee and opponent in traditional games like checkers or bridge, or can present entirely new types of games. All of these can be augmented or improved by multimedia. The moving figures and bleeps and bloops of video games turns into movie figures and digitized voices of a multimedia game.

Multimedia also is a great form for artistic expression. A well-equipped computer can take the place of a video lab and sound studio for much less. The musician can try adding visuals to his expression and the painter can try animation, and both of them can bring in a level of interactivity that previously was impossible.

From *Jump: The David Bowie Interactive CD-ROM*, © 1994 ION.

Jump lets you edit your own David Bowie music video, as well as create your own mix of the music.

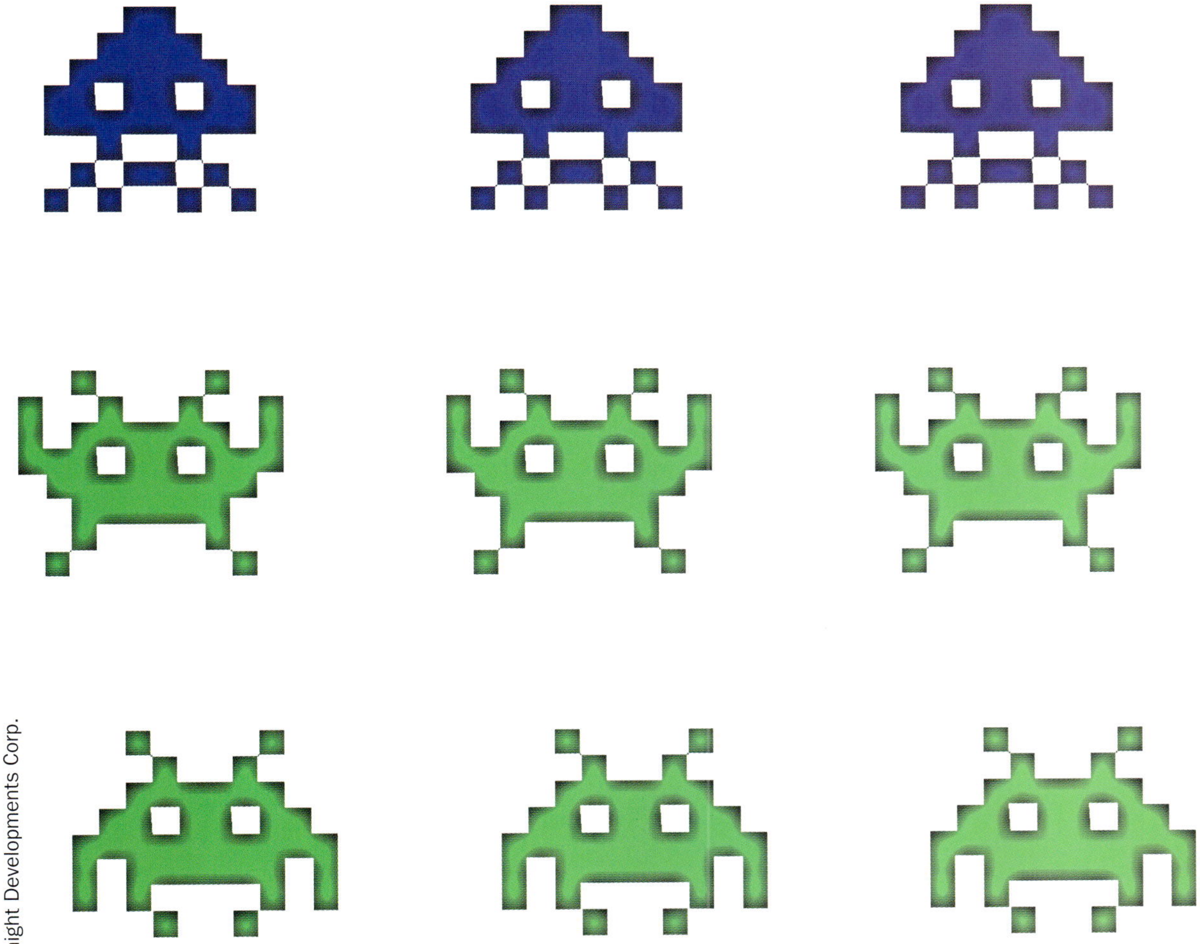

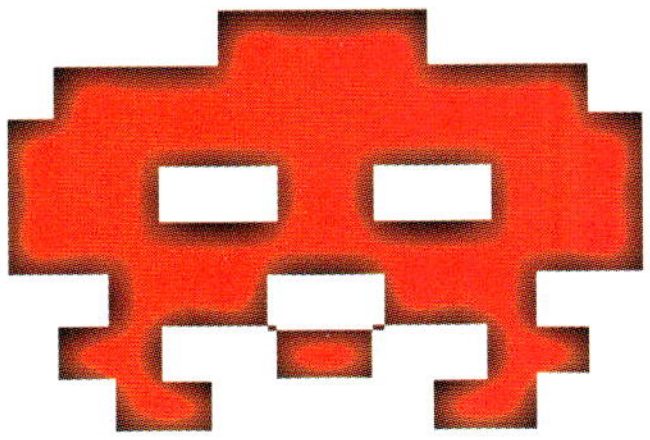

From *Amoeba Invaders*, © 1988 Latenight Developments Corp.

Let's face it, yesterday's attacking monster force doesn't stand a chance against today's!

From *The Fortress of Dr. Radiaki*, ©1994 Merit Software.

Multimedia Games

To a certain extent, video games have always been multimedia. Even *Pong*, the first popular video arcade game, had moving images (very simple ones), sound (beeps), and text (the score display). The quality of all these things got better over the years, but for quite a while it was still all clearly computer dot images and computer-generated noise.

When games with laser disc players in them started appearing, there was a quantum leap forward in visual and sound quality. Unfortunately, with that advance came a leap backwards in how games were played and game complexity. A good example of this was *Dragon's Lair*, which had an endless stream of gorgeous animation by the Don Bluth Studios but to play you simply had to figure out which direction to hit the joystick and when. There was no strategy and no variation from game to game. Then there was the successful Japanese disc game where the game play was nothing more than rock, paper, and scissors. It did well because the on-screen opponent was a pretty woman who shed a piece of clothing each time she lost.

From *Mortal Kombat*, © 1993 Accolade.

While those same games are resurfacing as part of the CD-ROM revolution, there are a new breed of games better designed to take advantage of the new form of computing. The action games don't just play video from the CD, but mix player and computer-controlled items, using both digitized video and standard computer animation. This gives the playability of a traditional game with the richness of new technology.

From *Myst*® 1993 Cyan Inc. and Broderbund Software.

Other games are designed more for thinking than for quick action, allowing the user to enter a mysterious or fantastic world of adventure. Some of these are like interactive movies, where you have to take the hero's role to solve the mystery, rescue the prince, or negotiate the treaty. Others are more of a string of puzzles that must be solved to achieve your ultimate goal.

Multimedia as Art

Multimedia is an art form and an art tool. You can do video, text, and sound in any combination, and with the unique addition of active user involvement, this surely qualifies it as a separate art form. Or, you can have a multimedia-based program allowing you to edit sound or pictures on your computer, giving you expert assistance and power.

Different multimedia artworks take advantage of the art form in different ways. Some are basically works taken from some other form, with multimedia features added. Take, for example, this multimedia adaptation (right) of the comic book *Freex*. It still presents the material as a comic book, but with some minor animation added, as well as dialogue and sound.

In contrast (below) is *Myriam*, an original multimedia work. John W. Ratcliff and Rob Wallace created *John & Rob's Multimedia Kaleidoscope*, a tool which displays computer images with music and a viewer-controllable set of special effects, adding a level of interactivity to any piece of art. John (a computer game designer) put a digitized picture of an old friend (Myriam Levinson) into this display engine and released it on the computer networks. His hope is that someone will recognize Myriam and help him get back in contact with her. (If you have any information on her whereabouts, please drop him a note at his Internet address, 70253.3237@compuserve.com, and tell him we sent you!)

From *CD-ROMIX: Freex #1*, ® 1993 Malibu Comics Entertainment.

Multimedia in Business

Business used to be about objects, real physical things—you bought them, you grew them, you made them, you sold them. If you wanted someone to buy the object—whether it was a chair or a vegetable or a rifle—you simply showed them the object.

This is no longer the case. Today, business is more about information than it is about objects. Product tracking, manufacturing management, sales forecasting, stock indexing, advertising—these are all information efforts, gathering information, making information, growing information, and communicating information.

Communicating information is essential to any information effort, because information is useless if nobody knows about it. Communicating information is at the heart of multimedia.

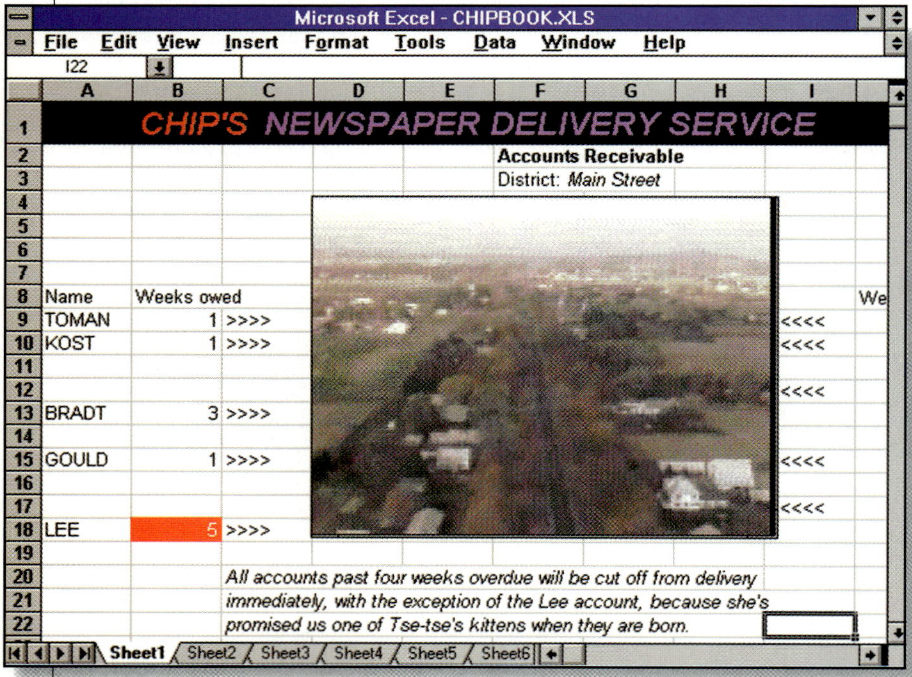

A *Microsoft Excel* spreadsheet. Video image © 1993 Jasmine Inc.

With the addition of object-oriented features to operating systems, you can now add multimedia features to traditional business programs. Spreadsheets, word processors, and databases can include sound, pictures, and video. Of course, sound and video only hold up when that material is presented electronically; there's no way to get an airplane to fly across the page on a printout, or to have a photocopied memo shout, "Get back to work, already!"

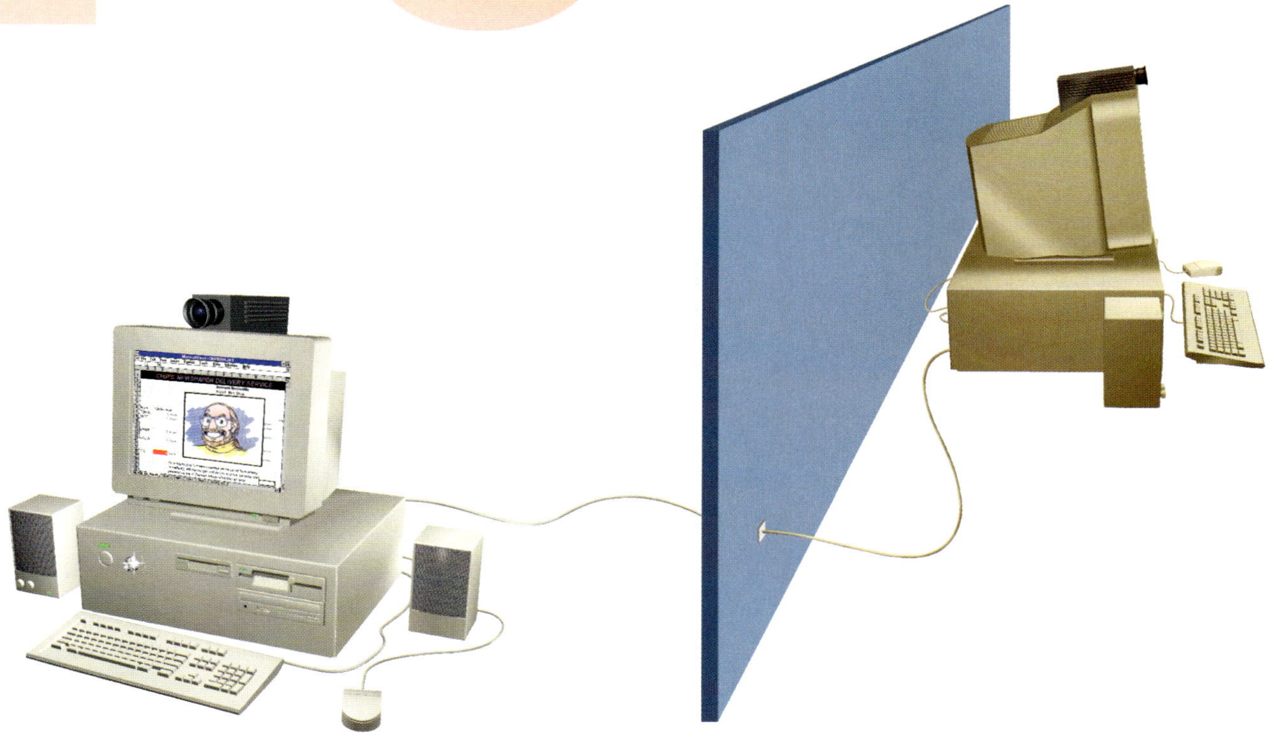

Live video is becoming part of the corporate multimedia scene. Computers with small video cameras on top can communicate via a network or over phone lines, so that two users who are exchanging data can see each other's face in an on-screen window. This allows for quicker and more natural communications than passing typed messages back and forth via fax machines. Of course, it's an open question whether this makes up for the time lost with people straightening their ties and brushing their hair each time they turn on the computer!

Multimedia Advertising

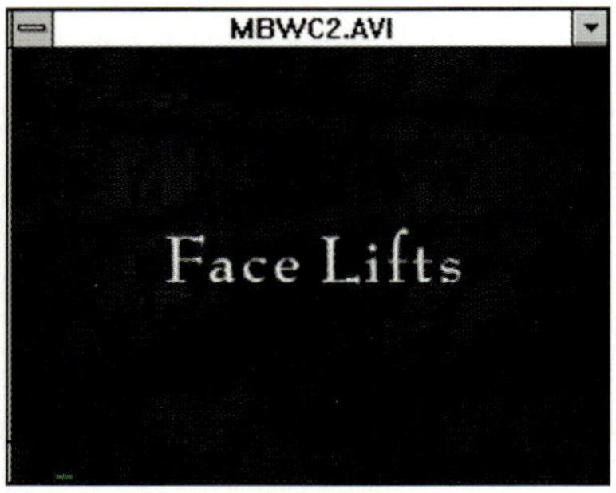

From *Classic Cartoons*, © 1993-1994 CDRP, Inc. and Alpha Video, Inc.

If you are being beaten, please seek out a local shelter or support group. They are there to help.

It seems that one hardly has to invent a new form of communication before it's used for advertising. There are some good reasons for this—advertisers have money to throw around, and they are always looking for any and all possible ways to get their message out. Something new and unusual will automatically attract attention, allowing their message to reach potential consumers.

Multimedia computing's attraction to advertisers is more than a novelty. Rather than flooding the potential customer with too much information (and probably boring him) or giving him too little (and probably failing to interest him), the consumer can be allowed to choose which information he or she wishes to view. In addition, by making the presentation interactive, you are getting the viewer directly involved in the advertisement, and keeping his attention.

A multimedia ad doesn't have to be interactive to be interesting. This public service announcement that Chestnut CD-ROM puts on some of their releases, is no less grabbing on a computer than on television, and it can be easily and cheaply distributed electronically.

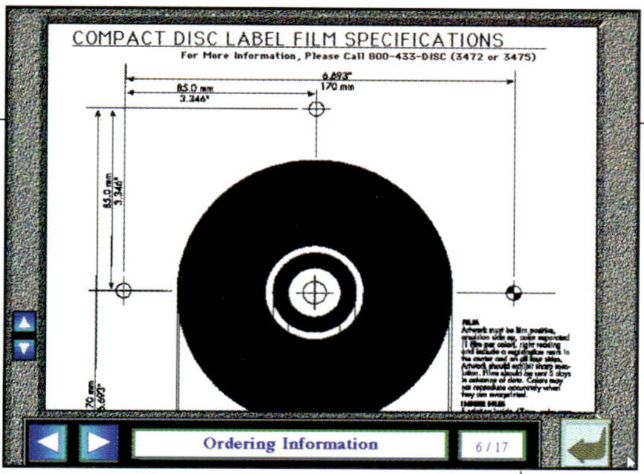

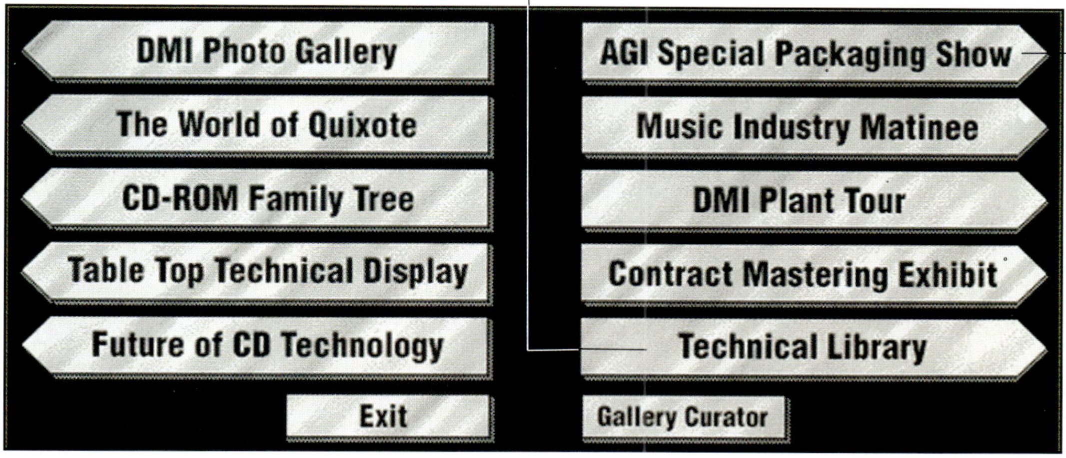

From *DMI Interactive Gallery*, © 1994 The Tuesday Group.

Of course, the computer industry itself is probably the biggest user of multimedia advertising. This CD-ROM from Disc Manufacturing, Inc. has an array of information that you can choose to view, including not only information about DMI and their CD manufacturing and packaging services, but also about how to set up your data for CD-ROM encoding. You even have access to electronic order forms to make ordering their services easier.

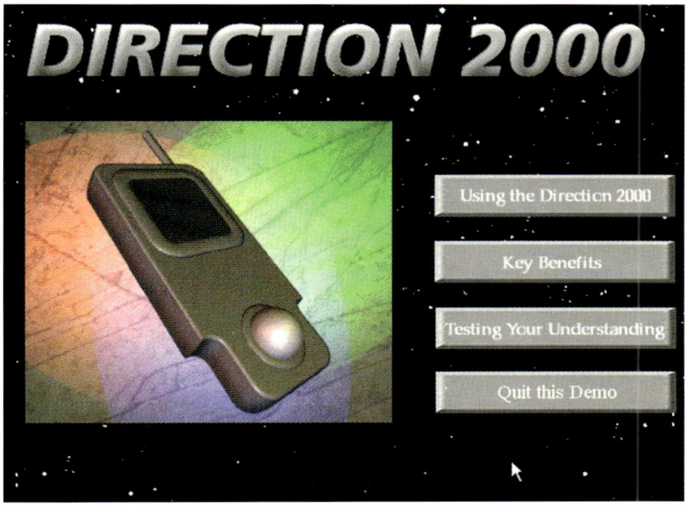

© 1993 MacroMedia, Inc.

Perhaps the product best suited to multimedia advertising is computer software. After all, you can be sure your ad is reaching only those with access to a computer, and you can demonstrate a program's ability directly. This ad for a personal, portable location and direction finder is a fake—it's really an ad for MacroMedia's *Authorware Professional* software, showing an example of the sort of multimedia presentation that you can make with it!

Multimedia Information Distribution

When you're in the software store looking at row upon row of games, tutorials, and home reference programs, it's easy to forget that these represent just a small portion of the CD-ROM market. CDs that house the huge mountain of information it takes to keep businesses rolling make up the larger portion of the market. Technical journals, law libraries, databases, and huge industrial catalogues are now available on CD-ROM, making them cheaper to produce, easier to use, and far easier to store.

Most of these are text-only, while some use still images. That way, they can be used on a wide variety of machines not equipped for multimedia. They're also easier to produce, and many business purposes don't really call for moving pictures and sound.

On the other hand, there are times when those glitzy elements can be useful. One example is the effort that the ABC television network used to promote its miniseries *The Stand*. Based on Stephen King's epic-length novel, and targeted to get epic-scale ratings, ABC wanted it to get plenty of press coverage by giving the entertainment reporters something more interesting and more useful than the usual pile of press releases and glossy photos.

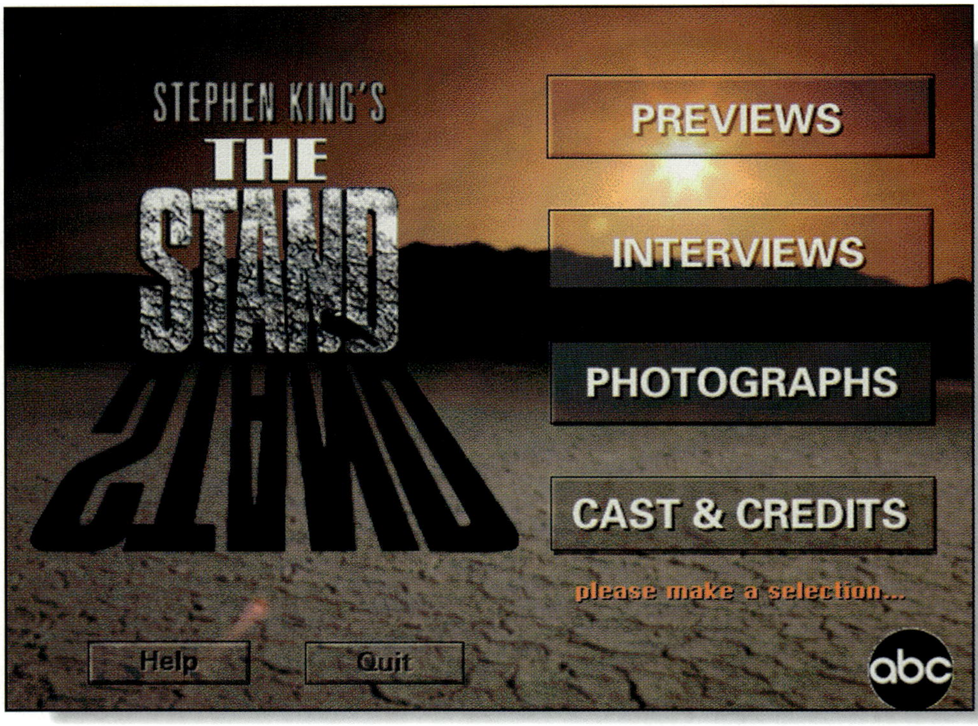

The disc used the **ISO 9660** file format, a method of organizing files so that a variety of different types of computers can read them. Separate control and display software was provided for Macintosh and Windows PCs.

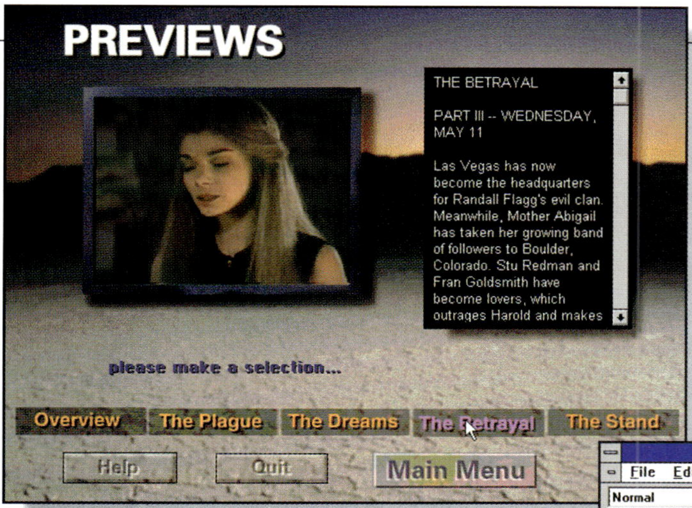

Numerous video clips were included, ranging from several seconds to several minutes each. This half hour of video was not broadcast quality—TV stations needing promotional clips would get a video tape—because it was created simply to give reporters a good feel for the series.

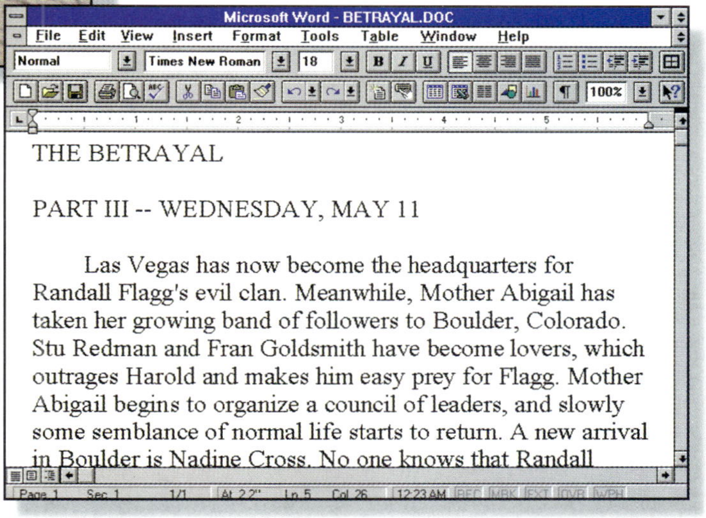

Interviews, credit lists, cast biographies, episode summaries, and other press release information was stored in standard word processor files. That way, it could easily be cut and pasted into a writer's column, or even directly into the newspaper or magazine's page layout program.

Dozens of publicity photos, in full print resolution, were included on the disc. With the electronic paste-up that most newspapers and magazines use these days, digitized photos are easier to use than physical photos, which have to be digitized anyway.

Frequent villain and occasional comic book writer Miguel Ferrer.

Of course, there are some limitations to a promotional attempt like this. This attempt was limited to reporters who had access to CD-ROM multimedia computers—which is presumably most of them, but there are others who could only be reached using a more standard promotions packet. There is always the risk that something could go wrong when using technology. In this case, thanks to the minor incompatibilities from machine to machine, some Windows users found that the multimedia display program froze while displaying certain videos.

Still, it appears that the advantages far outweighed the problems. With the help of this CD, *The Stand* got a plethora of publicity (including some commenting directly on the CD itself, making ABC look like a cutting-edge organization). The miniseries went on to get ratings which utterly devoured the competition during an all-important TV "sweeps week."

A Multimedia Showroom

One of the most difficult things about selling an automobile or other major product is getting someone to come take a look at it. Once you manage to do that, you've got their attention, and can show them all sorts of wonderful things about your product.

But what is a showroom anyway? It's a place where a potential customer can find out what products are available, look at them, get information about them, and find out how much they cost. A multimedia presentation can carry much of the same information, and can be sent to people on disk or even via modem, so they can get the information they want without leaving their homes.

To gain a competitive edge, Ford made a showroom that they can bring to the customer. The *Ford Simulator Showroom*, a disk available by phone order, may not be able to replace all the functions of a real showroom, but it can provide the customer with a lot of information about the product, and is a real attention-getter as well.

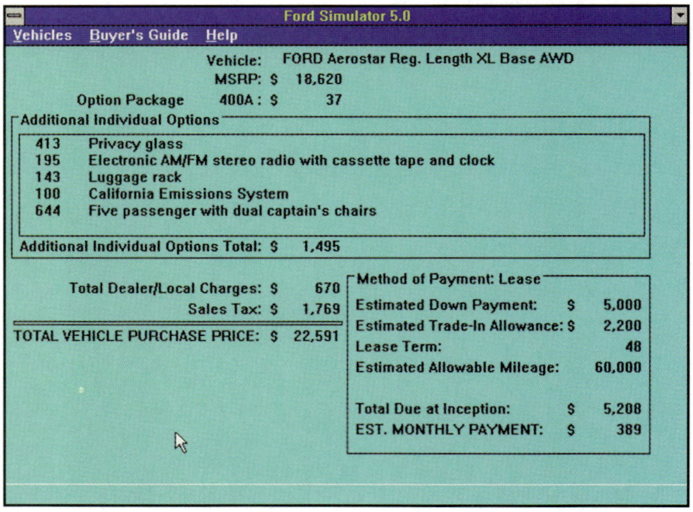

The *Ford Simulator Showroom* lets you view pictures and obtain information on any of the standard Lincoln, Mercury, and Ford cars and light trucks.

The paint job screen lets you see what the car looks like in your choice of the available colors.

There is no way that a simulation can replace the function of an actual test drive, and the simulator doesn't do this. Instead, a driving game features your choice of Ford cars, in an attempt to create a sense of excitement about the product.

At the click of a button, you get all the primary technical specifications of the car you're interested in.

A companion program on a separate disk lets you choose the options that you would want on your car, and see the sticker price, financing, and lease payments.

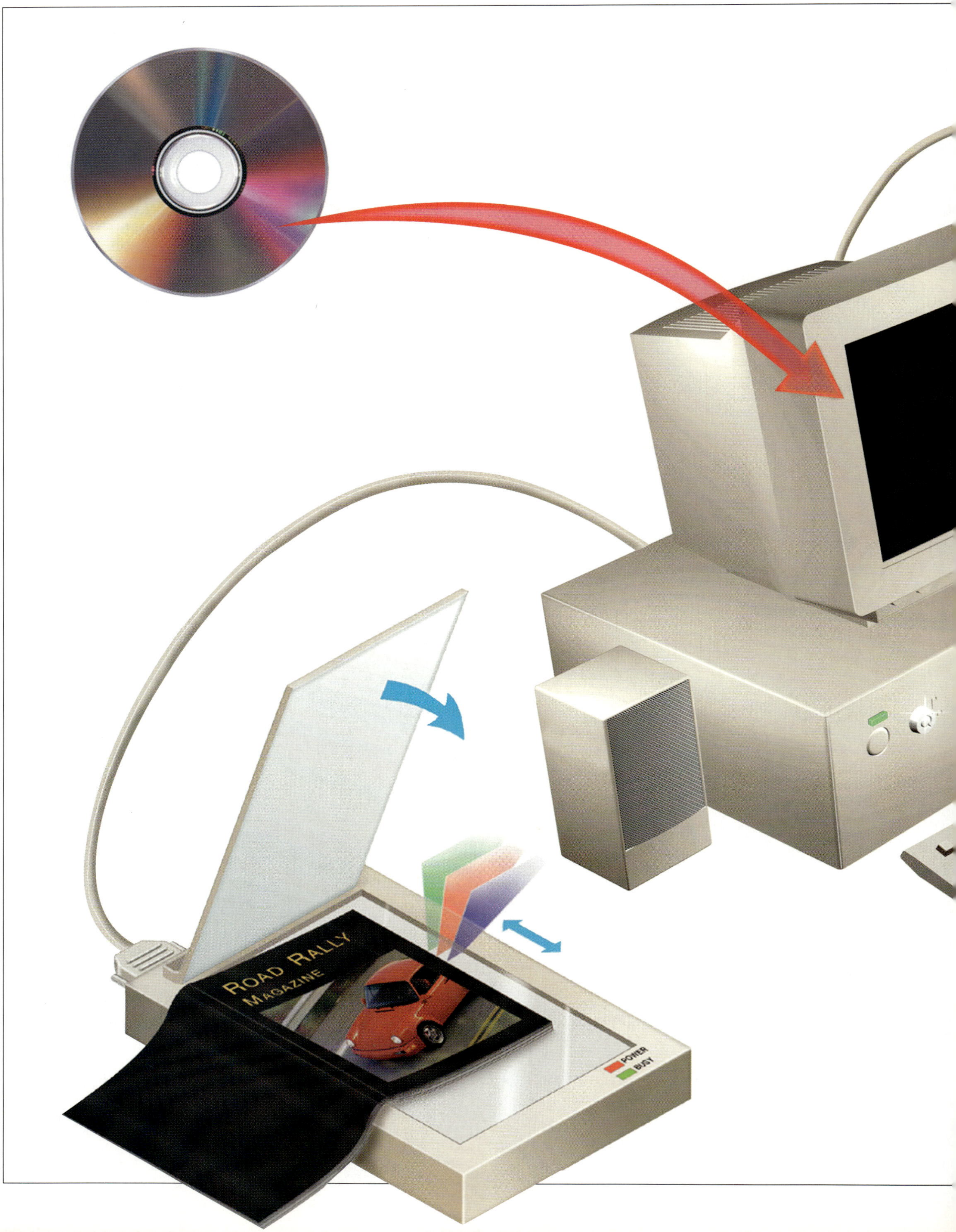
ROAD RALLY
MAGAZINE
POWER
BUSY

Part III

How Multimedia Is Created

Creating Sounds

Two types of sound can be used in your multimedia presentation. You can use sounds generated completely by computers, which is called **synthesizing**, or you can import sound from some outside source (like a recording or a microphone), which is called **digitizing**.

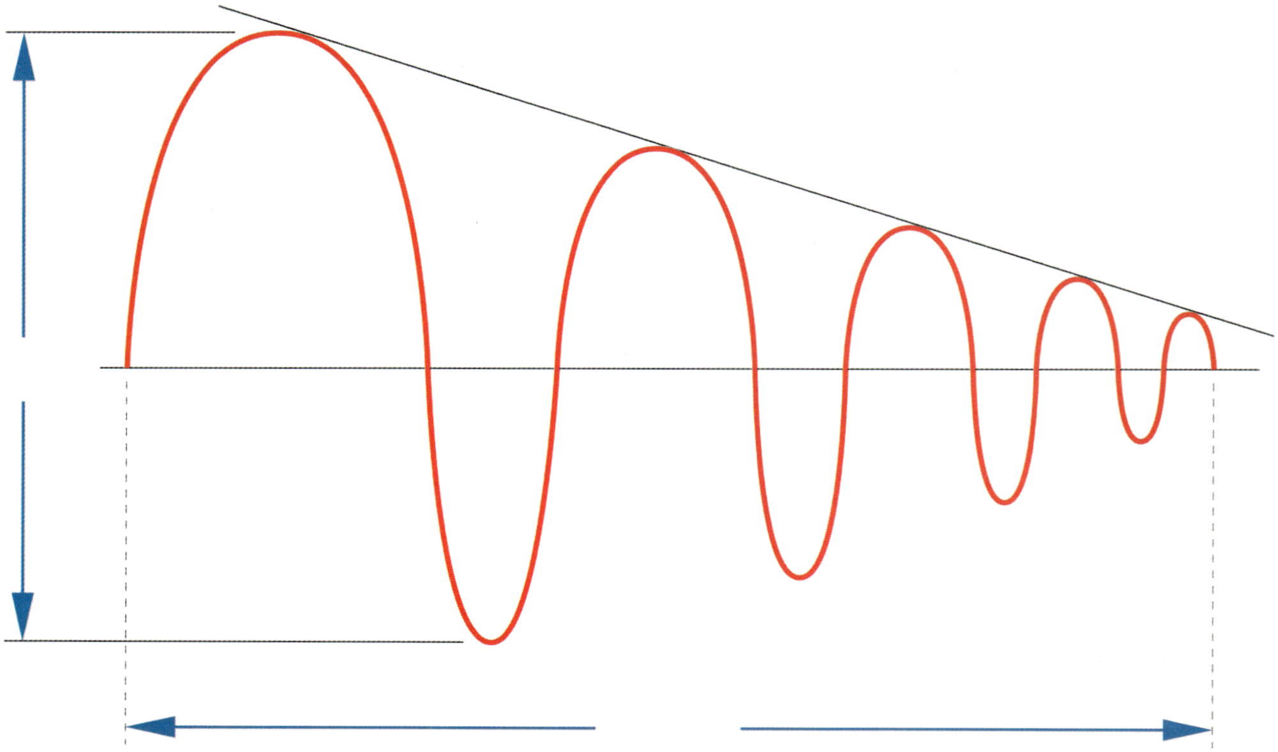

Sound is vibrations that travel through the air to your ear. The shape of the vibration determines the sound. With synthesized sound, the shape of the vibration is described by a mathematical formula which plots out the curve of the sound.

Early personal computers could only make beeping noises, which were synthesized; a beep is a short distinguished noise. Modern computers can support much more complex sound shapes, providing a much wider range of sound. Using a series of curves, even human speech can be synthesized. Still, synthesized sounds have a fake, electronic sound to them because they don't have the nuances and subtle variations of real instruments.

For digitized music, sound is played into a computer. (This is why your sound board has input jacks for a microphone and for other devices like tape decks or CD players.) Thousands of times a second, the computer records the position of the sound wave (this process is called **sampling**).

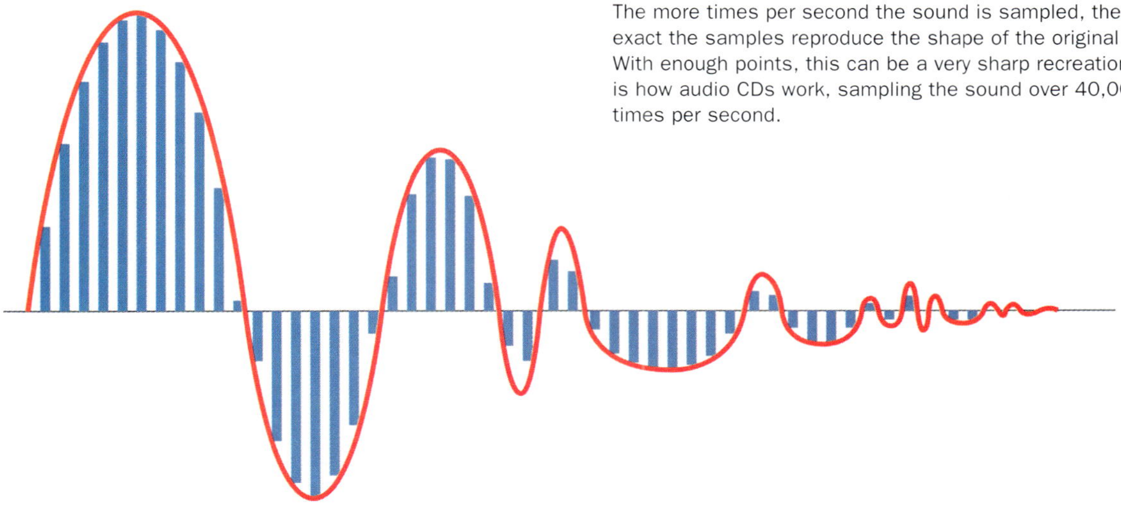

The more times per second the sound is sampled, the more exact the samples reproduce the shape of the original sound. With enough points, this can be a very sharp recreation. This is how audio CDs work, sampling the sound over 40,000 times per second.

Sampled sound can take up a lot of space. For the most part, that's why CDs were invented in the first place—digitized audio of that quality takes up almost 10 megabytes per minute, so a medium needed to be developed that could handle that much space.

There is new software available that allows you to take the digitized music data right off an audio CD. Most set-ups, though, have the CD player play the music and then redigitize it, which decreases the quality of the sound. You also have to be careful when you use sound taken from an outside source rather than that you create yourself because copyright laws exist to protect those who own the reproduction rights to that music. Check to make sure you aren't stepping on anyone's rights.

Sample Editing Software

Once you have a sampled sound (either by sampling it yourself from some source or getting a copy of a previously sampled piece) you can make all sorts of changes. A **sample editor** does for an existing sound sample what a word processor does for an existing letter.

The sound wave is displayed. You can point and select a portion of the sound, or use the magnification control to zoom in on it.

Like a word processor, you can use the editor to cut out and move parts of the sample. If you have a sample of someone saying "I am not a complete idiot," you could find the portion of the sound recording that makes the sound "not" and delete it. You could even insert bits from a recording of him saying "I'd like a cheese sandwich," and end up with "I am a cheese sandwich."

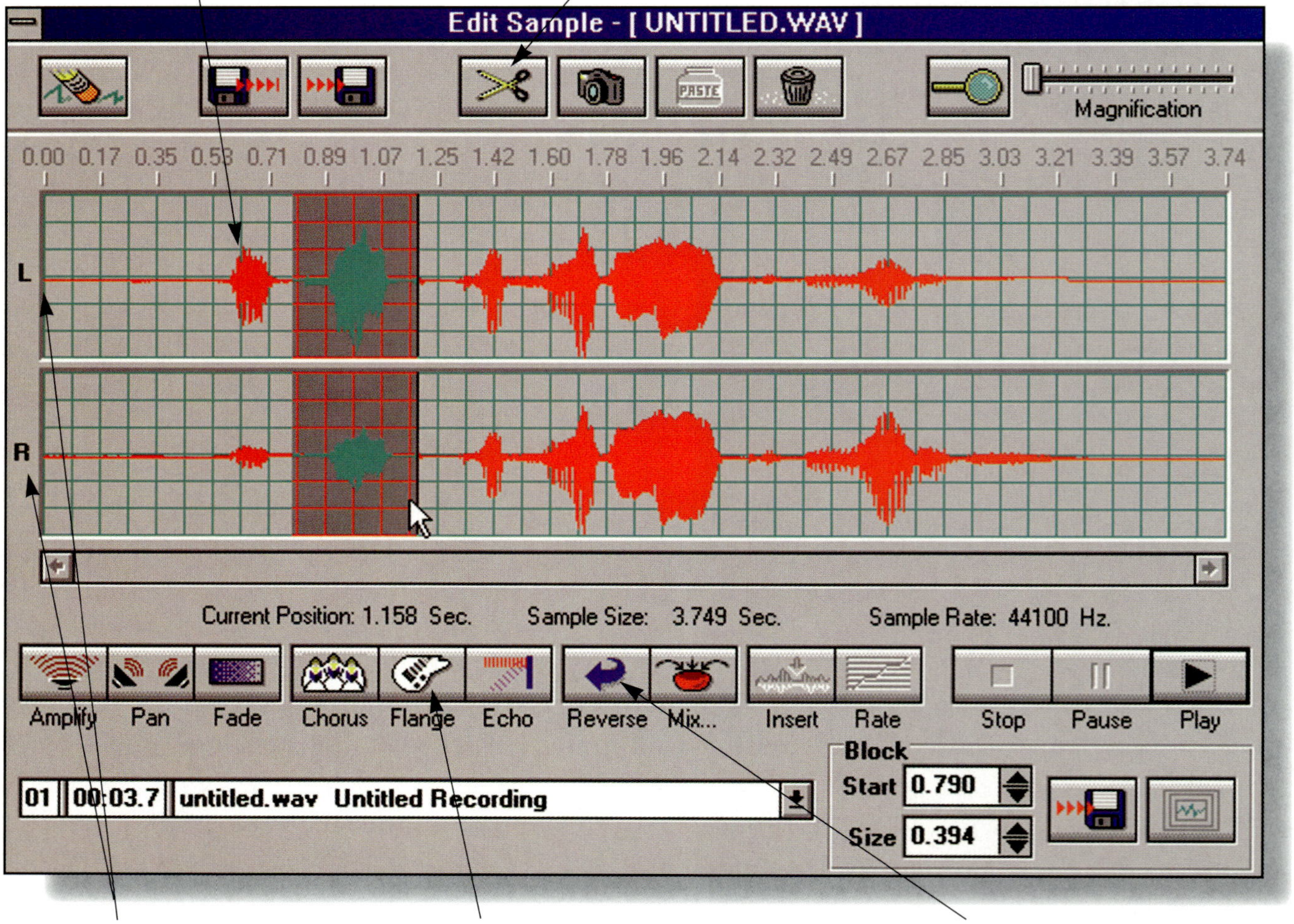

When working on a stereo project, you're really working with two samples: one for the left speaker, the other for the right.

Just as you can make words bold or italic in a word processor, you can augment sampled sounds by making them louder, or softer, or adding a fake echo or a twang. Since the sound is all stored as numbers, these changes are made by performing a series of mathematical calculations with those numbers.

Want to know whether there are really messages hidden backward on your records? Digitize them, reverse them, and find out!

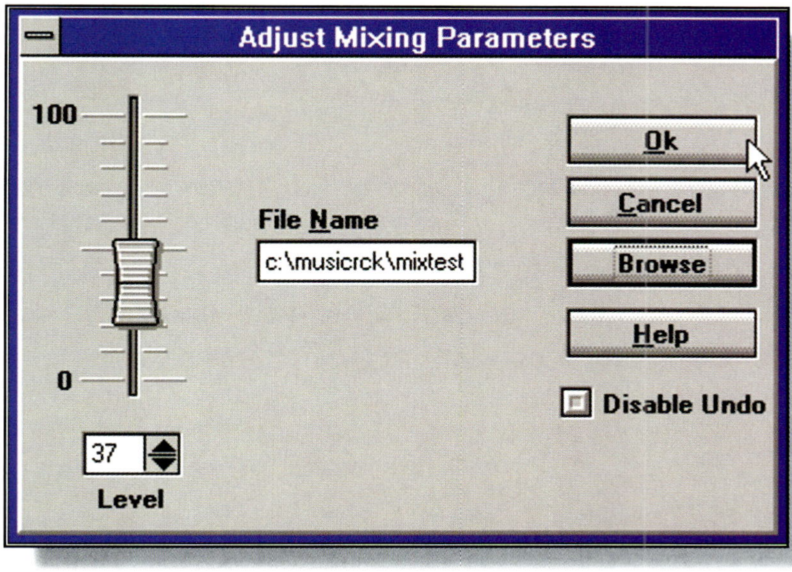

Mixing lets you layer samples on top of each other. When recording a song, musicians often record each instrument separately, and then combine them afterwards. This lets them make separate adjustments of volume and tone on each instrument.

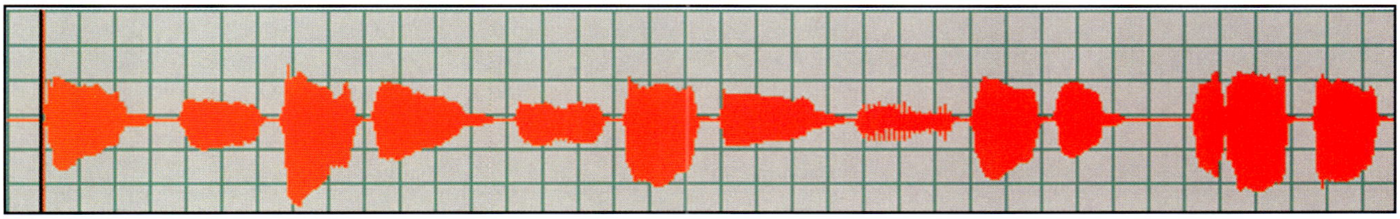

So you could record yourself singing a bit of a song…

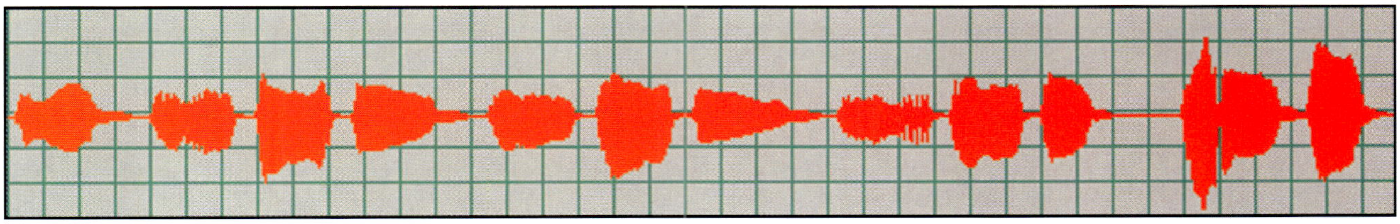

…and then record yourself singing the same song again…

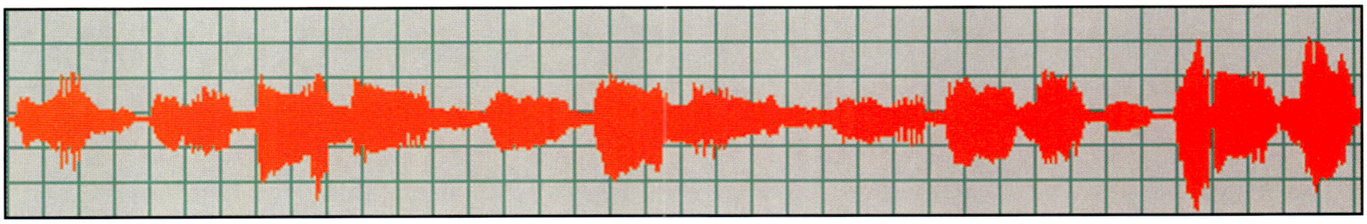

…and then mix them together, so you are singing a duet with yourself!

The standard file format for digitized sound in the MS-DOS and Windows world is known as **Wave**. Wave files (which have the extension .WAV) include data about the sampling rate and resolution in addition to the raw digitized sound data.

MIDI

The **Musical Instrument Digital Interface**, commonly known as **MIDI**, was designed as a standard way for computerized musical instruments and a computer to talk to one another. Using MIDI, a computer could control a whole room full of automated instruments through a musical performance, or a performer could jam on an instrument and have the computer automatically record the sequence of notes, so that it could be re-created at any time.

Now, the MIDI standard is often used for exchanging musical information between various programs and hardware components, all within a single computer. You can use MIDI **sequencers** (software to control MIDI sessions) to compose music on the computer, and the computer will be able to play it, using either synthesized or sampled instruments, or a mix of both. With a sample instrument, only a single note needs to be stored as a sample, and the computer can alter the pitch so that it's any note needed.

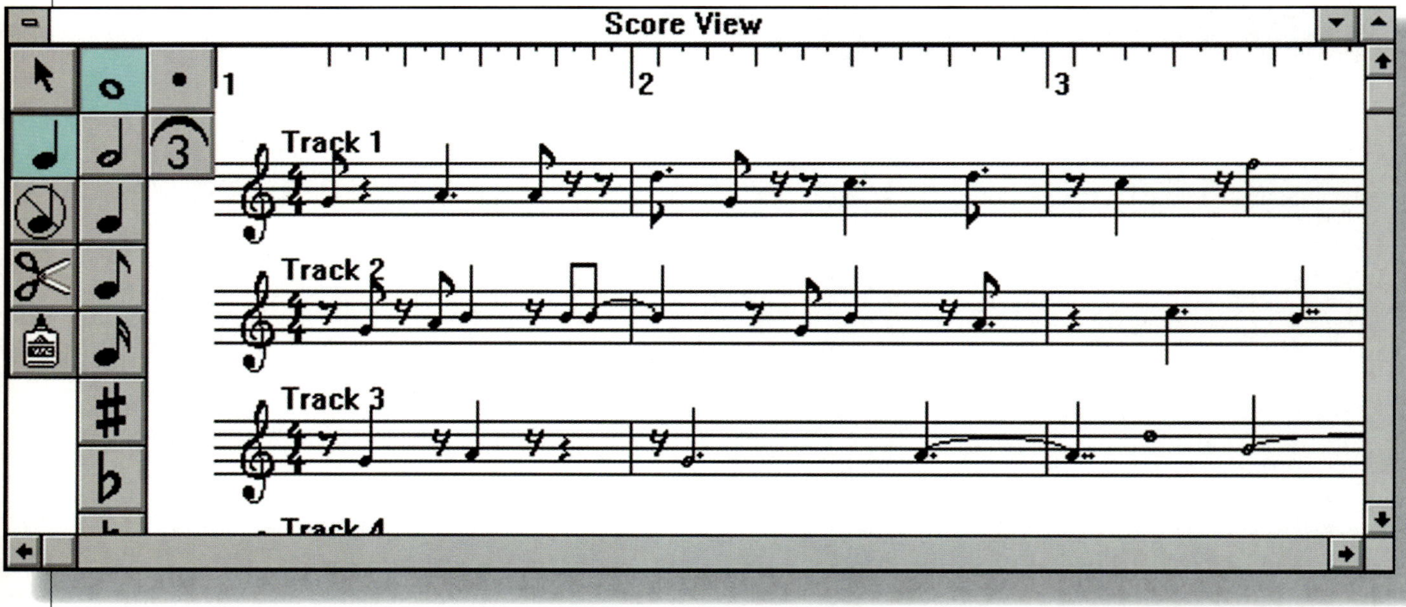

From *Recording Studio*, © 1994 MIDIsoft Corp.

Different MIDI sequencers take different design approaches. The MIDIsoft *Recording Studio* software, for example, lets you edit a musical score…

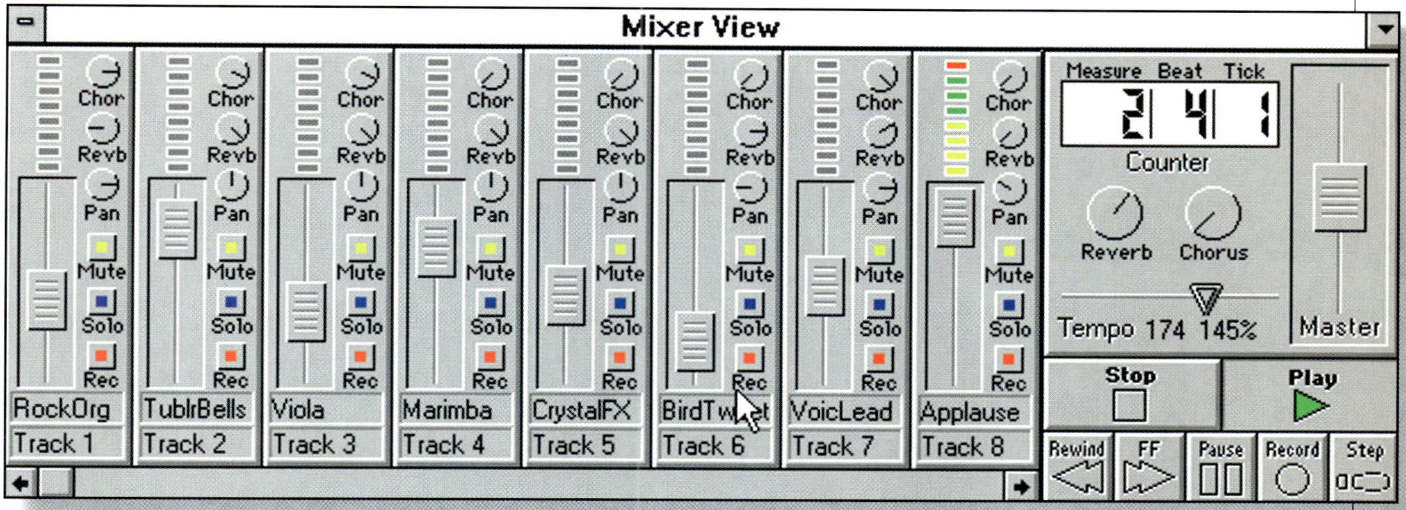

…and mix it with a control panel setting the types of instrument and volume for each track…

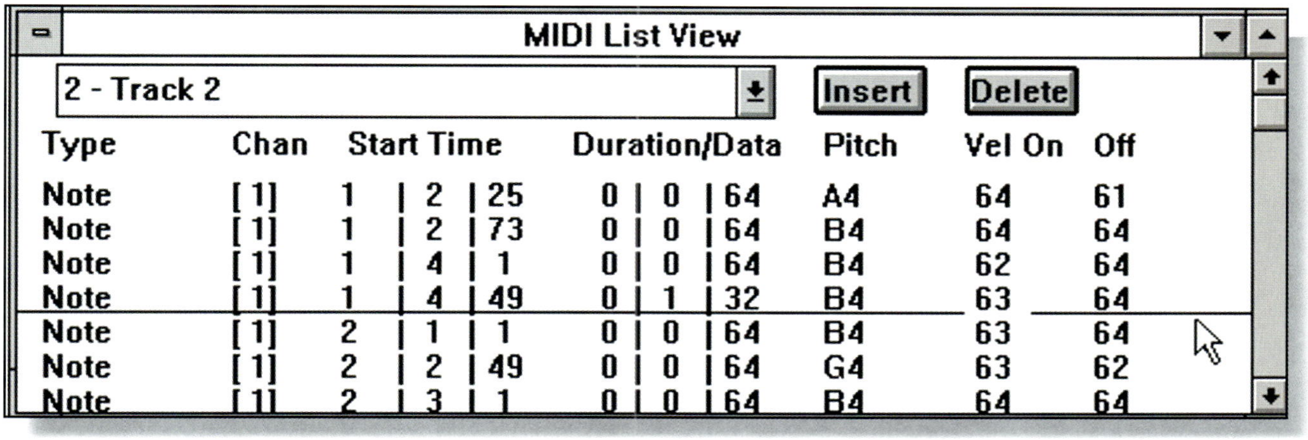

…to convert it into the MIDI commands that will control the MIDI instruments.

Most people don't have musical instruments hooked up to their computer. However, modern sound cards have the ability to create the sounds of many instruments. The lower priced ones synthesize the 128 different instruments that the standard Windows MIDI set-up now expects. Newer, more expensive sound cards have something called **wavetables**, which are stored digitized recordings of all of the instruments. Wavetables sound a lot better.

Compressing Sound

Sound information takes up *a lot* of disk space. Even if you are creating a multimedia application for CD-ROM, you have to keep an eye on how much space your elements take up. A CD-ROM only holds about 70 minutes of top-quality stereo sound, and that's assuming you don't take up room for anything else.

The first trick is to use MIDI scores rather than digitized music wherever possible. A digitized version of the same song will often have more life to it, but the MIDI version takes up a lot less storage room. With MIDI, you're not really storing the whole performance, just the sheet music for it, and that will usually take up less than one hundredth of the disk space.

But if the sounds you need aren't music, or are music but with vocals, then you'll be talking digitized sound. There are three basic factors that set how much space your sounds take up: stereo versus mono, sample resolution, and sample rate.

Audio CDs use 44 kHz, stereo, 16-bit digitized sound. This means that for each of two speakers, it's using roughly 44,000 samples of two bytes apiece every second. Two (speakers) times 44,000 (samples) times two (bytes) equals 176,000 bytes for each second's worth of data, or roughly 10 megabytes per minute. That's a lot of data.

Usually, you won't need stereo. Switching to mono recording cuts the data in half.

To cut the data in half again, you could either cut the resolution from 16 bit to 8 bit, or cut the rate in half. Generally, you get a better sound quality keeping the resolution high and cutting the rate, but if you're aiming for an audience with 8-bit sound boards, you'll want to go with the low resolution and higher rate. If you cut all the way down to 8-bit, 11-kHz mono sound, you still have usable sound in 1/16th the space of full CD quality sound.

Other methods of compressing sound are being developed, but they are not as pervasive as picture and video compression.

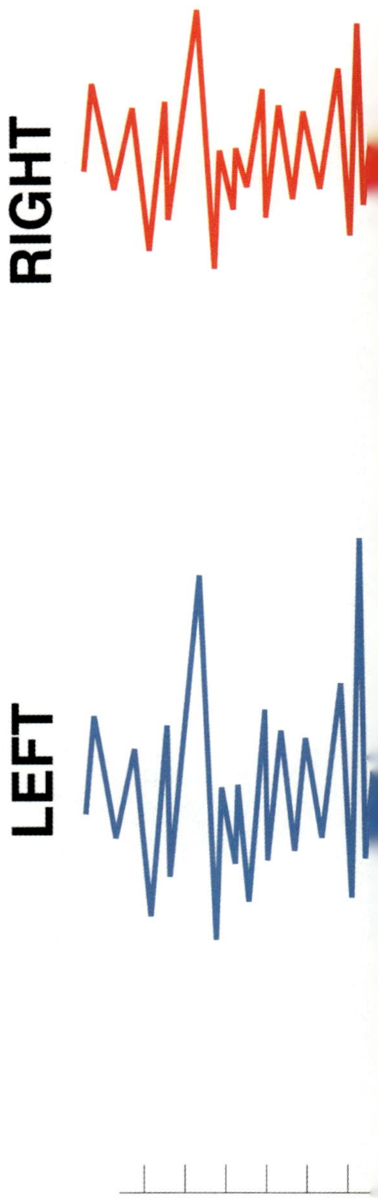

Stereo versus mono—When you record in stereo, you are taking two samples, one for each speaker. As such, stereo recording takes twice the disk space of a mono recording.

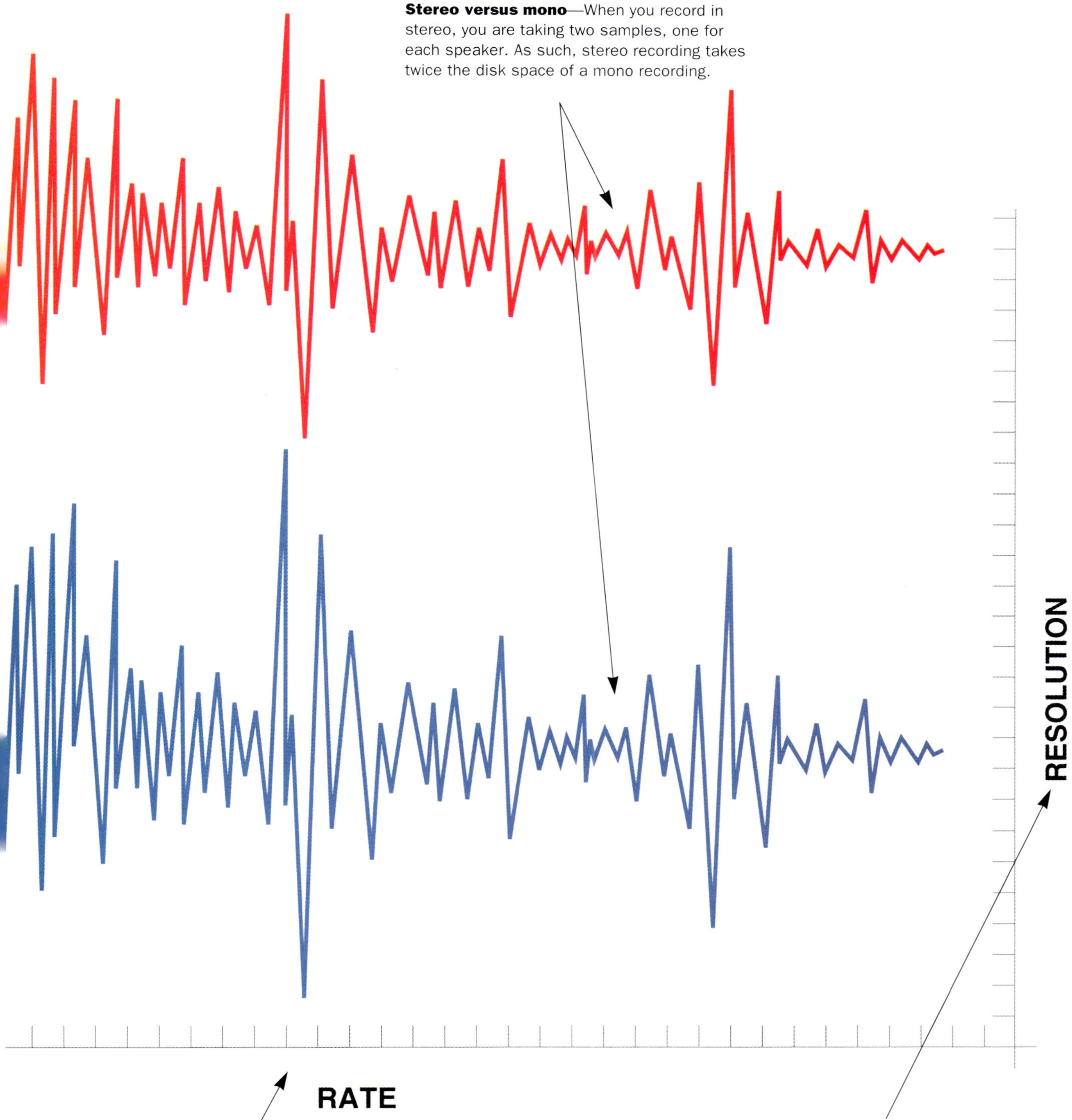

Sample rate—Today's computers and software generally sample the sound at a maximum of approximately 44,000 times per second (also known as 44 **kilohertz**, abbreviated kHz). Common rates used also include half that (22 kHz) and half again (11 kHz).

Sample resolution—You can use 8 bits (one byte) of data to describe each moment of the sample, or 16 bits (two bytes). Because 8 bits allows for only 256 possible values, and 16 bits allows for 65,536 values, the latter gives a much more precise rendering of the sound. However, many multimedia users have sound boards that can only reproduce sound at the 8-bit resolution.

Creating Images

Photographs, drawings, and other non-moving images are often undervalued in multimedia. They aren't as flashy as their moving image counterparts, nor as astonishing as fancy sound effects. When it comes to conveying information, however, still pictures are great, because they invite you to sit there and look at them for a long while until you absorb everything they have, whereas a moving image or a sound is quickly gone.

From *Best of MediaClips 2.0*, © 1991-1994 Aris Multimedia Entertainment, Inc. Photograph by Aris Entertainment.

© 1991-1994 Aris Multimedia Entertainment, Inc. Photograph by MediaMix.

© 1991-1994 Aris Multimedia Entertainment, Inc. Photograph by Aris Entertainment.

© 1991-1994 Aris Multimedia Entertainment, Inc. Photograph by Aris Entertainment.

A still image also takes up less disk space than a moving image, and requires less of the computer's processing power to display it. There are many computers out there without the processor power or advanced graphics capabilities necessary to show a video clip, but can display a still image without any problem.

From *Time: Man Of the Year*, © 1993 Time Inc. and Compact Publishing.

Images also can be used in many ways on a computer screen. Icons are simply images used to quickly display a complex concept, and including icons in your project can make it more user-friendly. Using a backdrop behind a menu or text screen can add a sense of richness to the project (although you do want to make sure that the image is presented in a way that does not distract from what you really want the user to be looking at).

Images from Outside

The easiest way to get images on the computer is to let someone else do the work for you. **Clip art disks** are filled with all sorts of general purpose and specialty images, so that if you find you need a picture of a car, just copy it off the disk. Of course, you're limited to the images that they offer, and in some cases there may be a **royalty** (cash payment) involved in using it.

The world is full of beautiful things but unfortunately, most of them are not on your computer for inclusion in your multimedia work. That "fully equipped multimedia computer" of yours may well be fully equipped to display other people's finished works, but to get your own photographs or hand-drawn artwork onto your computer, you're probably going to need more hardware.

If your needs are small, you may be able to rent the equipment or, in the case of a scanner, find a service bureau that will scan in your images for you. Upscale photocopy shops often provide scanner access.

Once you get the image on your computer, you are just beginning. Using the same programs you would use to create original art, you still can edit the pictures—changing colors, erasing portions, combining parts of various photographs, and so on.

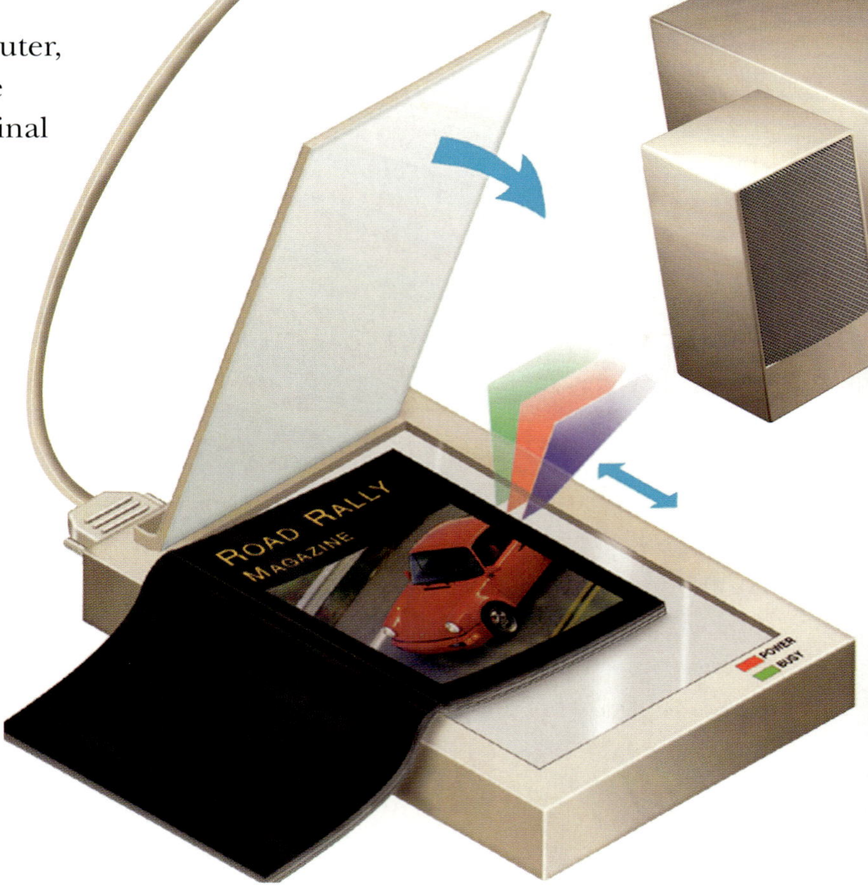

If the image that you want to use is on paper—either as a photograph or an original drawing—you need a **scanner**. These devices bounce light off of the page and convert the reflected information into a grid of values that the computer uses to represent the picture. Hand-held scanners and black and white models are available, but for quality work you'll need a flatbed color scanner. These are available in a range of sophistication and price.

Frame grabbers are the most common way of capturing original images in computer form. They allow you to connect your computer to any standard video source and store a single frame from that source. You can hook one up to a video camera and grab a frame of whatever the camera is aimed at, or you hook it up to your VCR and grab a frame of anything that you have stored on tape.

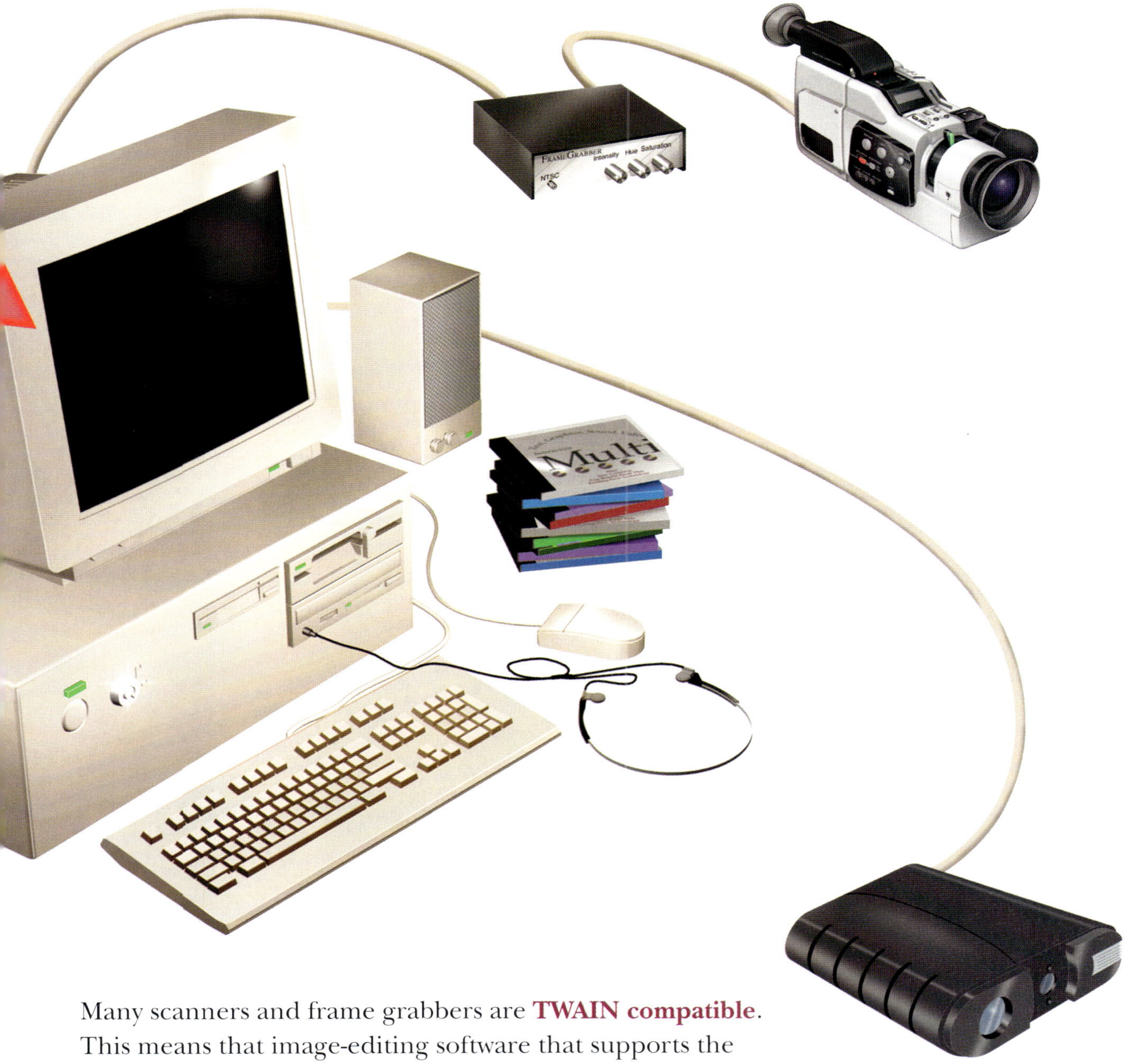

Many scanners and frame grabbers are **TWAIN compatible**. This means that image-editing software that supports the TWAIN standard can accept images directly from the device, saving you from having to load one program to get the image, save the image to a file, and then load a different program to edit it.

Painting and Editing

As wonderful as the real world is, it doesn't include every artistic image you might need. At times you will need to create original images or alter images that you get from elsewhere. For this, you want a **paint program**, which treats the computer screen as a canvas, and gives your computer the equivalent of brushes and other tools to create or change that image. Using a paint program, you can change each **pixel** (the dots that make up the screen image) one at a time or in huge moves that change the entire screen.

Paint programs come in a wide variety of prices and powers. A basic one, with the standard set of minimum functions, comes free with Windows.

The various art tools are easily accessed through icons.

The text tool lets you type words and numbers onto your picture.

The paintbrush lets you paint lines, while the roller fills up large areas instantly.

You can pick your "brush" thickness, so you can paint a single pixel at a time or fill in whole bunches of pixels at once.

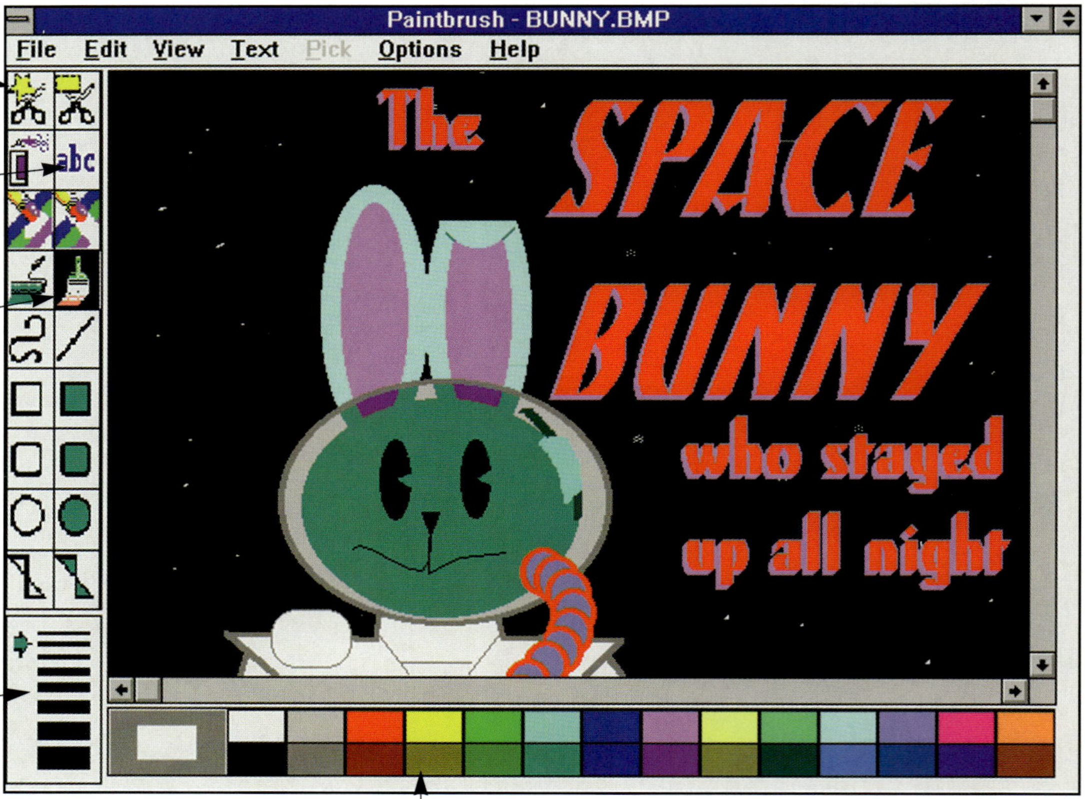

From *Paintbrush*, © 1993 Microsoft.

Paintbrush lets you work on images with millions of colors. The on-screen palette only lets you use a few of those to paint with at any one time, but you can change the palette to get other colors.

For advanced work, particularly for photo-retouching, you want an advanced painting program, like *Photoshop*, which is designed to handle rich use of colors and complex details of photographs. However, these programs are often more attuned to creating finished work for printed publications rather than for the screen. Since a single square inch on a printed page often has as many dots as an entire computer screen, the program has to be able to handle images many times the size of the screen. Because of this, the programs have controls and procedures that handle oversized images very well, but are more complex and difficult than what you need to edit images for the computer screen.

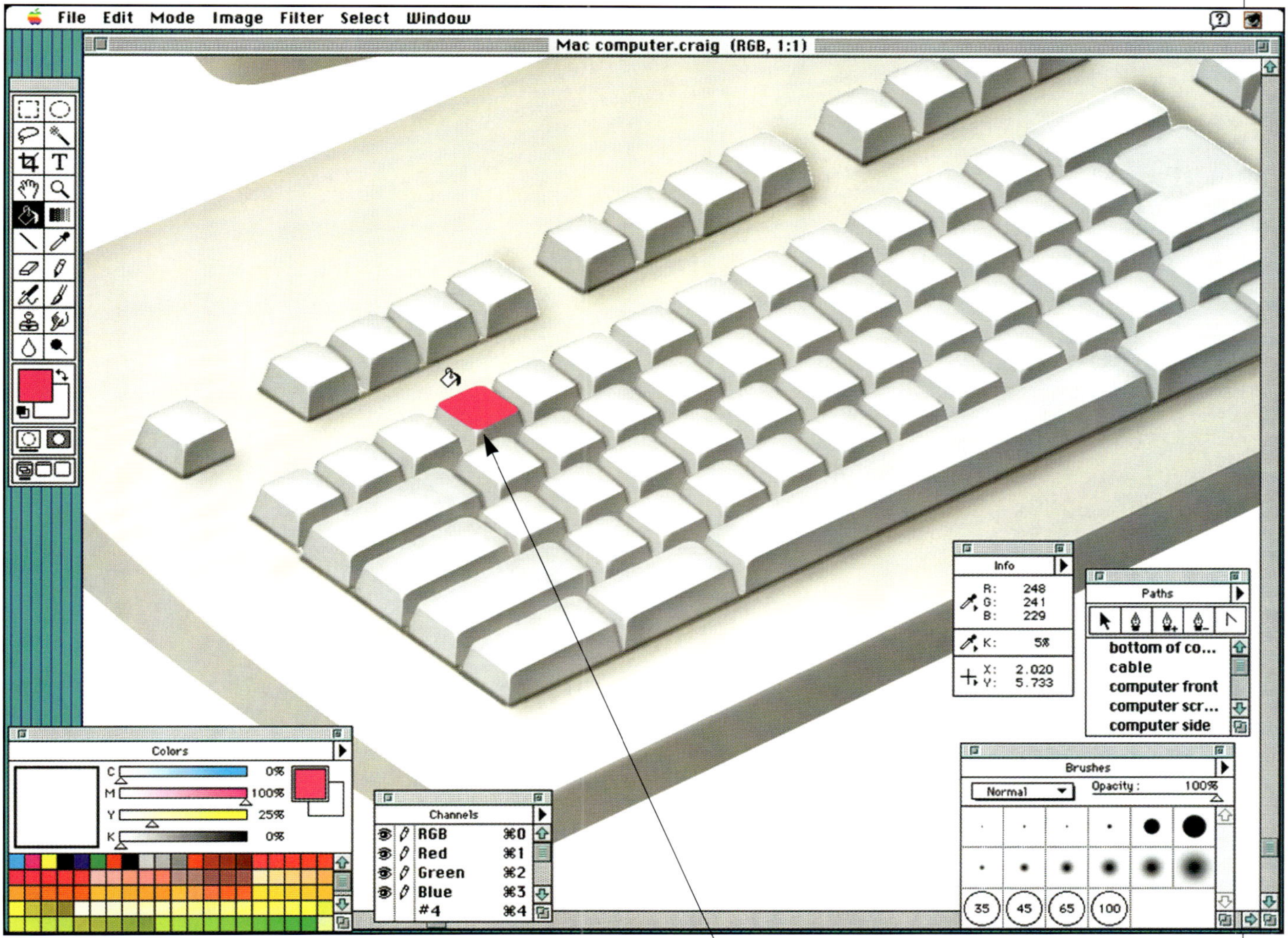

Advanced area-filling tools make creating areas of fading or changing color easy.

Faking Reality

Photographs are handy when you want a realistic image of something. Drawings are handy when you want an unrealistic image of something that may exist (like space) or may not exist (like space bunnies). But what can you do if you want a realistic picture of something that doesn't exist?

That's easy: you build it. Only you don't build it in the real world (that's far too much work). You build it in an imaginary world—inside the mind of the computer.

3-D modeling is the craft of designing 3-D objects within the computer. Once designed, the computer is able to render images of those objects very precisely, sometimes with a photographic sense of reality.

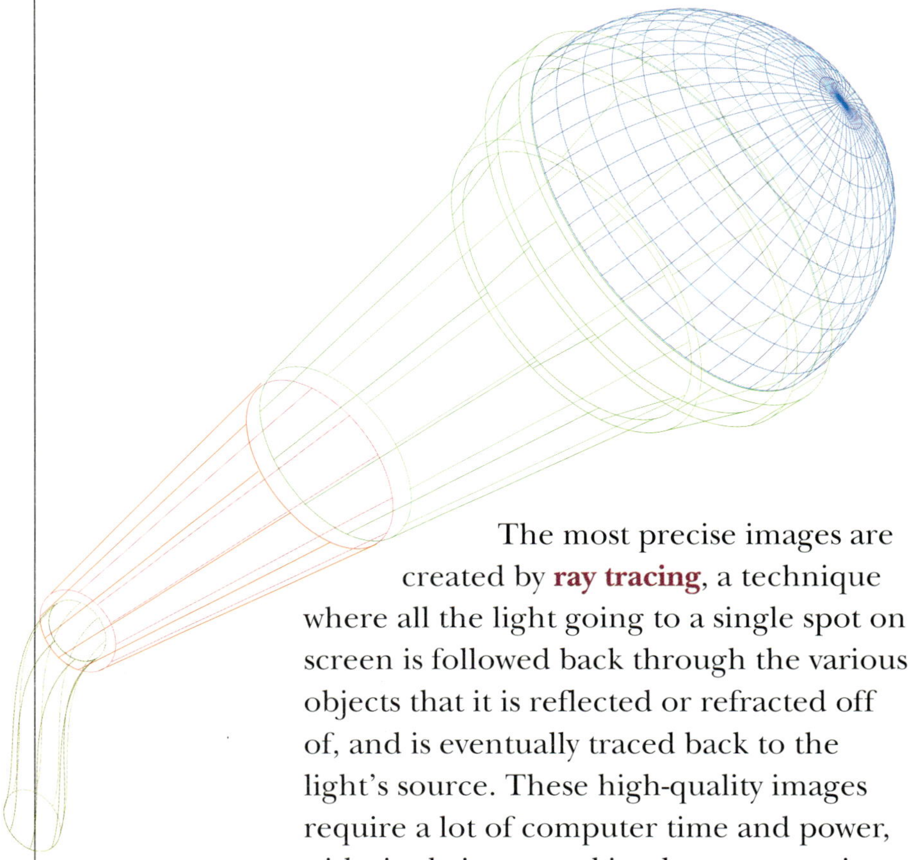

The designer builds the objects out of a set of **primitives**: simple shapes (squares, spheres, cones) that can then be altered and combined to build more complex objects. Generally, the shapes are manipulated as a **wireframe**, an outline of the object which can be viewed from different angles. The various pieces of the object are then given individual features—surfaces, colors, degrees of transparency, degrees of reflectivity—which define what the object looks like beyond the shape.

The most precise images are created by **ray tracing**, a technique where all the light going to a single spot on screen is followed back through the various objects that it is reflected or refracted off of, and is eventually traced back to the light's source. These high-quality images require a lot of computer time and power, with single images taking hours, sometimes days, to render. Other, less processing-intensive methods are constantly being improved.

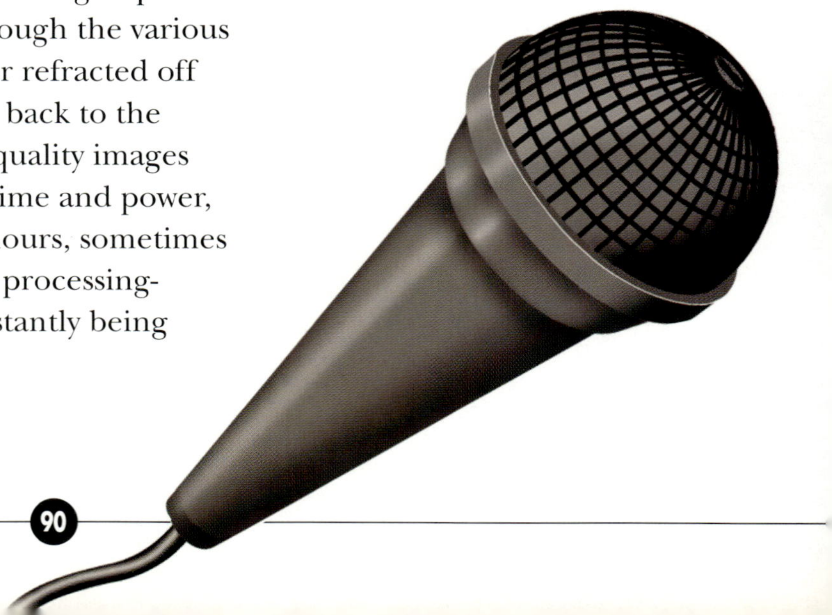

The light bulb is a light source. The computer figures how well lit any object is based on the distance from that light and if anything is blocking the light source. Of course, the light source itself doesn't need to be visible to be shining light on what we see.

From *Myst*, © 1993 Cyan Inc. and Broderbund Software.

The wood grain appearance of the shelf is an example of **texture mapping**, a technique where the surface of an object is defined by having a pattern, not as being a given color.

From *Myst*, © 1993 Cyan Inc. and Broderbund Software.

Because the object has been defined in three dimensions, you're not limited to rendering it from only one angle. The computer can position the point of view for looking at the object, just like a real photographer can move around an object and shoot it from different positions and angles.

Compressing Images

Pictures take up space (if they didn't, this book would sure be a lot shorter). A single pixel in 16 million color mode (also known as 24-bit color) takes up three bytes of data. Without any compression, a picture that is 640 pixels wide by 480 pixels high would take up 640 × 480 × three bytes, or 921,600 bytes of data. You couldn't fit two of those almost-a-megabyte pictures onto a single floppy disk. Even if you are producing for CD-ROM, which could hold about 700 such pictures, you would have to worry about the time that it takes to load it from the disc—a single-speed CD-ROM would take about six seconds to load that picture. Six seconds may be a small time in the overall scheme of the day, but when you're waiting for a computer to do something, it feels like forever.

Luckily, many systems for storing a picture will compress it at least somewhat. Most file formats include compression that notes when the same color is used for multiple adjacent pixels, and it stores the count of the number of pixels of that color rather than storing the value of that color repeatedly.

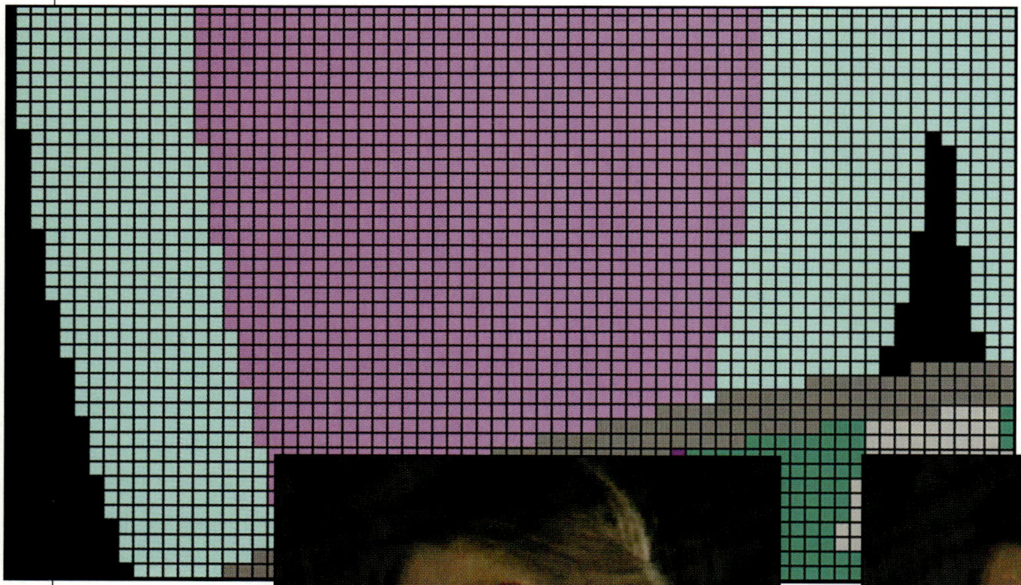

The top row of this enlarged section of a picture would be stored as one pixel of black, 12 of cyan, 27 of violet, 12 of cyan instead of as black, cyan, cyan, cyan, cyan, cyan, cyan, cyan, cyan, cyan, cyan, cyan, cyan, violet, violet... As you can see, the compressed version is more efficient. The computer stores a number that represents each color, rather than the color name.

A slight blockiness of color that is visible close up in 16-bit mode...

From *The Stand* promotional CD. © 1994 ABC/Capital Cities

...becomes blatant and stiff when reduced to 8-bit mode.

For most projects, you won't need the 24-bit color mode. Most video cards can't even support that much. Most photographs will look just as good to the naked eye in 16-bit mode (65,536 possible colors) and most computer art in 8-bit mode (only 256 colors). By using fewer bits for each pixel, you cut one or two thirds off your file size.

Another path toward smaller files is smaller pictures. That may sound obvious, but by putting a border area 50 pixels wide around your shot, the picture size is cut by a third. You may be able to use a lower resolution screen mode, where the screen is made up of only half as many pixels, and you can fill the screen with half as much data. Again, though, the pictures don't look as sharp.

Photographs don't tend to have a lot of repeated colors in them, so they don't compress well using those methods. The Joint Photographic Experts Group has developed the **JPEG** file compression scheme that keeps photographs looking sharp in much less space. JPEG-compressed files (usually stored with the .JPG extension) actually have less information than the original photographs, because the compression actually loses some of the detail you want. However, you can choose how much compression you want on a scale from 1 (maximum compression, most detail lost) to 100.

At a compression rate of 75, you still have a very clear, usable image...

...and even as far down as five, the image is still recognizable (although not something you'd want to impress anyone with)...

...but woe to anyone who expects to bring their image down to one. You get a very small file, but also a very useless picture.

Creating Video

Video—genuine moving pictures of real things—is the headline attraction in the world of multimedia. Oh, you can have pictures and sounds doing all sorts of wonderful things, but when you can see Bogart kissing Bacall, or the Cubs losing a game, or the flagella of a paramecium waving about wildly, then you know that you have multimedia. Anything less is just computing.

Video also is the bane of multimedia's existence—it's difficult to master and expensive to produce. Video eats up the most powerful machines available and quickly spits them back out again. It gobbles up processor cycles like they were M&M's, and it looks upon disk space just like a school of piranha looks upon a cow attempting to cross a river.

Today's cutting edge systems can do just about anything you may want with sound and still images, but they are barely up to the task of displaying extremely crude video. The days of affordable video perfection will come, but for now, you must be content to watch the technology bloom.

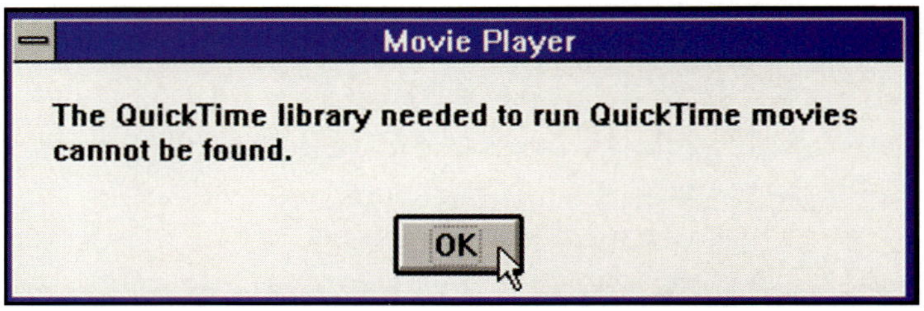

If there are any incompatibilities between how your system works and how the video routines expect your system to work, no matter how small, it will find them.

Just how much data does this involve? A full screen picture, in 24-bit color mode, takes up about a megabyte. Standard television uses 30 full screens every second (although TV, unlike most computer video, uses two passes to make up each picture, putting odd numbered lines up with one pass, even ones with the next). To match that smoothness, you would need to pass 30 megabytes of video data through the system every second. Even a double-speed CD-ROM drive can only put out *one one-hundredth* of that much data per second. Even if it could put out the full 30 megabytes per second, an entire CD-ROM would store only a little more than 20 seconds of video.

The magic of video is the same as that of film: Show a series of still pictures (or **frames**) quickly enough, and they produce the illusion of motion.

If the machine can't keep up with the massive amounts of data needed to display this series, it might slow the video down…

…or skip frames…

…or try to reproduce it much smaller than desired—shattering the illusion.

Capturing Video

The video information coming out of the tape deck is **analog video**. It hasn't been broken down into a series of numbers, and is just a wave signal indicating which of an infinite number of colors make up the point on the screen currently being described.

Odds are you won't be recording video directly onto your computer—there are too many things that can go wrong with computer video capture, and besides, your computer is too heavy to lug around. You want to use a good video tape camera, using the best video format that you can (both Hi-8 and S-VHS have greater picture quality than VHS). But if you're creating small-frame, limited resolution pictures, don't worry about getting the best professional equipment because you lose most of the detail anyway.

There are high-end professional video tape decks that are excellent for this sort of work, but on a simple project you can get adequate results with one of the better consumer-grade video decks. If you want to do complex video mixing (overlaying of pictures, quick-cut editing), or your goal is to use your computer to edit video for tape or broadcast, you need a professional editing deck, as well as other professional video equipment.

There are many powerful video editing software packages available for the Macintosh and a fair number for the PC. It's important to find one that not only lets you do what you want, but also matches your own level of understanding of how video works, because some of these packages are designed with full-time video pros in mind.

If you're dealing with high-resolution video, you will need a really good hard disk. You'll need a big disk, measured in gigabytes (thousands of millions of bytes, rather than the hundreds of millions of most hard disks), and it will have to be very fast to keep up with the data that keeps pouring out. You can get hard disks designed especially for the video market. They aren't only large and fast, but they also minimize the interruptions that hard disks need for their own internal workings—interruptions that can disrupt a steady stream of data.

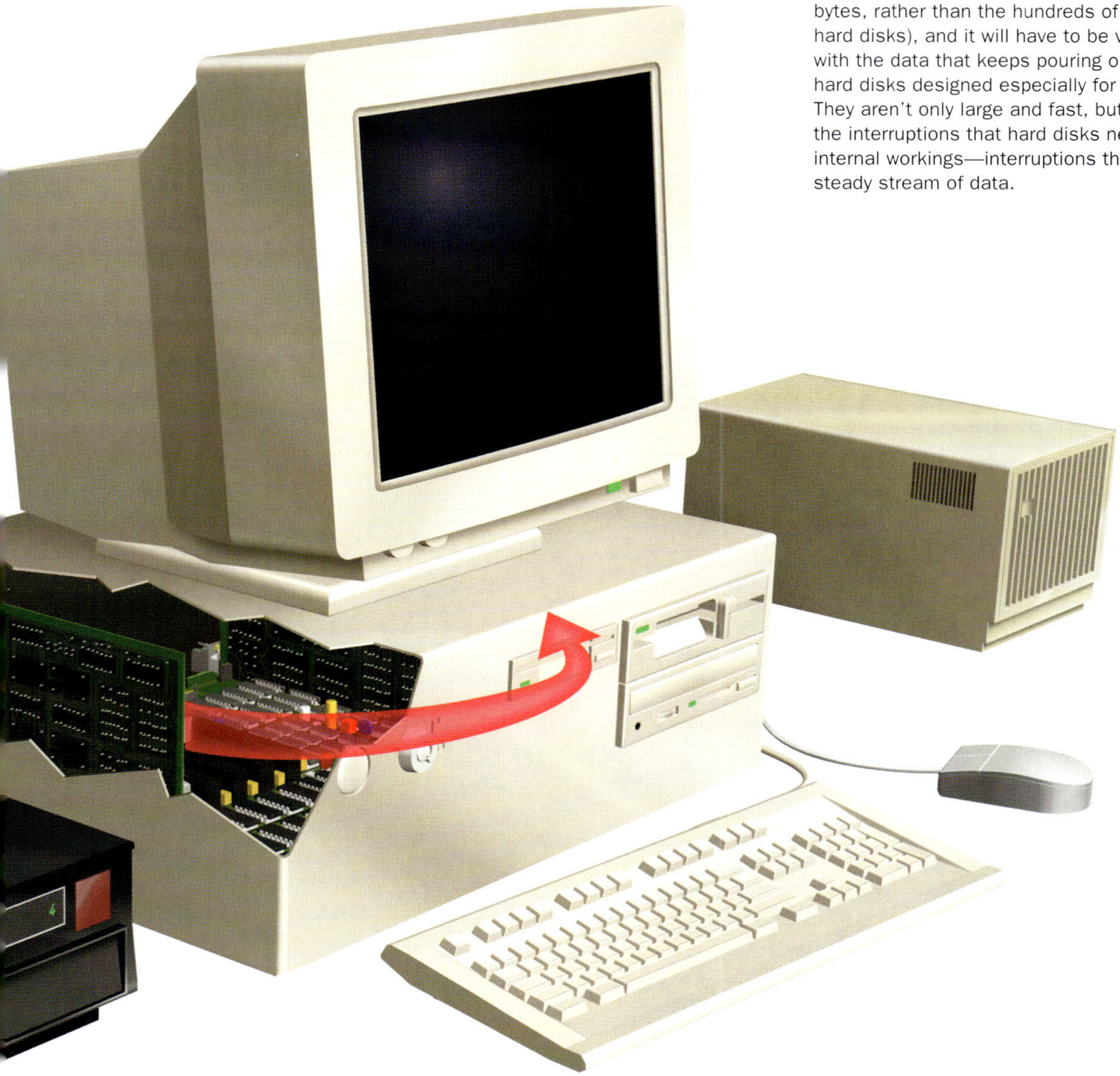

e **video capture board** is the heart of the process. This board takes the incoming alog data, translates it into a grid of pixels with numerically described colors (**digital deo**), and compresses it. Boards that put out very small videos (about 1/16th of standard screen size) at very slow rates (15 frames per second) and with a smaller range of lors start at a little more than $200. Boards that can put out full-speed, full-screen, 4-bit color video cost thousands of dollars.

ie better-quality boards put out each frame as a still picture compressed using the PEG compression scheme described in Chapter 11, "Creating Images." With a moving cture, it's harder to notice the data loss than with a still picture.

Reducing Video Data

There are a number of tricks that will let you reduce the amount of disk space your videos use, and tell you how much power your computer will need to play them smoothly. The first choice for many is to simply reduce the number of frames per second. This makes for a jerkier video, but 15 frames per second is generally good enough if you don't need perfectly smooth motion. Often, you'll find that you can use fewer frames and still meet your needs.

You also can reduce the resolution of the video. By giving this video a big frame, the active video area is actually less than a quarter of the pixels of the full screen, and takes much less data.

From *Movie Select*. © 1993 Medior Incorporated. Scene from the movie *Patriot Games* © 1993 Paramount Pictures.

From *QuickTime Movie Player*, © 1992 Apple Inc.

Apple's QuickTime video player software, popular on both the Macintosh and Windows computers, is just one example of a video driver that lets you play video clips bigger on screen than the actual dimensions of the stored video. Each pixel is effectively multiplied, resulting in a filled screen but a blocky and fuzzy image. Although it does save disk space, it requires so much processor effort to expand all of those pixels that on systems without a special video accelerator, the computer just can't keep up.

Another popular option is to reduce the picture's **screen depth**—the number of bits of color information being stored for each pixel. Many systems (even ones promoted as multimedia systems) can't support the 24-bit, 16.7 million color modes, and have a maximum of either 16-bit, 65,536 color modes or 8-bit, 256 color modes. With those systems, the extra stored colors would just be wasted anyway.

Eight-bit color is reasonably good, although it appears grainy and some patterns appear to superimpose themselves over a screen.

Four-bit, 16-color video is a bit much, unless you *want* it to look abstract. There's also a tendency for colors to jump and flash in odd ways, making it hard to watch.

Using your eight bits for blacks, whites, and grays instead of color can give you a very sharp, classy-looking image. It's not as flashy as color, but it also doesn't have that grainy appearance.

Four bits of gray is usable for some applications and easier on the eyes than 4-bit color, but it's fairly crude.

Compressing Video Data

So you've decided on the width, height, frame rate, and depth of color of the video, but you still want to make it smaller. That's when video compression comes into play. There are a number of different **codecs**—compression/decompression systems—that can severely reduce the amount of disk space that a video requires. These codecs reduce the precision of detail in a picture, but try to minimize degradation of the video quality while maximizing reduction of the video data.

Some codecs try to find elements that are repeated in multiple frames, saving space by describing them only once. Others try to redescribe the picture as a set of natural-seeming curves called **fractals**.

Motion JPEG, the most popular codec for video editing work, compresses each frame using the JPEG technique described in Chapter 11, "Creating Images." However, it doesn't attempt to save space by not repeating elements frame-to-frame. Motion JPEG is considered **symmetrical** because it takes the same amount of time to compress a frame as it does to decompress.

Every few frames, one frame is considered a major frame. About two major frames per second are considered **I-frames**. MPEG simply stores the whole I-frame as a JPEG-compressed still.

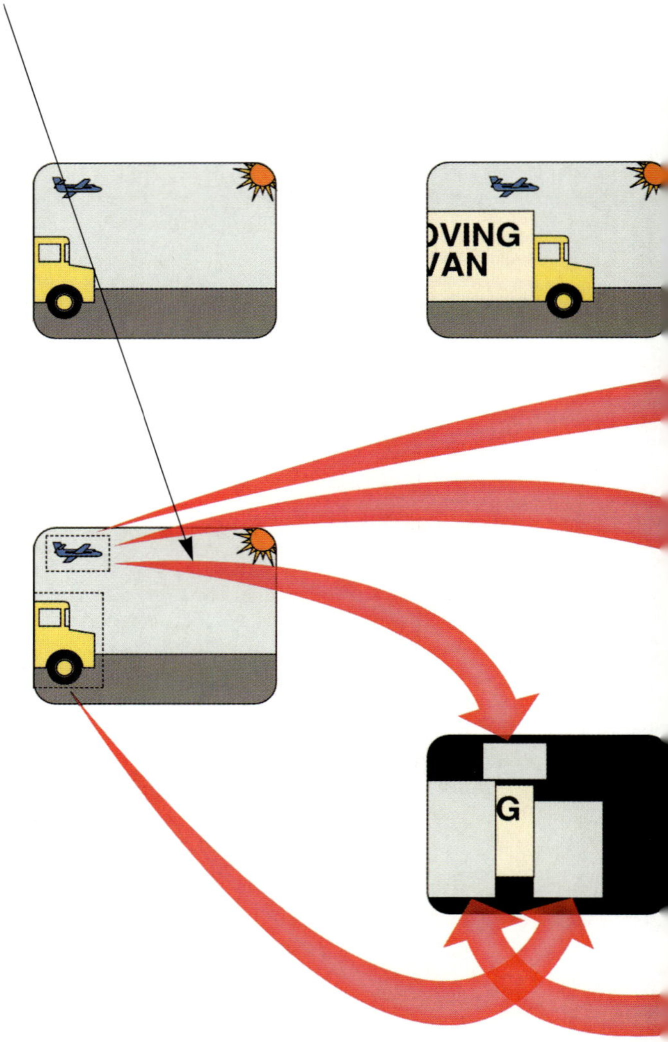

While some codecs can both compress and decompress on a standard multimedia computer, others need very expensive equipment. Most companies hire service bureaus to handle the compression. Some codecs require special hardware for the decompression. While that limits the potential audience for the videos to people who have that hardware, these codecs are the most powerful, making much smaller files with better looking pictures than their all-software cousins. The king of the hardware-dependent codecs is **MPEG**, created by the Motion Picture Experts Group.

The big future for MPEG appears to be in television. Satellite and cable systems will be using MPEG to fit more channels in the same bandwidth. Test systems are already in place to allow you to order an MPEG-encoded movie and have the data sent to a special cable box, allowing you to watch anything you want.

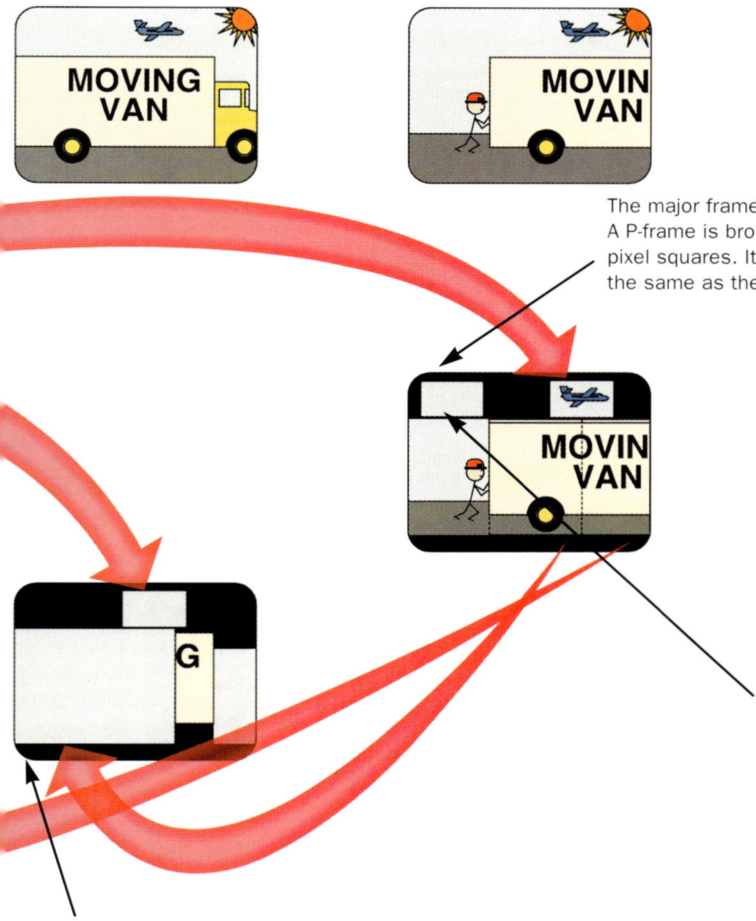

The major frames between I-frames are **P-frames**. A P-frame is broken down into a grid of 8-by-8 pixel squares. It doesn't store the pieces that are the same as the previous major frame.

When the system finds a group of four grid squares (called a **metablock**) that matches *different* pieces of the previous major frame (because an object or the camera moved), it just stores an indicator saying which block from the old frame is in the same position. This way, for the P-frame they only have to store the information for the blocks that are completely new.

The other minor frames are called **B-frames**. B-frames are broken down into a grid, like P-frames. Any grid piece that matches *either* the preceding or the following major frame isn't stored. Any metablock that matches a section of either major frame is stored to indicate where the metablock is from.

Creating Animation

Animation comes from the Latin word meaning *bring to life*, and that is just what animation does for a multimedia project.

When you hear the word animation, most people think of cartoons in which Mickey Mouse and Superman are given life through a rapid sequence of still drawings. Animation, however, refers to any illusion of motion. In computer terms, this includes the following:

- A pointer flying across the page
- A company logo plummeting down from above
- A lone space bunny fending off an entire armada in a computer game

From *Classic Cartoons*, © 1993-1994 CDRP Inc. and Alpha Video Inc.

Understanding the basics of traditional cartoon animation helps you understand computer animation. The characters moving along in a scene are on **cels**, paintings on a clear material. A series of cels are made of the character in different positions.

From *Classic Cartoons*, © 1993-1994 CDRP Inc. and Alpha Video Inc.

The unmoving parts (such as the grass and trees) of the scene are on a single background painting. Each clear cel is put on top of the background and photographed, so that the character on the clear cel appears to be interacting with the background.

By putting one cel at a time on top of the backgrounds and photographing a single frame for each cel, you can create a series of pictures that, when played back rapidly, make it appear as if the character is walking across the background. Separating the picture's moving parts from its stationary parts means the entire background doesn't have to be redrawn for every frame. Even the cels can be reused against a different background.

Sheep image from *Classic Cartoons*, © 1993-1994 CDRP Inc. and Alpha Video Inc. Background image from *Best of MediaClips 2.0*, © 1991-1994 Aris Multimedia Entertainment, Inc. Photograph by David K. Brunn.

You can include animation in your multimedia presentation by doing it the old-fashioned way, which includes photographing all the painted cels and backgrounds and bringing them into your computer as video. This has been done in games like *Space Ace* and in packages such as the *Classic Cartoon* collection featured in these figures. These days, however, even Disney is replacing some of the traditional animation steps with computer processing. If you're putting together a computer presentation, you should be doing the same.

Traditional and Character Animation

Some computer animation is created like traditional animation. Backgrounds are drawn and moving elements are drawn separately as a series of small pictures. The small pictures are then superimposed on the background to create the animated effect.

By taking a series of characters designed to look like rotating letters and moving them across a black background, a fancy moving-sign display becomes animated.

There are two basic ways of storing this type of animation:

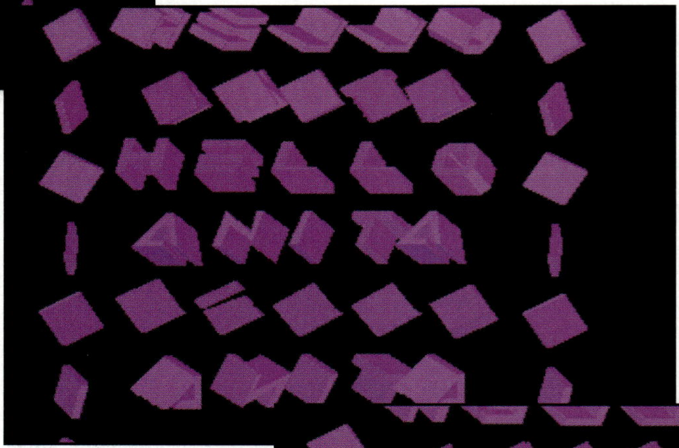

1. Stamp the moving elements onto the background when you create the animation, storing the animation as a series of still drawings.
2. Store the background once, and store each of the moving elements as a small series of pictures with information about the path that it takes when it moves across the screen.

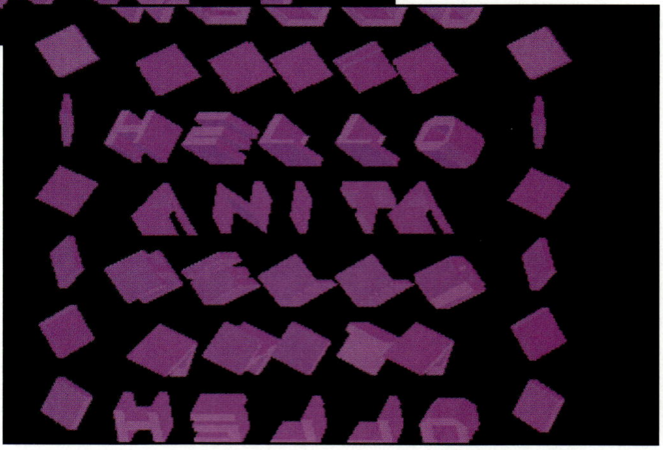

Before you select your storage, you must consider various factors. You first have to select the tools you want to use to create and display these animations (few animation programs support both). You also have to consider the graphics power of the machine on which you intend to show the animation. If you have a lot of moving elements on the screen at the same time, it may be hard for your computer to keep up.

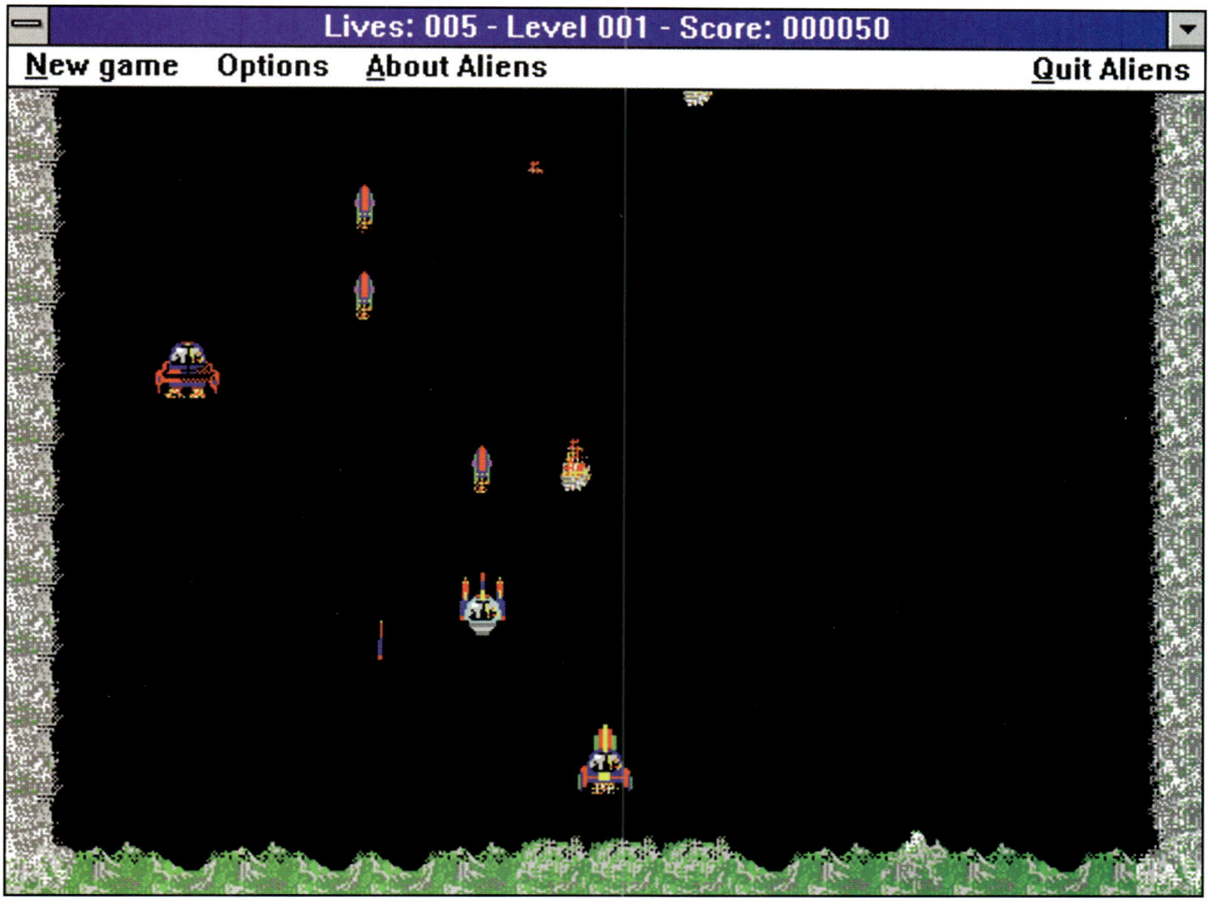

From *Aliens: The Game* by Marc Tebeka

When the user will control how the elements move, it's imperative that the background and moving elements are stored separately. After all, an arcade game is nothing but a bunch of predesigned characters moving over a background in response to user control.

Some computers and most game systems use animation built around a **sprite**, which is a single, small, moving graphic. A sprite may be animated within itself, but it doesn't have to be. It could just be a still picture that moves against the background. In a game, your spaceship might be one sprite, your missiles another sprite, and each enemy spacecraft is one sprite.

With built-in **collision detection**, the computer hardware detects when the paths of two sprites have crossed (for example, when your missile has hit the enemy spacecraft). The hardware can be set by the software to let the missile sprite cross on top of the enemy craft sprite, pass beneath it, or contact the program to let it know that the ship has been hit.

Modeled Animation

Just as you can create images of an unreal world using 3-D modeling, you also can bring such a world to life using 3-D animation. In defining a world, the initial setup is the same as it is for still images. Instead of picking a camera angle, you pick a camera path. You also have to define how the objects move. If you have a robot walking across the room, you must define not only what path he takes, but also such things as how his arms and legs move in relation to the rest of his body and how his head turns and his eyes blink.

Clearly, this is a painstaking effort that involves a lot of details that must be perfect or your image will look wrong. Also, if rendering a single modeled frame can take hours, it's easy to see that every second of modeled animation can tie up a computer for days. The results, though, can be amazing.

The details in these figures (from the popular game *The 7th Guest*) show the power of modeled animation. In this game, you must explore a strange old house, seeking clues to a frightful mystery. The same realism involved with this haunted house also can be given to a new architectural design, which enables you to see the inside of a building before deciding to go ahead with the plans. Or, in another of several such examples, it could show you the inner workings of a product not yet manufactured.

From *The 7th Guest*, © 1992 Virgin Games, Inc. and Trilobyte, Inc.

Of course, there is nothing to stop you from mixing techniques. Some sequences in *The 7th Guest* put video footage on top of the modeled animation, creating a set of inhabitants for this non-existent mansion. Standard computer animation is used to augment some of those scenes.

Not every type of modeling takes hours per frame, however. Simple, limited modeling of a limited number of objects can be done, allowing a number of frames to be generated each second. This way, the camera angle and the moving elements can change based on the user's control. This once was limited to the simple geometric shapes used in flight simulators, but more powerful software designed for today's faster computers can do much more.

From the virtual reality walk-through *3-D House*, © 1993 Charles Carr.

Some programs cheat, such as the amazing graphic PC game *Doom*. *Doom* uses on-the-fly 3-D modeling for the buildings and room designs, but the details inside the buildings—the objects to be picked up and the zombies to be defeated—are all just flat drawings that look the same from any angle. Other programs have items that are designed in 3-D but rendered from every possible angle when the program is designed. This way, they don't have to be rendered as the program is being run.

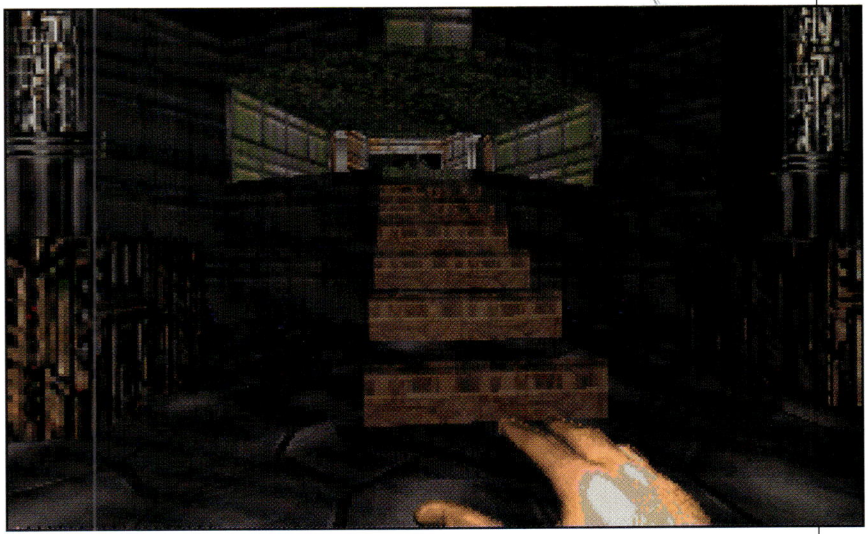

From the shareware game *Doom*, © 1994 Id Software.

It really doesn't matter what tools you use or how you cheat, just as long as you get the results that you want.

Bringing the Elements Together

So you've recorded a lot of audio. You've digitized tons of video. You've drawn dozens of pictures, and created amazingly intricate 3-D animations. You've written the finest prose known to humankind, all perfectly designed for being treated as hypertext. Now it's time to figure out how to bring all those elements together, how they're all connected to one another to make a whole project, right?

Wrong.

You should have figured that out before you started doing all that work. You have all the pieces for something, but for what? It's as if you had purchased all the lumber, concrete, roofing tiles, nails, drywall, gutters, carpeting, and wiring to build your new house, and then you start planning what the house will look like. You should be working with a careful plan from the very beginning, so you know what you need and what you can use.

Multimedia should be about more than just using different media—it should be about using them *effectively*. Effective use is something that doesn't happen accidentally. The more you plan in advance, the better off you will be.

This doesn't mean you can't make changes in the plan along the way. Often, you will find things to add that will improve the project, or things that aren't really needed that can be removed—just like you add a patio or change the den into a nursery even after you've built a house.

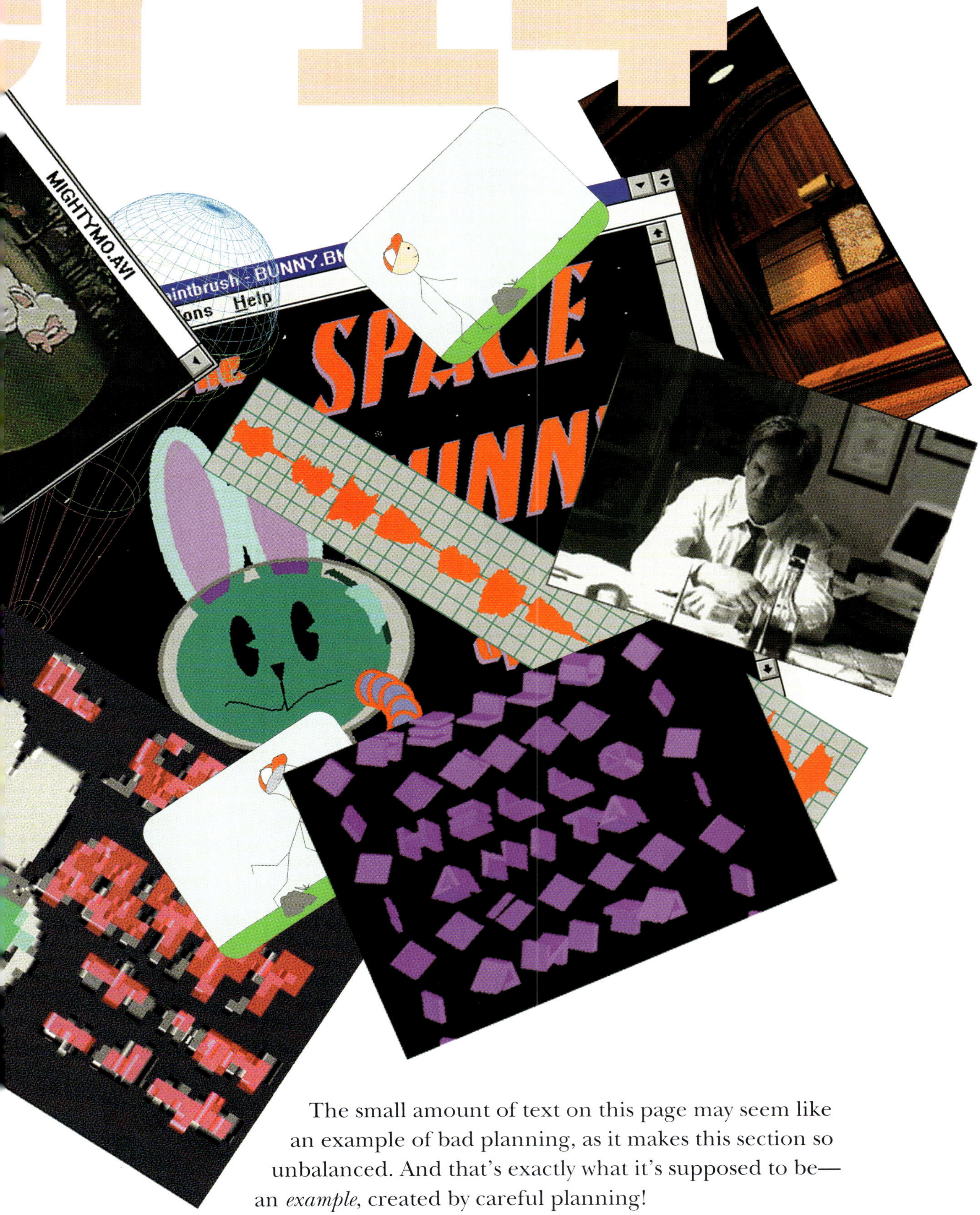

The small amount of text on this page may seem like an example of bad planning, as it makes this section so unbalanced. And that's exactly what it's supposed to be—an *example*, created by careful planning!

Breaking Down the Presentation

The key to organization is dividing what you are working with into parts. You build the structure of your project from the individual pieces that you wish to present.

There are several ways of breaking down a project logically, and you can use one or more of these organizational techniques on a given project. The way you organize all depends on the type of project and your personal style of working.

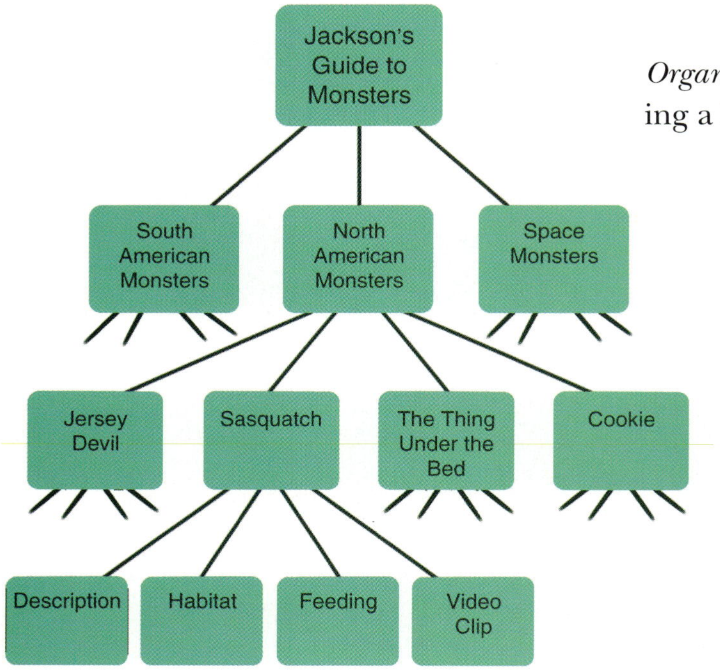

Organization by topic. This is a lot like organizing a book. You break the material you wish to present in your multimedia project into logically grouped chapters, and then into even smaller sections. This gives you a good sense of what information you need to present, which makes it easier to figure out the best way to present it. However, this may not leave you with much information about how the user will go from one part of the presentation to another, so you may wish to combine it with one of the other methods.

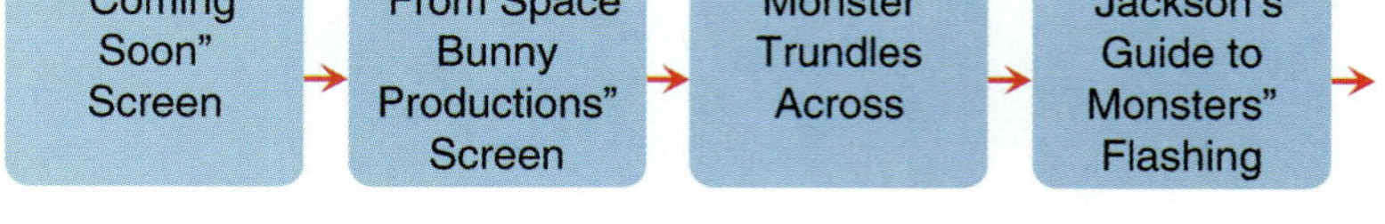

Organization by scenes. If the presentation you have in mind is a particularly visual one—with a lot of screen content and perhaps not much user interaction—you may want to organize by scenes. This is how a movie or play is broken down into scenes—when you change to a different location, it's a new scene. Start by deciding which screen displays you're going to have, and what changes you want those screens to go through.

Organization by decision points. An interactive multimedia program expects the user to input information or make a decision at times, such as when an adventure game asks you what room you want to go into next, or when a sales program lets you pick which product you want to learn about. By separating your project into the segments between decision points, and charting out what screen or sequence each decision will lead to, you can create a flow chart which lets you see the different paths your user can take through the project.

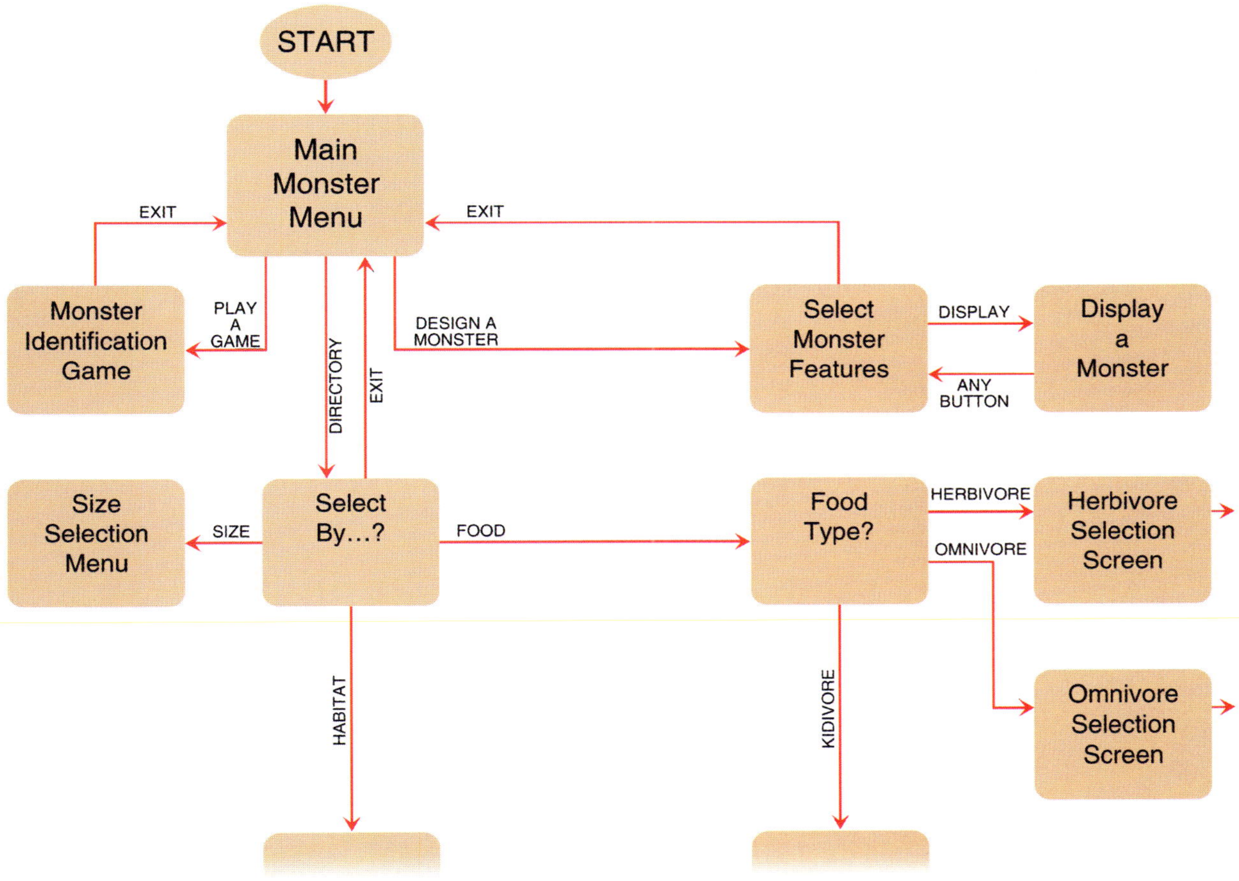

Ultimately, you need to know what information you will display, what the scenes will be, *and* where the decision points will lead, before you can assemble your project.

Designing Your Storyboard

The **storyboard** is a chart of scenes and decision points for your multimedia project. A good storyboard is a useful tool, because it gives you a clear picture of the entire project, one that is easy to share with others who may be helping you.

Most storyboards for multimedia projects are one of two types: the chart-type, and the card type. Each has strengths and weaknesses.

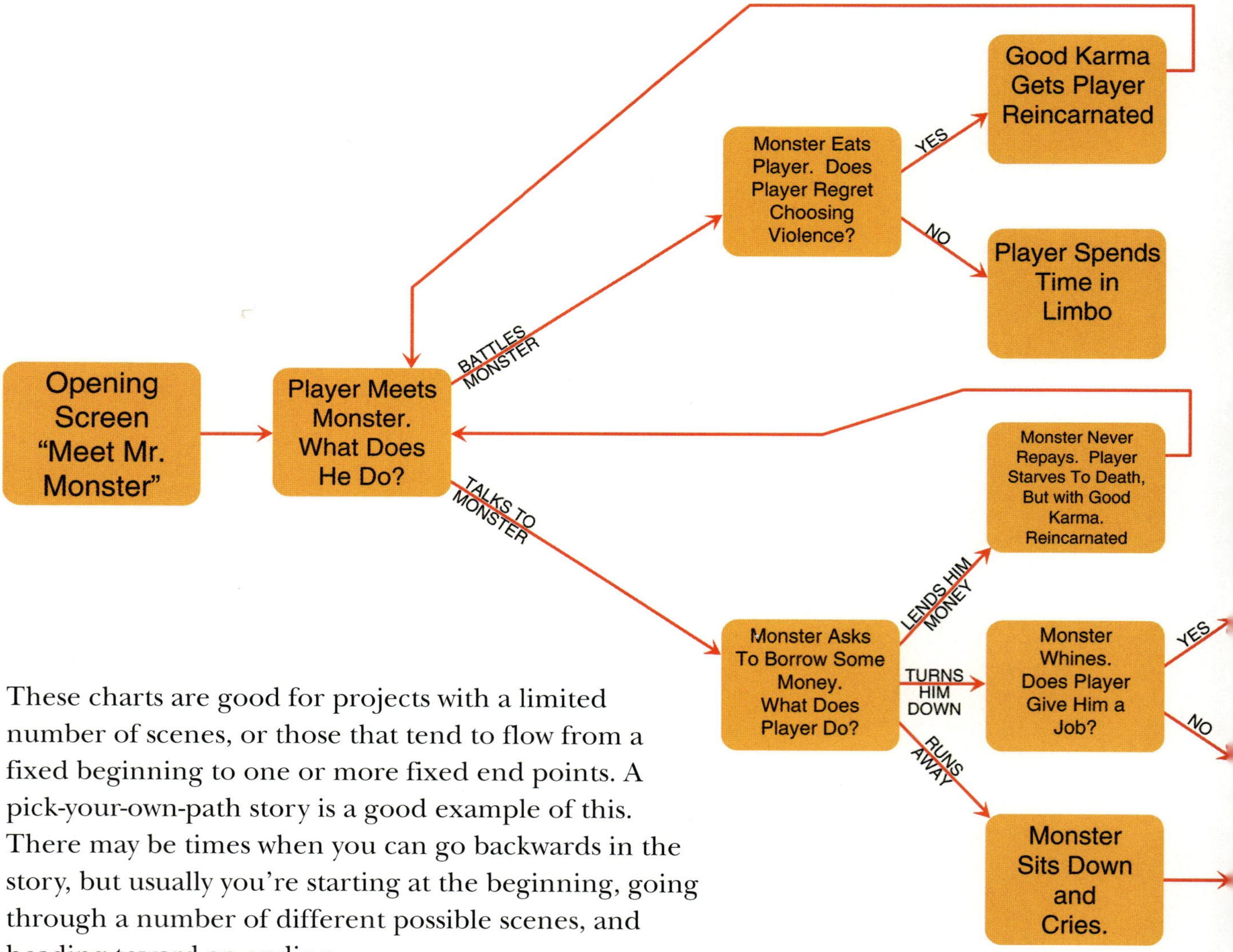

These charts are good for projects with a limited number of scenes, or those that tend to flow from a fixed beginning to one or more fixed end points. A pick-your-own-path story is a good example of this. There may be times when you can go backwards in the story, but usually you're starting at the beginning, going through a number of different possible scenes, and heading toward an ending.

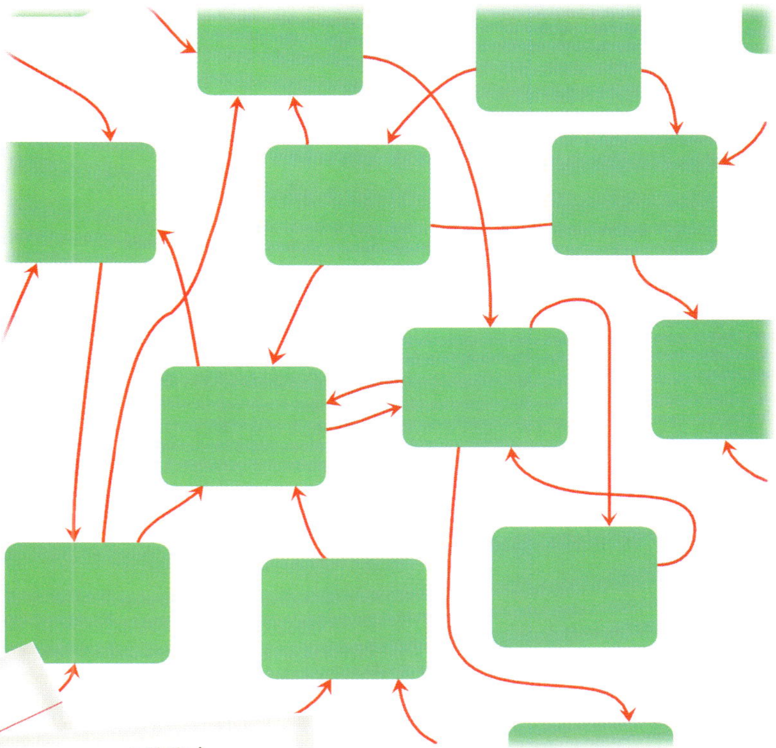

Projects with many scenes interconnected in many ways (such as a hypermedia encyclopedia) will have charts that are big and messy. This makes it hard to see how anything is connected to anything else, which ruins why you had a chart in the first place.

Card-based storyboards are good for more complex projects. You have an index card (or a computer simulation of an index card) for each scene. On the card, you keep track of what the scene is, what happens in that scene, where you can get to the scene from, and where you can go to from that scene. You also give the scene a number, so you can keep the cards easily sorted. This way, you can have a huge number of scenes, each neatly organized. If one scene changes or is eliminated, you don't have to redo an entire chart, and you can quickly find the scenes leading into and out of it.

Multimedia Slide Shows

In order to turn all your files into a complete multimedia presentation, you need a **multimedia authoring package.** There are many different examples of this type of software package, covering a full range of complexity and capability.

The simplest of these packages are frequently referred to as **slide show software**. This generally refers to display packages that use little or no user input, beyond perhaps hitting a key to get to the next screen. The software packages may be good for creating a show of your computer artwork or making a store window display, but they'd be useless for more complex projects.

A good slide show program (such as *PCX Supershow*) offers a lot of features to make your display as interesting as possible. Many such programs offer the capability to move text across the front of your still images, or to play a sound file while changing from image to image. Some of them have a rather impressive array of **fades** (techniques for going from a picture to a blank screen) and **transitions** (techniques for going from one picture to another).

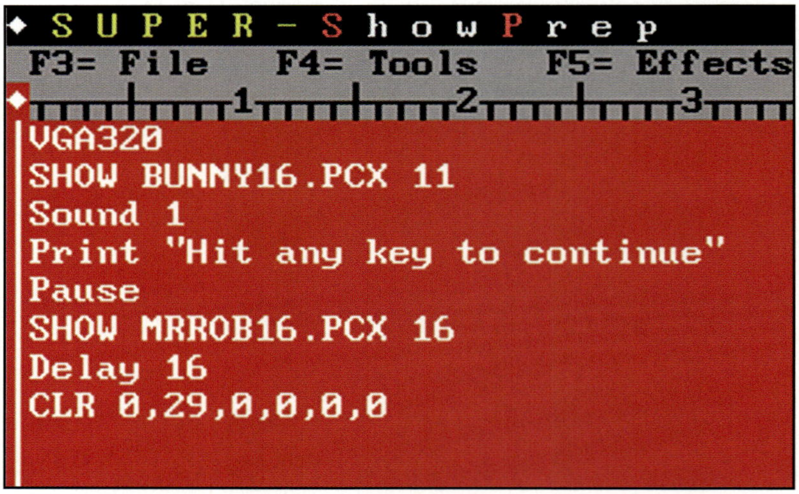

All screens from *PCX SuperShow* © 1992 PC West.

Different programs have different ways for you to design your slide show. Many have you create a script, listing which files to display and what special functions to perform. This simple script for the *PCX SuperShow* slide show program displays one picture, puts up a message, plays a sound, waits for the user to hit a key, switches to another picture, waits 16 seconds, then clears the screen. The program's script editor even allows you to pick the commands from menus, so that you do not have to have them memorized.

Bringing a picture on with a fancy wipe effect can add extra excitement to a still picture.

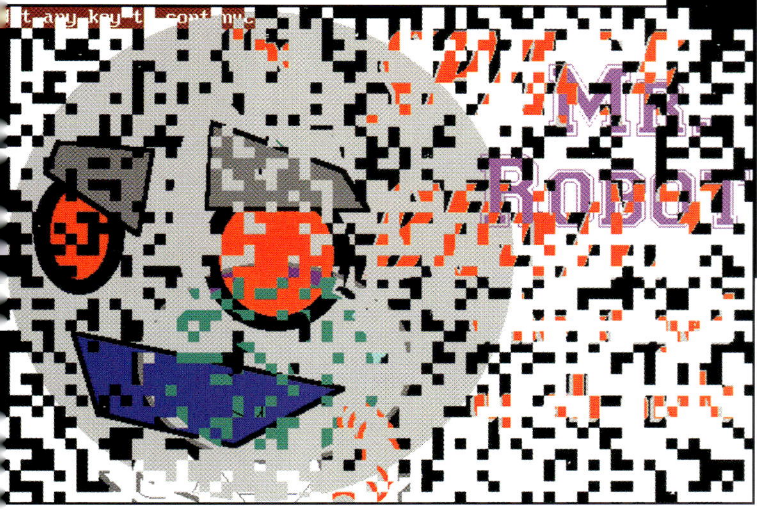

By using a nice transition, you keep your presentation from looking sudden and jerky, and you can hold the viewer's attention.

When your presentation is done, fading away to an all-black screen can make the presentation end less abruptly than just dumping the user back into the operating system. Of course, you also can create a slide show that doesn't end but just loops back to the beginning and repeats itself endlessly.

Slide show programs tend to be quite affordable. There are some good ones available as **shareware** (software you can legally copy from a friend or bulletin board and try it out before you decide whether you want to purchase it) or even **freeware** (software you can copy from somewhere and are never expected to pay for). As such, it can cost you nothing to have a slide show program on hand, and you never know when you might need it.

Multimedia Authoring Systems

There are dozens of different authoring packages designed to let you put together a full, interactive multimedia presentation. Most of the packages, in an effort to make creating your project as easy as possible, let you build your project simply by putting together a version of your storyboard that the computer can interpret.

Some of these authoring packages (including the popular *Hypercard*) are based around the card-style storyboard motif. This is a very flexible way of describing your multimedia project, but for many projects, it may not be the simplest or most natural.

This package lets you include icons that represent entirely separate routines. This way, a main chart shows you how all the screens link together, and each individual screen has its own chart for all the different functions and elements that make up that screen.

The storyboard is represented as a series of events (putting up a new screen, playing a sound, adding a button to the screen) and decision points that route you to different paths.

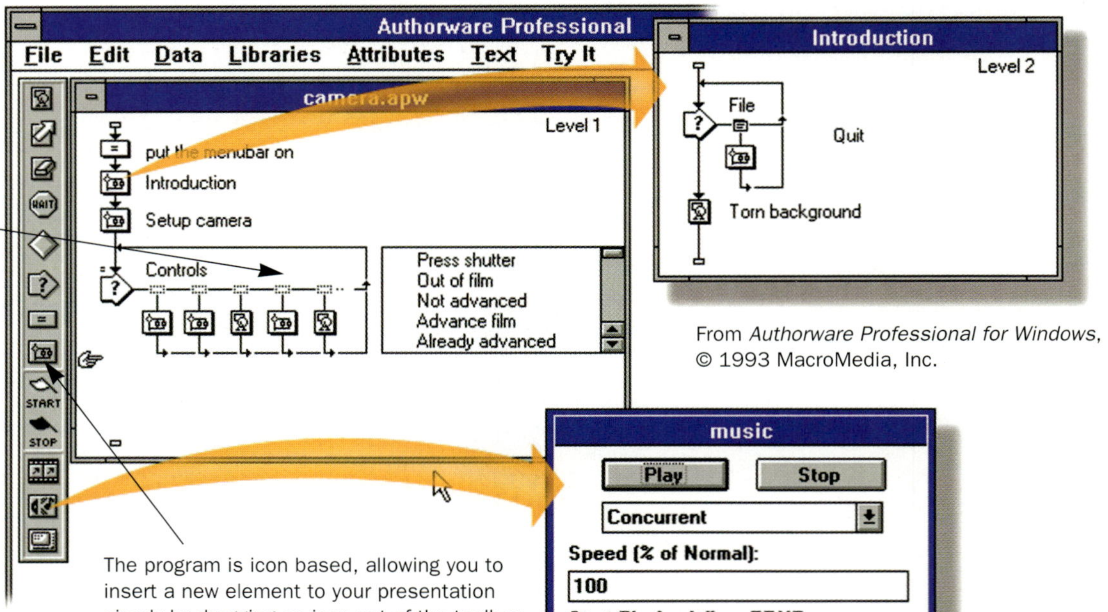

From *Authorware Professional for Windows*, © 1993 MacroMedia, Inc.

The program is icon based, allowing you to insert a new element to your presentation simply by dragging an icon out of the toolbox into the proper place in the diagram.

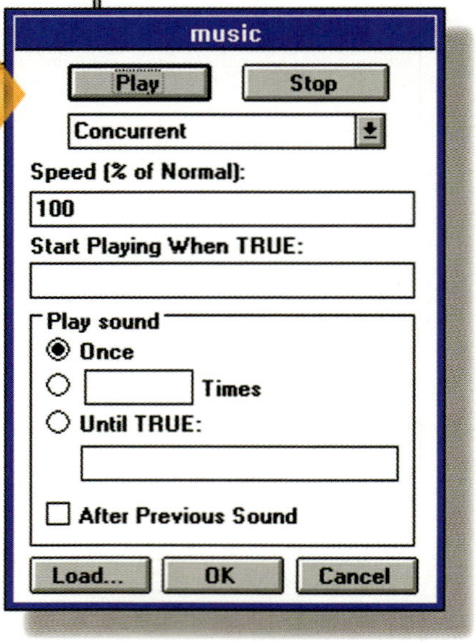

Whenever you insert a new element, the authoring program will ask for a description of that element. For example, it's not enough to say you want to add a sound, you have to tell it *which* sound, and how to play it.

Authoring packages, such as *Authorware Professional* use chart-style storyboards in order to make the process easier to follow. Each package has different storyboard-structuring and display features, and is organized a bit differently.

In contrast is the program *Action!*, which can only break the presentation down into linear series of screens, but describes the events on each screen as a timeline. This makes it easy to precisely coordinate things like moving text and sound.

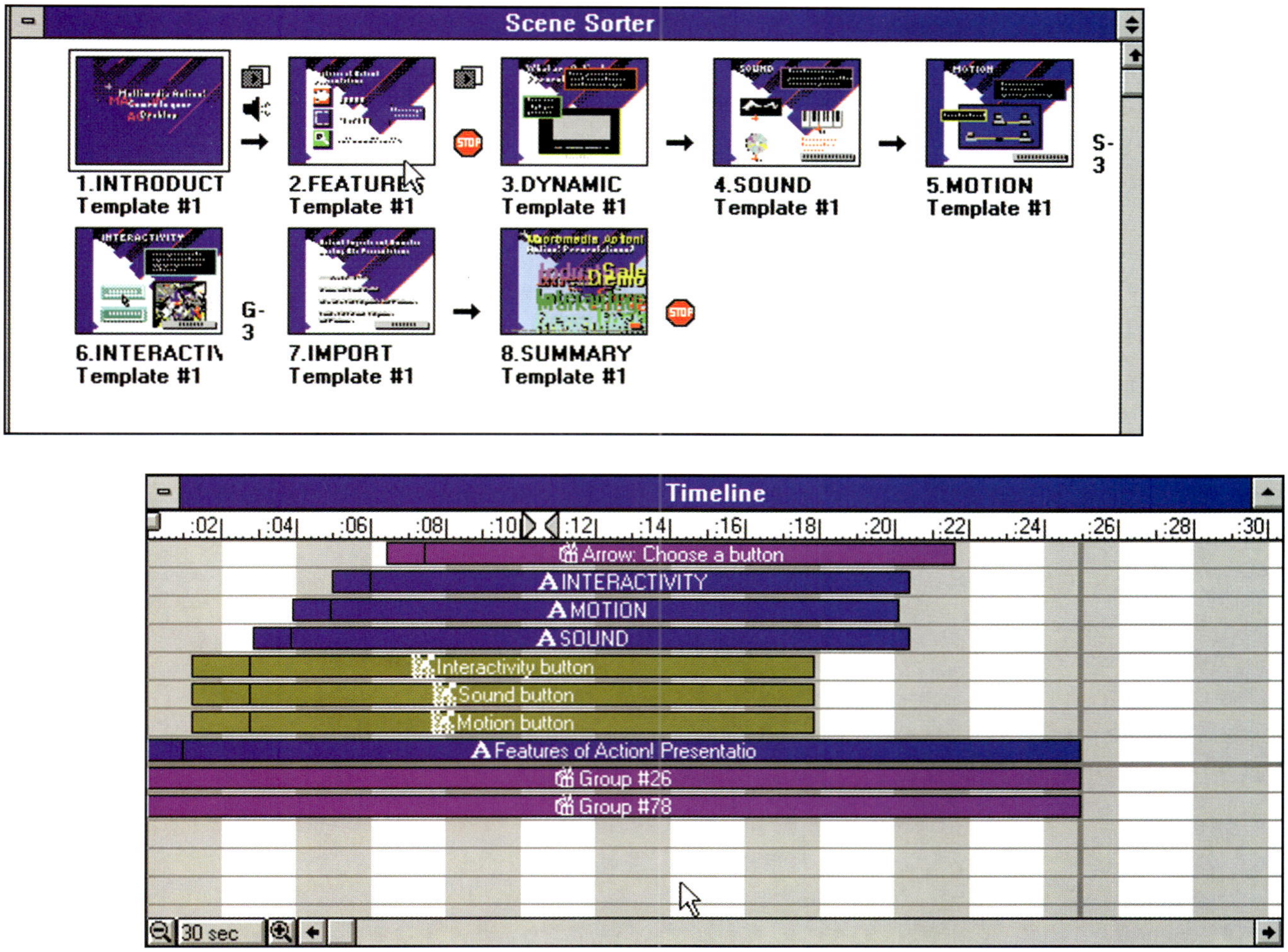

From *Action!*, © 1992 MacroMedia, Inc.

Multimedia Programming Languages

Icon-based authoring packages are fine, if your project uses only the features that have icons, or icons you can design with their limited logic systems. But what if you want to include something different or unexpected to your project? What if you want to throw a tic-tac-toe game onto one of the screens, or create your own nifty way of making one screen disappear and the next appear? Then you'll need to create your own original computer programs.

A **computer program** is a series of commands to the computer. A very complex process like word processing or playing *Doom* is broken down into small individual steps that the computer can understand. A **programming language** is a set of commands that can be used to make up a program, and the grammar that must be used for the computer to understand these commands (called **syntax**). The difference between working with an icon-based authoring system and working with a programming language is like the difference between building a bookshelf from a kit, and building a bookshelf using a pile of lumber and a workshop full of good tools—the kit may be easier, but if you're good at using the tools, you can make the exact bookshelf you want. A good programmer can make exactly the project he or she wants, rather than just the type of project an authoring package was designed to create.

Some multimedia authoring packages are simply **programming libraries,** which in effect add new commands to an existing programming language. This might be special commands that display video, play sound, or perform some other multimedia function.

Programming languages also pop up in some icon-based authoring packages and most card-based authoring packages. This lets you create systems that interact in whatever very complex ways you may want to design.

All screens from *Multimedia Toolbox* © 1991 Asymetrix Corp.

Multimedia Toolbox from Asymetrix is a card-based authoring system which allows you to build your screens by combining graphics, text, standard interface buttons, and other items.

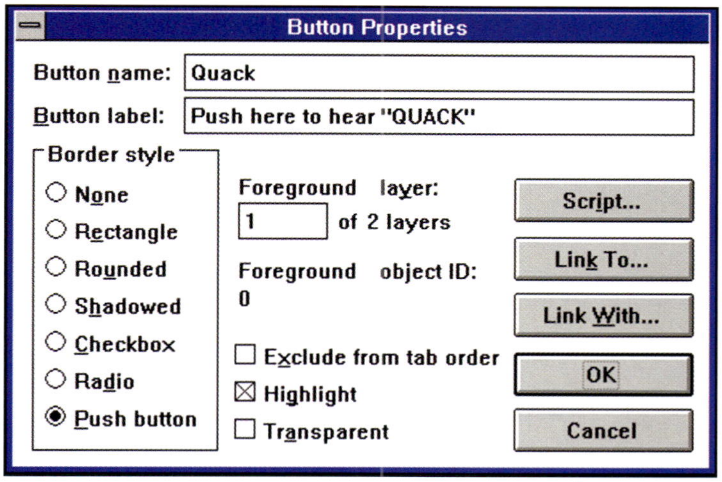

When you create a button, you can define a number of attributes to the button—what it looks like, what it's named, what it says on it, and so on.

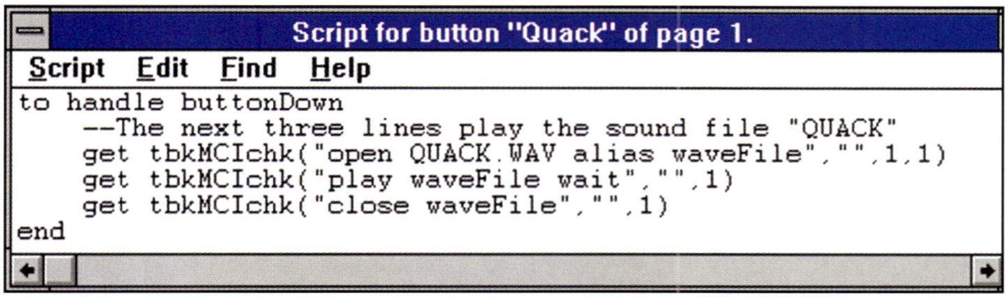

Where a simpler, less powerful authoring system might let you choose from a handful of effects (go to another screen, play a sound, change the current screen), this system lets you write a program as short or as long as you need. This may make it a little harder to tell the system to do something simple, but it allows so much more flexibility. A simpler system might just have a menu selection "play sound" that will associate the sound file with that button. Playing the sound here is broken down into the three major steps the computer has to go through—opening the sound file, playing the sound in that file, and closing the file. These same three commands could be used towards building a multimedia application that lets you edit sound, something that the simpler system would not let you do.

Multimedia authoring tools come in widely differing styles and complexities. No one tool is right for every project or every user; you will have to find the tool that is best for you!

Wise Multimedia Design

Working in multimedia can be frustrating—it is complex and a lot of things can go wrong. To be a master of multimedia, you really have to have a firm grasp of each individual medium.

Working in multimedia also can be a lot of fun. You have a toolbox full of fun tools to play with, and you can build almost anything.

Car image © 1994 Jasmine Multimedia.

It is important that you don't fall so in love with multimedia that you lose track of the goal of your project, and start making it fancy and media-laden just for the sake of doing so.

Your primary goals should be not only attractiveness, but also clarity of use and presentation. You don't want people to be confused about what you are saying, and you don't want people confused about how to use the program.

While you should try to check for these problems yourself, it can be particularly helpful to get someone to look at your project and give you feedback. In some ways, you are the worst person to check your own project, because you don't have to try to understand your own program—you already know what it all means. The users only have the clues that you left them in the program.

Appropriate Media

Sometimes, choosing which medium to present information in is easy. If you're doing a presentation about your son's rock band, the music will be stored as sound. If you're doing a piece about the paintings on the Sistine chapel, you'll want to use still images.

On the other hand, sometimes multiple possibilities present themselves, and a choice must be made. What you use depends on what you are presenting and who you are presenting it to.

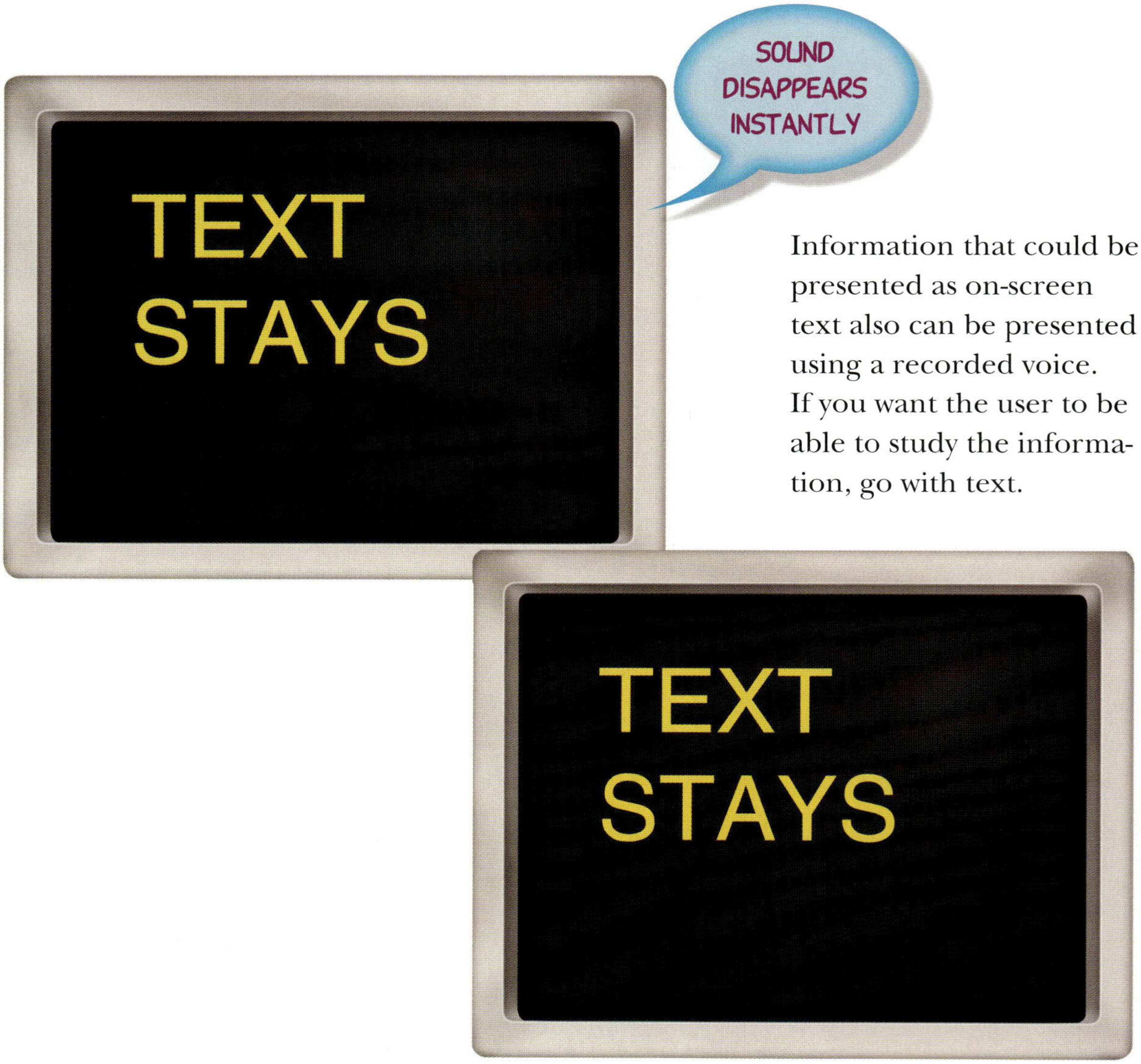

Information that could be presented as on-screen text also can be presented using a recorded voice. If you want the user to be able to study the information, go with text.

Image from *Best of MediaClips 2.0*, © 1991-1994 Aris Multimedia Entertainment, Inc. Photograph by David K. Brunn.

Recorded voice is also great for giving additional information while a still picture or video is being displayed…

…but you want to avoid spoken word at the same time as you are presenting new text on-screen.

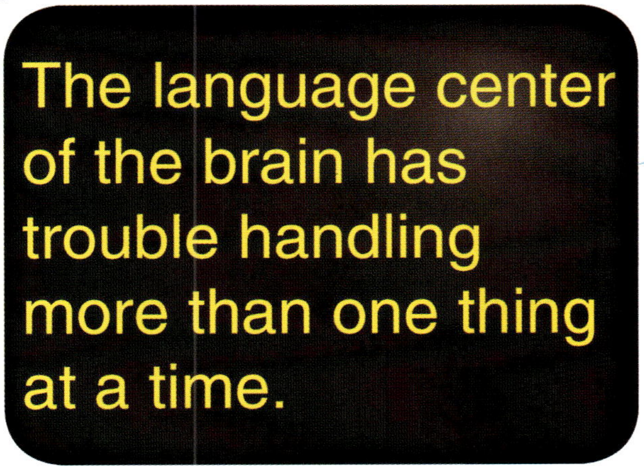

Moving video is a great attention grabber, but if the user has to spend too much time waiting for the system to stop getting his attention and start giving him information, he's going to stop caring about the information.

From *Word for Windows*, © 1994 Microsoft.

Uncluttered Screens

The usually well-organized screen from Microsoft's *Word for Windows* has been severely tampered with here to make a point. A cluttered screen like this makes it impossible to find anything.

If you really need to have a lot of functions, you will be better off to have only a half dozen to a dozen possible commands on the main screen, and to hide the rest in pull-down menus. Pick the commands that people use most often. Or, if you are willing to do some advanced programming, you can do what the designers of *Word for Windows* did, and allow the user to choose which elements appear on-screen.

Useful Interfaces

An interactive system should be designed to respond to the user's desires. The interface elements of your project can allow that control, or can limit and frustrate the user.

Clicking any of these buttons gets the program to play video of the interviewee's response to the question.

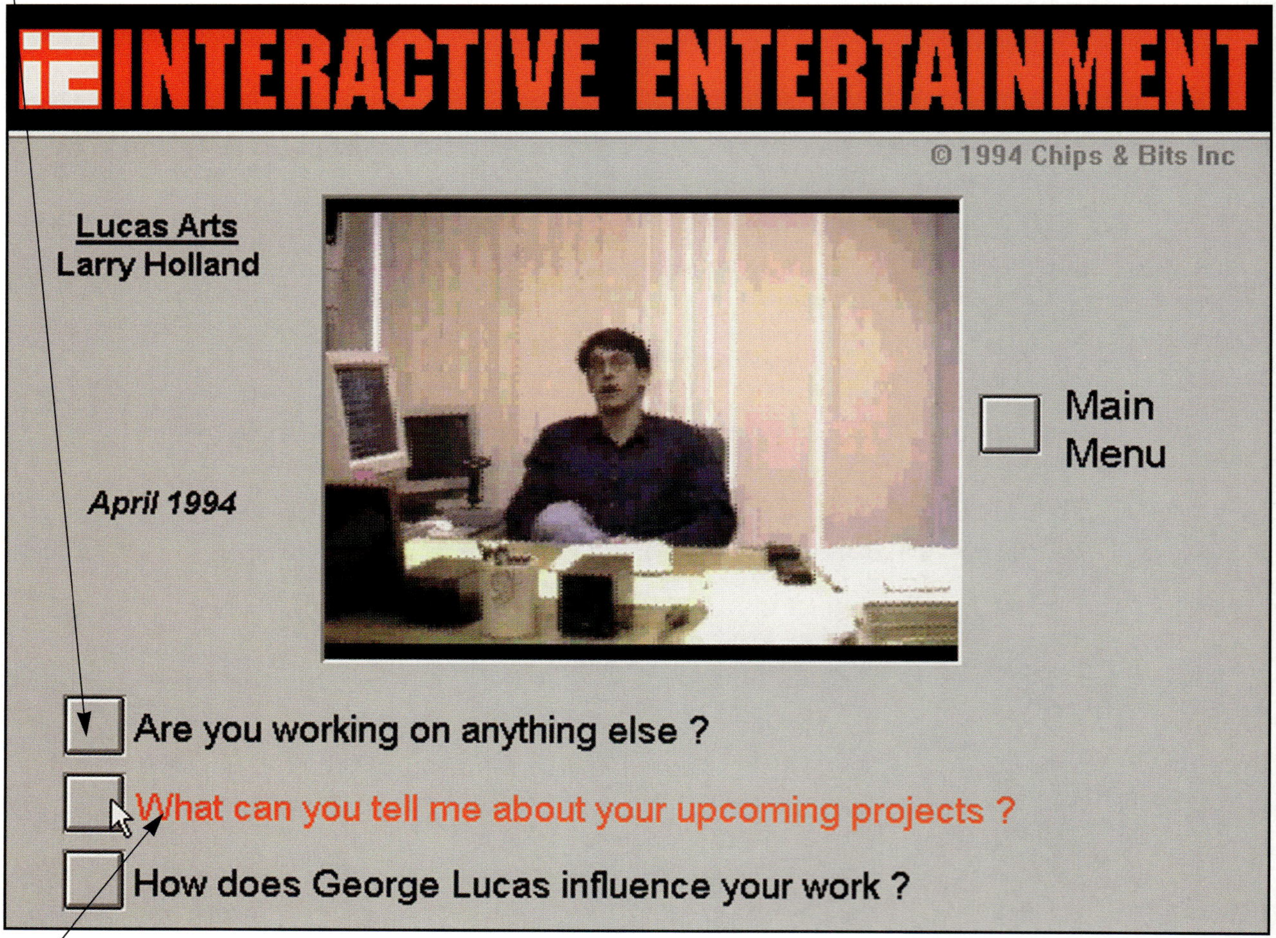

Red indicates questions you have already asked.

Interactive Entertainment is blazing new trails as one of the first CD-ROM-based multimedia magazines. Any new trail has a few unexpected twists and turns in it, and while they have provided some very interesting features, the magazine's staff is also going through a learning process about what works and what doesn't.

The magazine includes interactive interviews, where you get to select questions and hear the responses. Unfortunately, it only allows you to select one of the three questions displayed at a time. There's no easy way to say that you want to hear all the answers, nor to say that you aren't interested in any of the three questions.

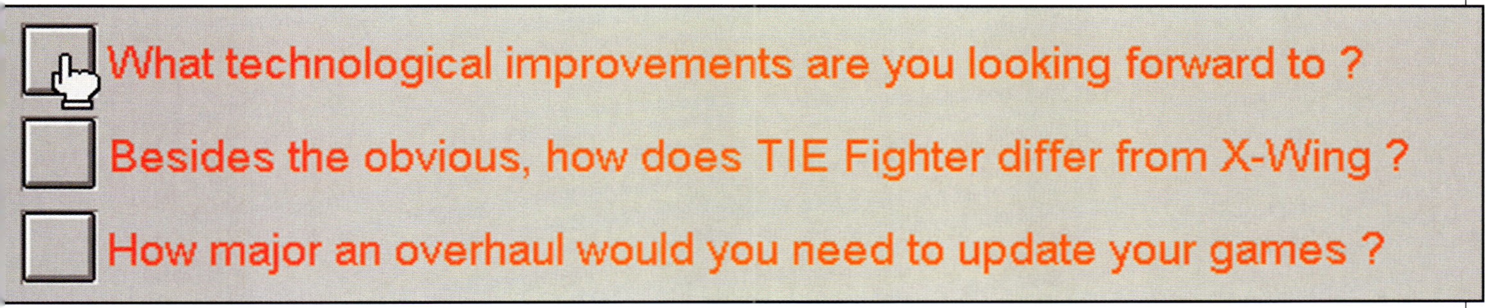

After you ask one of the three questions, all three are replaced by another set, so if you want to ask more than one of the three, you have to wait for those questions to come around again. Sometimes, you have to ask questions that you don't want to ask, or even that you've already asked, in order to get to another set of questions. This frustrates the user, and turns a good concept into more of a multimedia novelty.

Testing the interview format with readers might have quickly revealed this deficiency. Simply adding another screen button to allow the user to skip ahead to the next set of questions would have removed the need to ever ask a question that you don't want to ask. Even better would be if this button could abort the video in mid-answer, if users find that they are not really interested in the answer.

Good Interface Tools

One of the nice things about hypertext (which, you'll recall, is the ability to select a word or phrase from a text display and get more information on that topic) is that it offers the user the ability to get further information without filling the screens with *click here for more information on subterranean waffle houses* and similar messages. Once the user has used any hypertext product, he quickly recognizes the ability elsewhere, and doesn't need to have everything explained.

Actually, that's a good reason for using all sorts of standard interface elements. Scroll bars, VCR buttons, and close gadgets are things that your user will likely have encountered in some other product. Just to be safe, you should include an explanation of them in your help system and documentation (after all, everybody has to run into these things for the first time at some point). However, most experienced software users like to skip the help and documentation, and this will let them do so without getting confused.

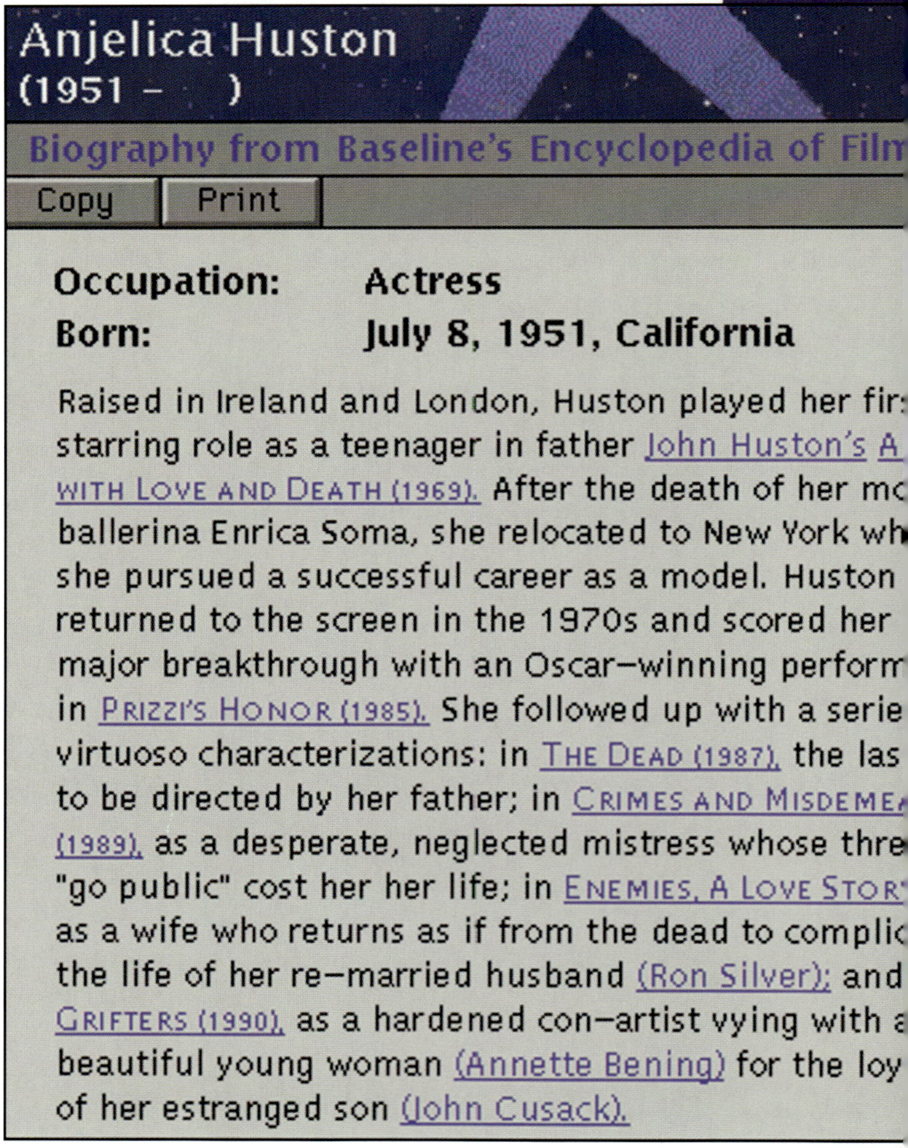

From *Microsoft Cinemania*, © 1994 Microsoft.

There are situations where you need to invent an interface tool to do something no other tool can do. However, when you can use an existing interface element, it's better for both you and your user that you do so, rather than reinvent the wheel.

Effective Color

Color can be a friend or an enemy, depending on how it is used. Carefully chosen color can highlight important parts of your presentation. Poorly chosen color can make it look ugly and can hide things.

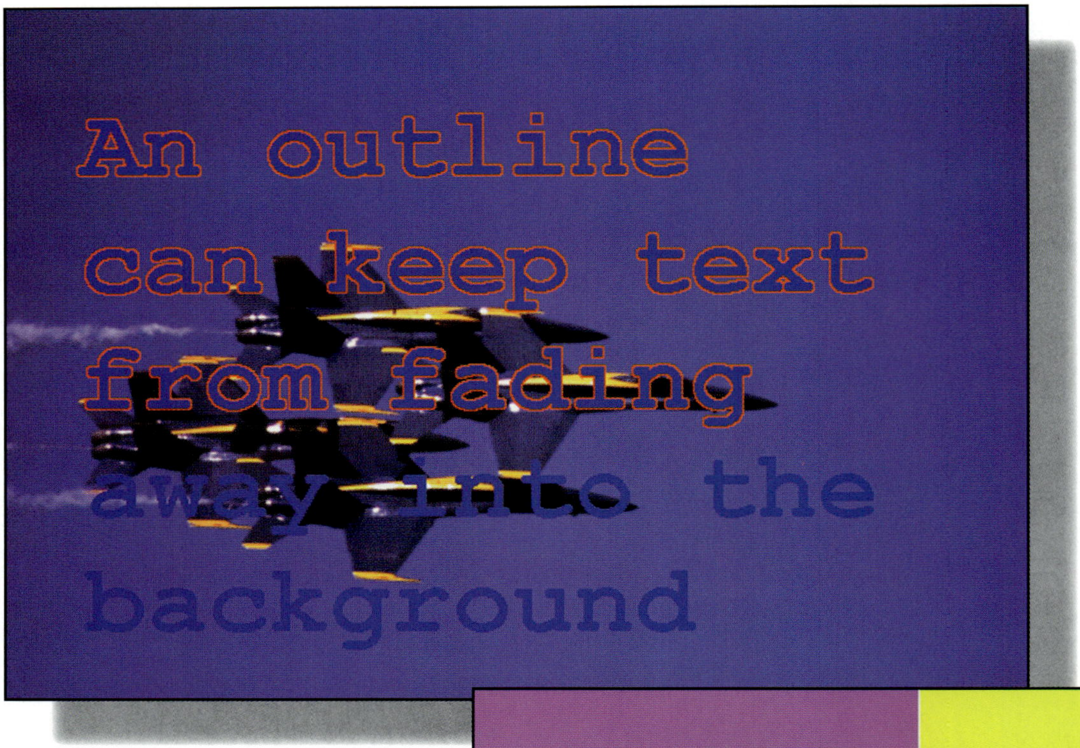

Background image from *Best of MediaClips 2.0*, © 1991-1994 Aris Multimedia Entertainment, Inc. Photograph by David K. Brunn.

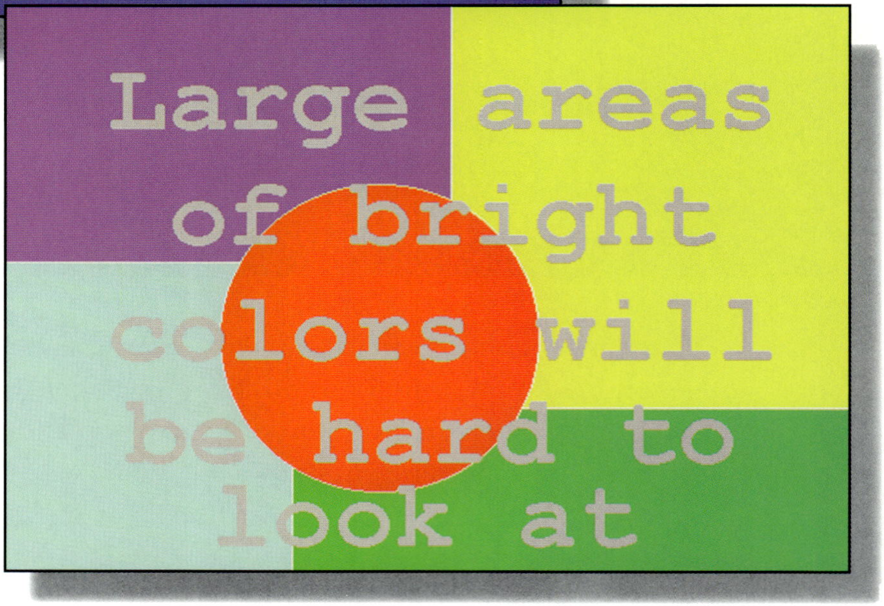

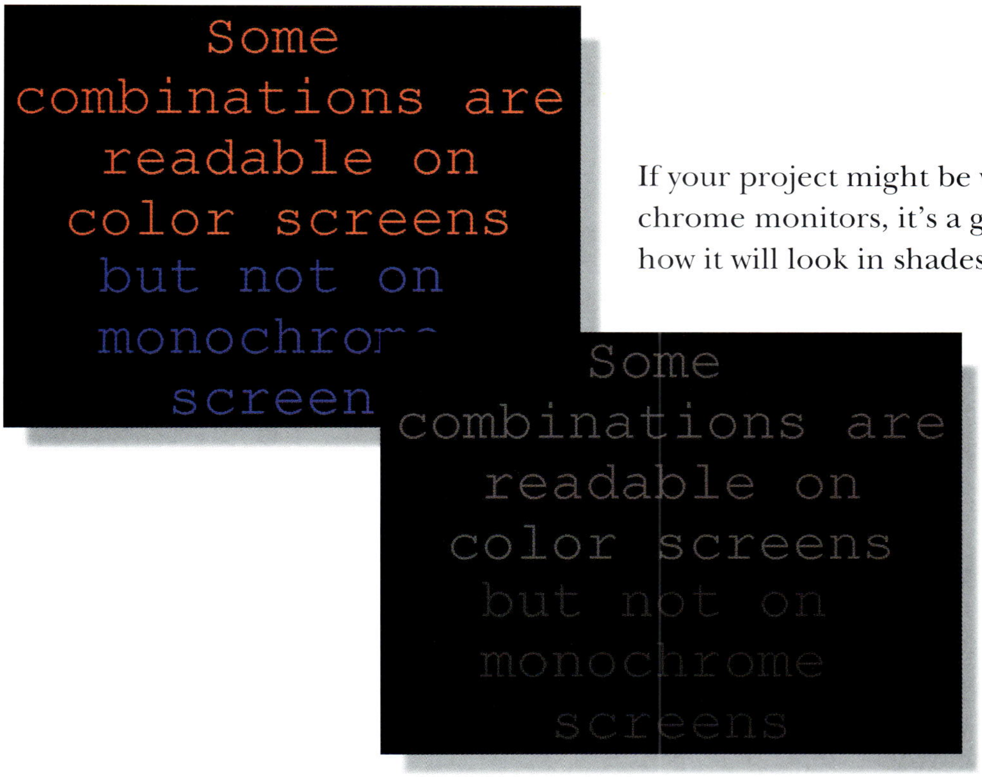

If your project might be viewed on monochrome monitors, it's a good idea to see how it will look in shades of gray.

If you're showing a series of pictures, make sure they all use the same palette, or fade out between pictures. Otherwise, you may get a *flash* of a picture with the wrong colors.

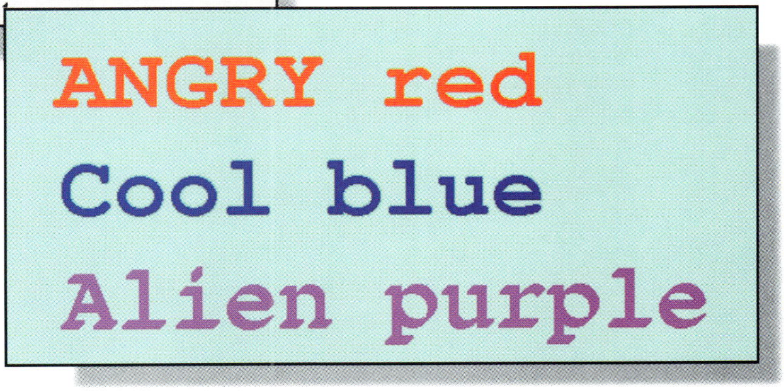

Color has mood. Take advantage of it.

Helpful Help

A multimedia project does not have to be very complex before a user might not understand fully what he is supposed to (or what he can) do. A useful help system becomes important in such cases.

A help system that no one can find, however, is not very useful. There are a number of standard ways for users to ask the system for assistance.

The popular spreadsheet program *Lotus 1-2-3* established the F1 key as the standard way of accessing help information. While it is not an obvious way for a new user, it is standard, and you may want to implement this in addition to other methods.

An on-screen button that the user can use to access help at any time is a good idea, serving as a constant reminder that help is available. Make certain the button is clear and recognizable. The question mark has become the standard (if not completely obvious) icon for such a button.

If your project will allow the user access to pull-down menus, you should include a Help menu. Windows programs use a standard help system with some very fine functions. The Help menu is generally the last menu on the right.

Other programs use a button marked Help. This is probably the best solution, unless you are working in a multilingual environment. It's clear and obvious, and that's just what a person looking for help needs.

One simple, brilliant feature of the Amiga computer is simply an additional key on the keyboard. This way, the programmer always knows where the user will expect to find help. Unfortunately, it is not a feature that other systems have copied.

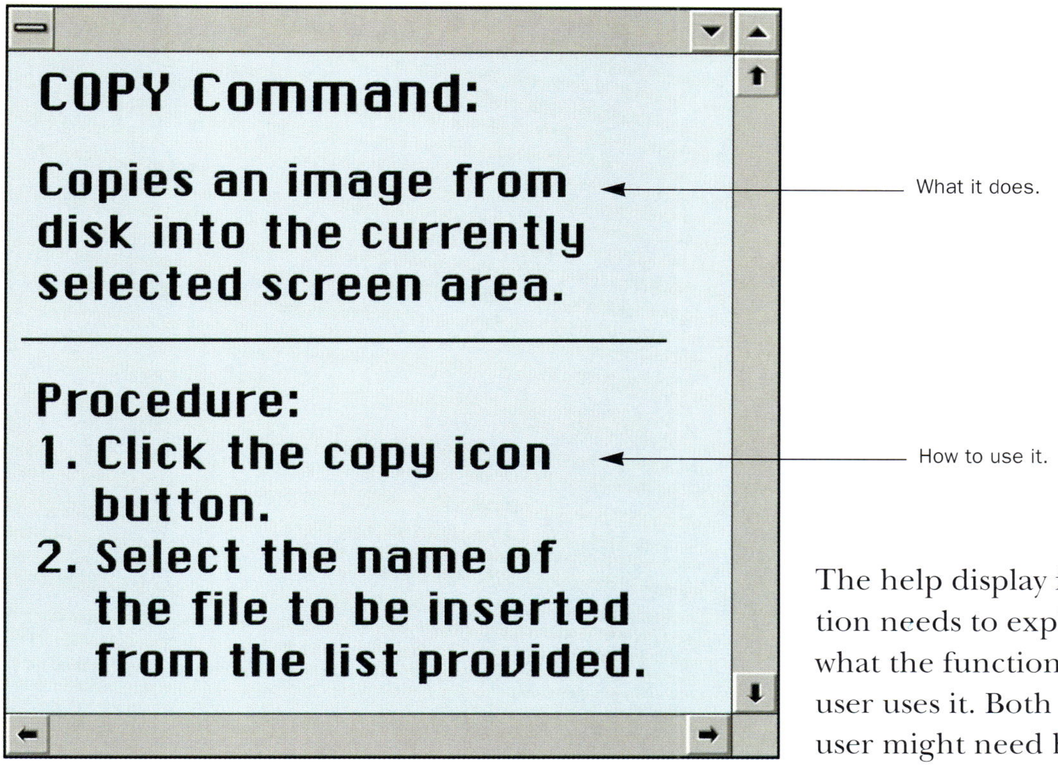

The help display for a given function needs to explain two things—what the function is, and how the user uses it. Both are items that the user might need help with.

Of course, always remember multimedia's goal—it is better to show than to describe.

Context-sensitive help automatically brings up the right help screen for the current screen or function. It's a very useful feature.

Many help systems include some degree of hypertext, making it easier for the user to find the piece of information needed.

When putting together an index of your help topics, try to include not only what you name the function, but also what it might be called by someone looking for the function. The help screen for your *clear* function, for example, might also be indexed as *erase*.

Making a CD-ROM

CD-ROMs look so perfect and are so full of data, that it's easy to assume that making a new CD-ROM is something only huge multinational corporations with boatloads of money and an army of engineers could do. The truth is very different.

In reality, it takes little skill and not nearly as much money as you might suppose to create a new CD-ROM. If you've learned how to copy files from your hard disk, you can learn how to prepare your files for placement on a CD-ROM. As you'll see later in this chapter, the cost of producing a CD can be quite affordable.

But being able to make a CD does not mean it is necessarily the right thing to do. Remember that a CD-ROM has some significant limitations:

- *It's slow.* Even the quad speed CD-ROM drives are far slower at finding and reading data than a modern hard drive; currently, people with CD-ROMs only have a single- or double-speed drive.
- *Most computers still don't have CD-ROM drives.* This is changing as more new machines come with a drive as standard equipment, and as people continue to put new drives in old machines. But we're still a long way from the time when you can assume that anyone who wants to use your project has a drive.

As such, if your project takes up just a few megabytes of disk space, you're probably better off distributing it on floppy disks and telling the users to install it on their hard drives.

On the other hand, there are definitely times when you want to use a CD-ROM because of the following advantages:

- *They store a lot of information.* Users are not going to want to install hundreds of megabytes of data on their hard drives, so CDs make sense for large projects.
- *They're cheap to make in quantity.* If you're looking at mass-producing a project that would take up 10 floppy disks, you will find that you can release it on a single CD for a fraction of the cost.
- *They're reliable.* A CD-ROM that is not abused should be able to hold its data for decades, surviving through storage conditions which could cause a floppy disk to lose its data.
- *They're harder to copy than floppy disks.* Any system that can read floppy disks also can copy them, leaving them wide open to the many software pirates who are out there. However, very few of the systems that have CD-ROM readers also have the capability to make CD-ROMs, and the expense of making a single copy is high enough that it makes piracy much less tempting.

File Preparation

To be able to make your own CD-ROMs, you have to be able to take the files that you wish to include and organize them so that they are ready to be placed onto your CD. Generally, this involves creating an **image file** that contains all of the data and structures for your CD.

There are a number of software packages available that are designed to do this. Generally, such packages would be included with CD-ROM recording devices (which will be discussed in the section, "CD-ROM Recording Hardware," later in this chapter), but you also can get them separately, so that you can create the image on your PC for someone else to turn into the actual CD.

This software is constantly being enhanced and upgraded, both to improve ease of use and to enable the handling of the expanding sets of standard formats for CD-ROMs. The examples here are from *QuickTOPiX for Windows 2.00*, the latest revision of a popular CD publishing package from Optical Media International.

First, you have to select what files you want on your CD-ROM and how they are going to be organized. CD-ROM file structures are generally similar to hard disk structures, but they may have some additional limitations. For example, if you are using the ISO 9660 standard format, you can have directories nested no more than eight deep. You also are limited to the short file names that MS-DOS machines use, even if you are using a Macintosh and are used to using longer, more descriptive file names.

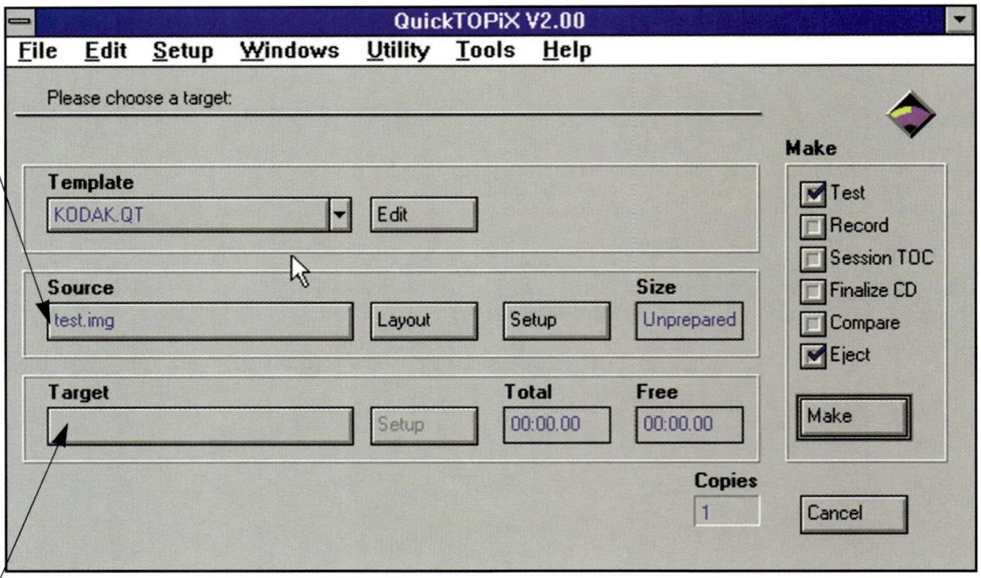

Next, you have to select the output device that you are copying these files to. This could be an image file on your hard disk, a direct recording on a CD-ROM, or one of several accepted standard tape formats for the image file.

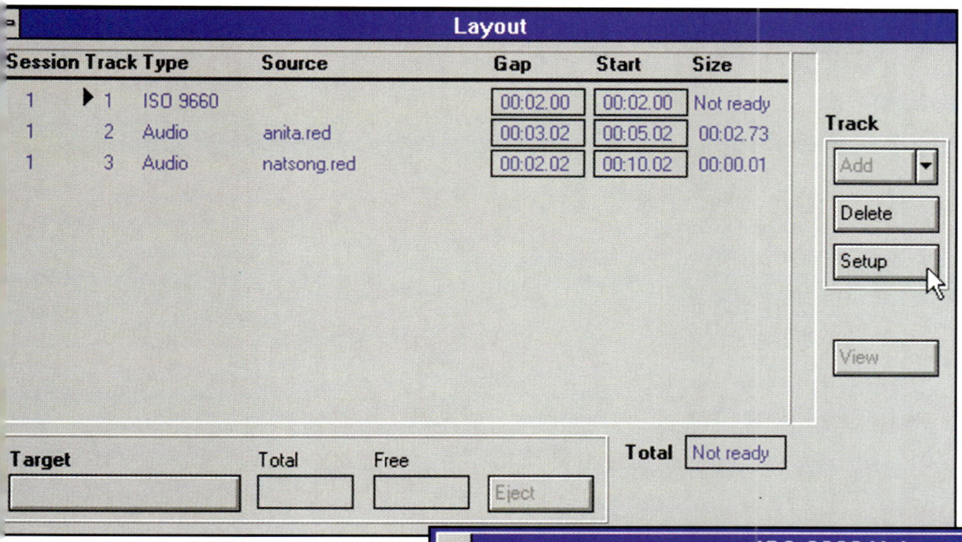

Some of these programs permit you to mix standard audio CD tracks with computer data tracks on a single disc. Many game manufacturers take advantage of this, allowing you to take the program disc and stick it in your CD player in order to listen to the music from the game.

The ISO 9660 standard provides for a large amount of special header information, which this software allows you to enter. (Not all of the header fields are applicable to all projects.)

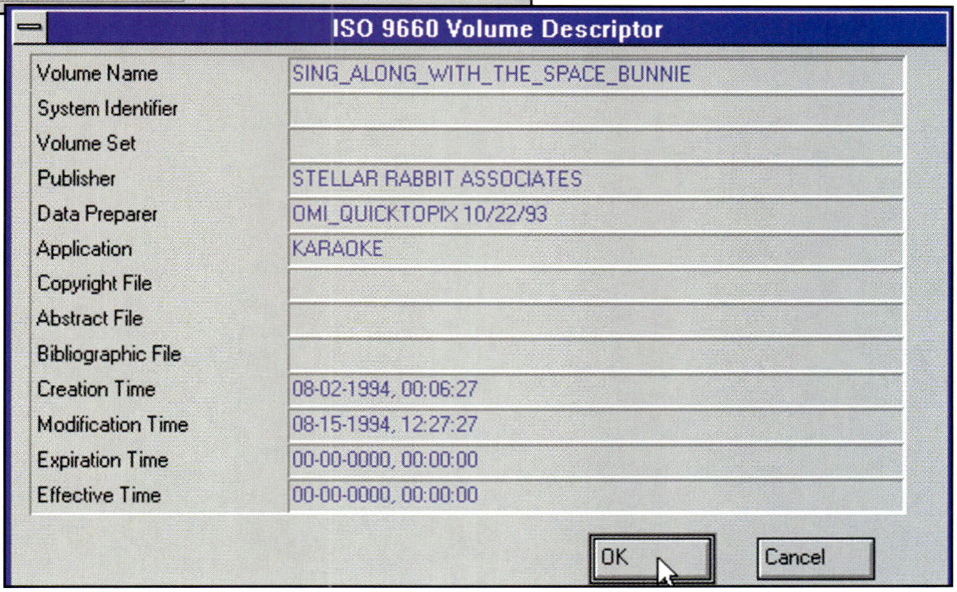

All screens from *QuickTOPiX for Windows 2.00*, © 1994 Optical Media International.

It's one thing to put together a CD-ROM, but it's another thing to do it well. It really does make a difference how you arrange your files on CD-ROM. To make it easier for the user to understand, you should put thought into what you name your files and how you divide them between different directories.

Perhaps more importantly, the order that you put your files on the disc will affect the speed of your project. When the computer stops reading from one file and starts reading from another, the distance between those two files on the disc has a major effect on how long the computer takes before it starts reading data from the new file. By keeping the files that the computer is going to be switching between, you can make your project run much smoother.

CD-ROM Recording Hardware

As noted earlier, the ROM in CD-ROM stands for **Read Only Memory**, because you can only read information from the disc, not store information onto it. However, there is a special variation on CD-ROM called **CD-R** (for Compact Disc-Recordable), **CD-WO** (for Compact Disc-Write Once) or, alternately, **CD-WORM** (for Compact Disc-Write Once, Read Mostly) that you can record data on using a special recording drive, often referred to as a **CD writer.** Once data is recorded onto a CD-R disc (which costs around $20), it can be used as a standard CD-ROM in any CD-ROM drive.

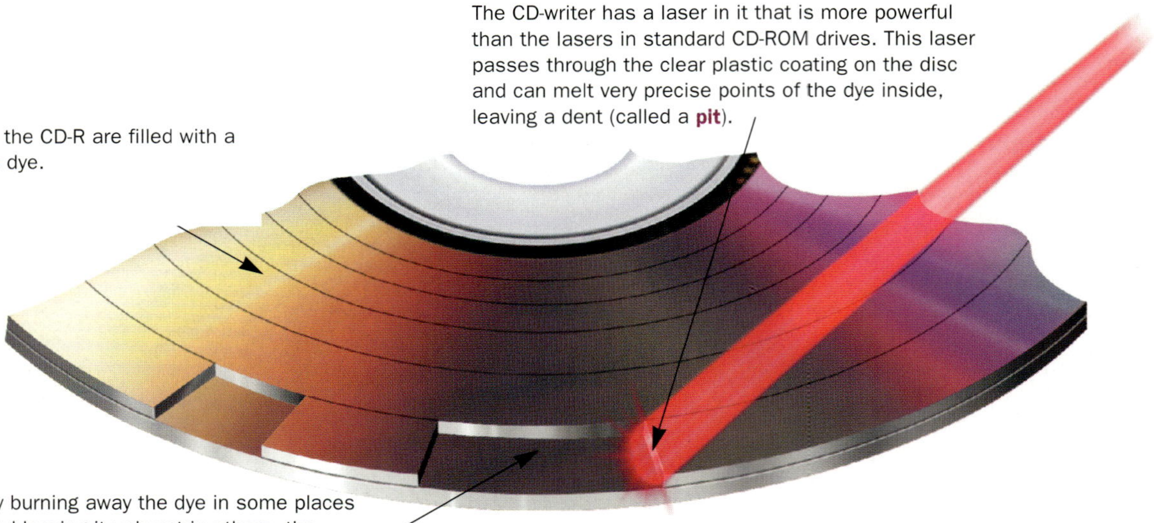

Because there is no way to fill in the pits on an area of the disc that data has been recorded onto, you can't write data onto an area of the disc that has already been used. This is why some of the names for this technology refer to *write once*, because you can only write once to each section of the disk (as opposed to a floppy disk, for example, where you can keep erasing and reusing tracks of data).

If you're going to keep adding data to your disc, you have to make it a **multisession** disc. This means that the disc has a special directory structure that creates a separate area for each disc recording session. The down side to making a multisession disc is that many CD-ROM drives aren't able to understand the directory structure, and can only handle single session discs.

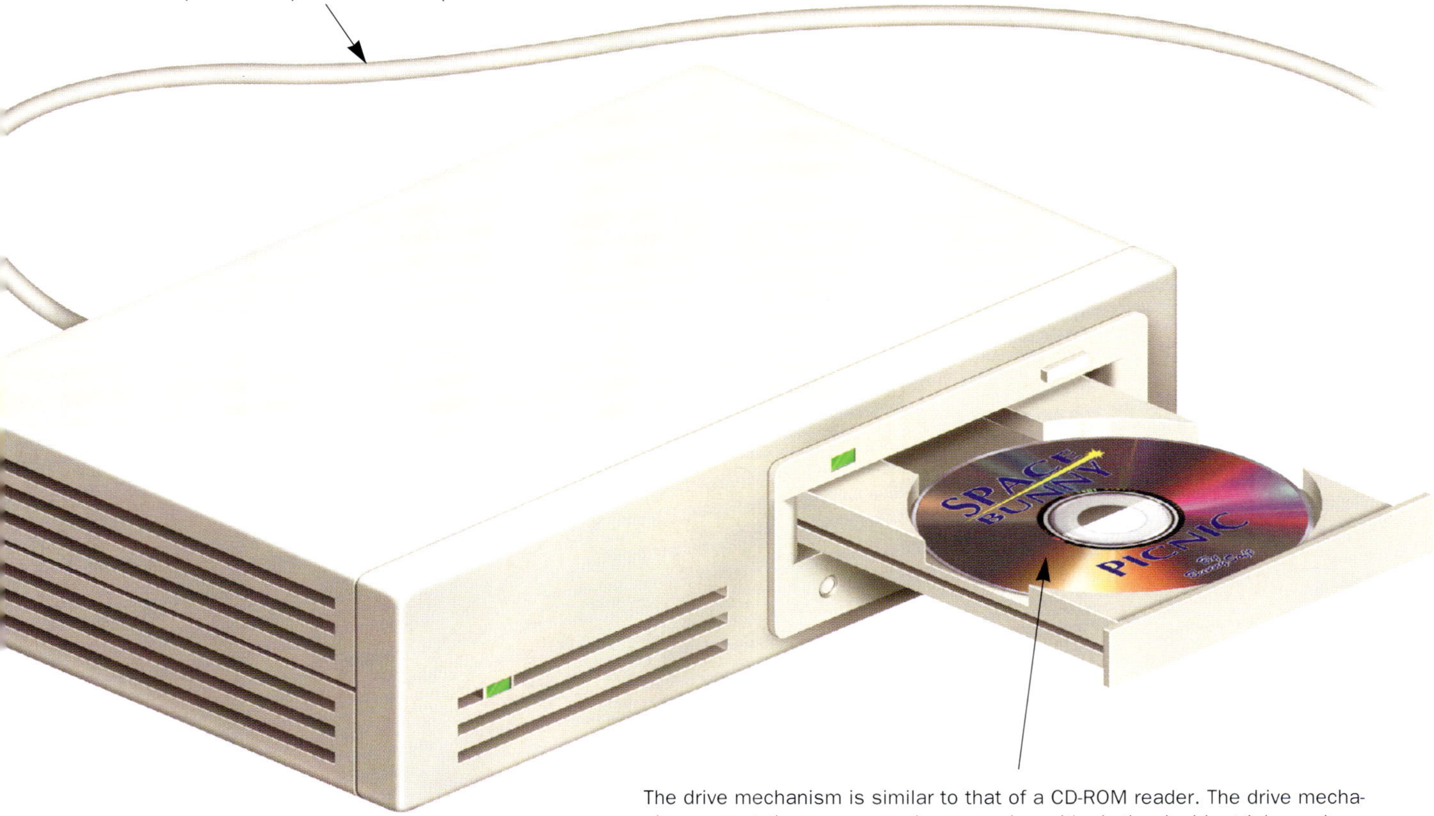

CD-writers start at about $4,000, which is certainly too expensive for most home users, although quite reasonable if you have a small business that is going to be producing CDs frequently. The price of the recorders should continue to decrease over the next few years. Other, often better alternatives are to rent them from computer rental outlets, or to find a service bureau that can take your files and create the disc for you. These bureaus generally prefer to get the files stored on tape, so you'll need a tape backup drive, preferably one that uses **DAT** (Digital Audio Tape format) tapes.

CD-ROM Reproduction

Making one-at-a-time discs using a CD-R system is good if you only need to make a single disc or very few copies. Making many copies this way, however, can be both time consuming and expensive. At $20 for each blank CD-R, you can see that it is not the way to go if you're trying to make a game that will sell for $35, for example.

There are a number of companies now that mass produce discs. For around $1,000, they will take your files already arranged for reproduction on tape or on a CD-R, and turn them into a master disc which is used for reproduction, and set up the machines to reproduce your disc. Once that is set up, the cost of the actual discs is around $1.50 each. (Please note that these prices are all rough estimates, and will vary depending on the special requirements of your disc and on the individual disc manufacturer you deal with.)

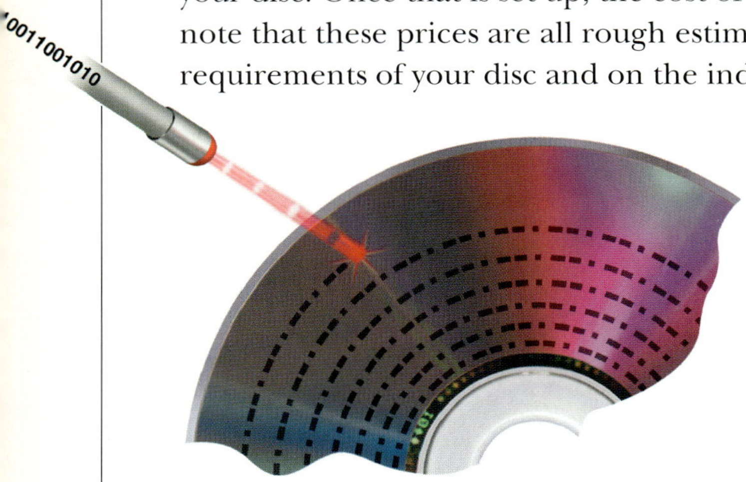

Your files will be laser-burned into the coating of a special glass disc called the **master**.

The coating where the laser struck is washed away, leaving pits. The disc is then coated until the pits are just the right depth—a depth that is measured in *millionths* of an inch!

The master is used as a mold to make **stampers**, which have a reverse image of the disc, with bumps wherever the master has pits.

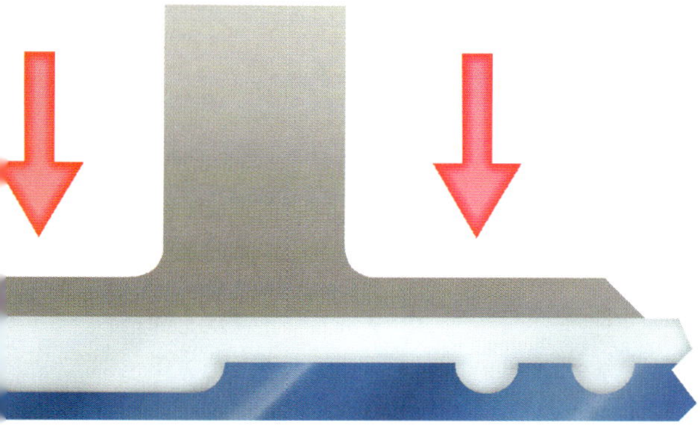

The stamper is used to form plastic discs. These discs will be reverse images of the stamper, which means they are positive images of the master.

The plastic is then coated with a thin layer of shiny aluminum to make it reflective.

Polycarbonate, a clear plastic, is used to coat the shiny disc and protect it.

Finally, the artwork is screen-printed onto the disc.

After that, your disc will be packaged. If you supply the little booklets and the backing cards that go in the normal CD containers (called **jewel boxes**), they can put the discs, booklets, and backing cards into the jewel boxes and shrink-wrap the whole thing into a nice little package for about 35 cents per disc!

You don't have to use jewel boxes for containers. There are a number of other packaging options available. Some discs come in simple plastic or cardboard sleeves, which don't provide nearly as much protection but are a lot cheaper. Others come in jewel box alternatives that are designed to provide the same level of protection while being more ecological than those big chunks of plastic. Be sure to ask your disc manufacturer about different packaging options.

PRESIDENT LAPPIN CITED CONSTITUTIONAL CONCERNS WHILE VETOING THE CONTROVERSIONAL CULTURAL UPLIFT BILL, WHICH WOULD HAVE CREATED STRICT GUIDELINES FOR CONTENTS OF MUSIC LYRICS...
The News Source
FREEDOM LOVERS EVERYWHERE ARE CELEBRATING THE PRESIDENT'S VETO OF THE LATEST MUSIC CENSORSHIP BILL!
HiPP NooZ
ENSURING A CONTINUING FRAYING OF AMERICAN MORAL FIBER, PRESIDENT LAPPIN VETOS THE OVERWHELMINGLY POPULAR...
AVN
American Values Network
SOME PEOPLE THINK THAT SOME SONGS ARE BAD FOR YOU. BECAUSE OF THIS, CONGRESS (THE PEOPLE WHO MAKE UP THE LAWS)...
What's up?
NEWS for KIDS

Part IV

Multimedia of the Future

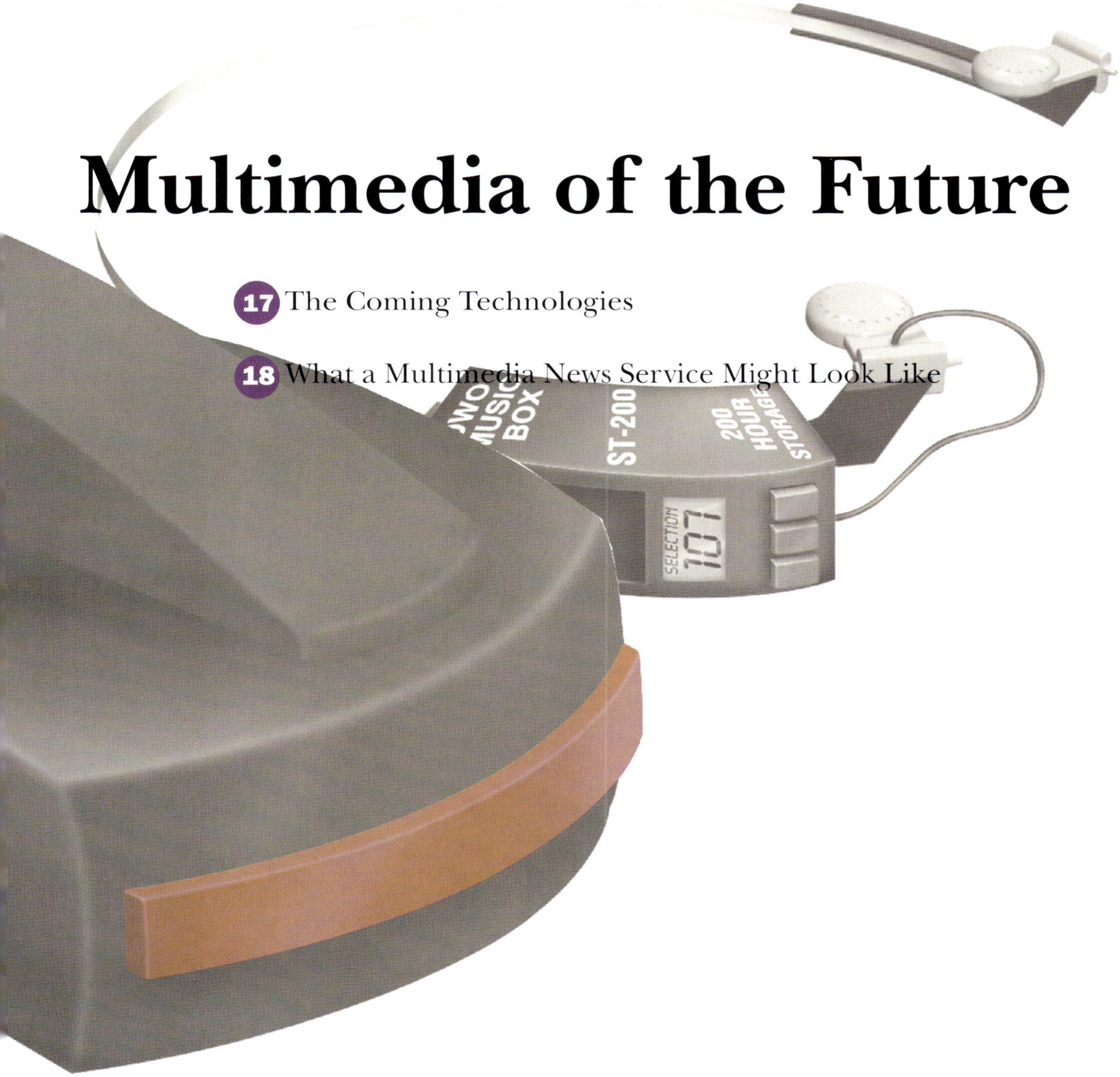

The Coming Technologies

Computer technology is constantly changing. In fact, computer sages note that every part of your computer is out of date, because there is always an improved version coming in the next six months, and a complete new technology that will wipe it out in the next two years.

What does this mean on a practical level? Don't wait to buy your computer until that great something new that you heard about actually comes out. By the time it does, there will be another something great to wait for, and you'll never get around to buying that computer. (Don't waste your time kicking yourself when the same computer you bought is 25 percent cheaper six months later, either—that's just the way computer prices go.)

The future is going to be amazing. It's less than 20 years since the first complete personal computers came out, less than 15 years since the IBM PC and the Macintosh hit the scene, and probably less than five minutes since some new development that will eventually be included in every personal computer was created. Technology changes so fast that you can't even begin to guess what it will be like in our lifetime. About the best you can do is look at what's already on the drawing board.

Multimedia computing is evolving so quickly that soon the concept will disappear altogether! The ability to handle sound and video will just become an assumed part of computing, like handling still graphics today, despite having come relatively late in the development of the computer.

Science fiction writers—the traditional predictors of the future—often show us just how off-base computer predictions are. For a long time after computers started doing wonderful feats (now being duplicated by a $20 calculator), these writers were writing about how the future would reveal computers so powerful that they would take up an entire city block. Size meant power to them.

In reality, though, as computers get more powerful, they get smaller. Obvious advantages to the smaller size are convenience and lower costs. More importantly, though, computer components are becoming so fast that the speed of electricity traveling down a few inches of wire is often a limiting factor. By building smaller circuits and smaller microprocessors, they shorten the already minute journey that those items have to take.

Monitors, on the other hand, are getting larger to match the more visual nature of modern computing. Because monitor technology and TV technology are very much the same, advances in either are advances in both. On the other hand, because TV is an older technology as compared to personal computers, the huge advances are fewer and farther between. The push towards sharp images on flat screens will continue, and some developments point toward a much shallower monitor, perhaps no thicker than a piece of cardboard, which will take up less space and may even be hung on the wall like a painting.

As processor chips get more powerful, there likely will be more and more use of special graphics coprocessing chips, which can handle complex visual updates while the main processor is crunching other sorts of data. New technologies may allow processor circuits to be built molecule by molecule, allowing hundreds of millions (instead of the current mere millions) of miniconductor devices in the same space.

Memory and Storage Advancements

Both the amount of immediate memory for computer operations (**random access memory**, often abbreviated **RAM**) and the amount of long-term memory for storage (disks) affect the ability of a computer to handle multimedia. Luckily, both seem sure to continue to grow faster, larger, and cheaper (at least the amount of storage per dollar). The same money that bought 1,000 bytes of RAM 15 years ago can now buy over a million bytes of faster, more reliable memory. Early PC hard disks cost close to $1,000 per megabyte; now they cost about $1 per megabyte and go over 10 times as fast.

RAM, particularly the RAM on the video card, plays a large part in how sharp a picture can be displayed. More RAM also means that more information can be put forth without having to access the disks, which are much slower. RAM may soon no longer be a separate component, but rather integrated with the processor into a single chip. This will have significant advantages in terms of space, because the space taken up by the RAM electronics is small compared to that taken up by the chips casing, the board the chip is mounted on, and the wiring to connect it to the processor chip. More importantly, it should slash the amount of time it takes for the processor to get information from RAM.

Despite its ability to store over 600M of information, the speed and storage of the CD-ROM drive are already limiting factors for multimedia applications. The speed problems are being addressed with faster CD-ROM drives being released (thus driving down the older ones). However, with the appetite that video applications have for disk space (or **real estate**, as software professionals call it), 600M is no longer that huge. There are already games out that require more than one CD-ROM, and any gains made by compression technology are more than balanced by the public's demand for more video and better quality.

New **blue laser CD-ROM drives** can read more data off a single disc. You won't be able to use these discs in one of the current CD-ROM drives, but you may be able to use one of the red laser CD-ROMs in a blue laser drive, so you will still be able to use your software and play music CDs with them.

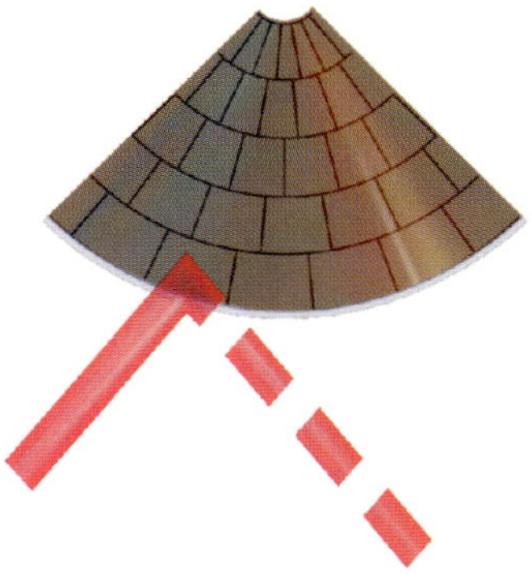

Current CD-ROM drives bounce a red beam of light off the CD to read the data.

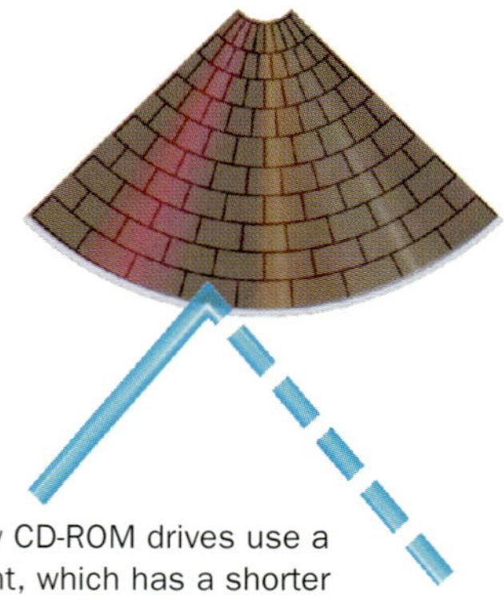

The new CD-ROM drives use a blue light, which has a shorter wavelength. It will be able to read much smaller pits on the CD surface, so that more data can be stored on a single disk.

IBM has found ways to fit about 30 times as much data onto the same size hard disk. Just like current hard disks, they will store data on magnetic platters. However, instead of storing the data as magnetic polarity (as is currently done), they will use another, subtler property of magnetism. While it takes time for technology like this to come to market—and even more time to become affordable—it will happen, and where you now have a 340M disk you will instead have a 10G disk. And you'll still find ways of filling it up.

Many experts think the future for data distribution and storage is **non-mechanical media**, all-electronic devices without any moving parts. While that might sound fancy, read-only storage like this is already in common use—video game cartridges. Modern video game cartridges often hold several megabytes worth of data, but total storage amount will have to go way up and prices way down before they make a good medium for computer data.

Non-mechanical media have a number of advantages over mechanical media:

- Quicker
- Smaller without being overly delicate
- Faster data transfer
- More reliable (moving parts wear out)

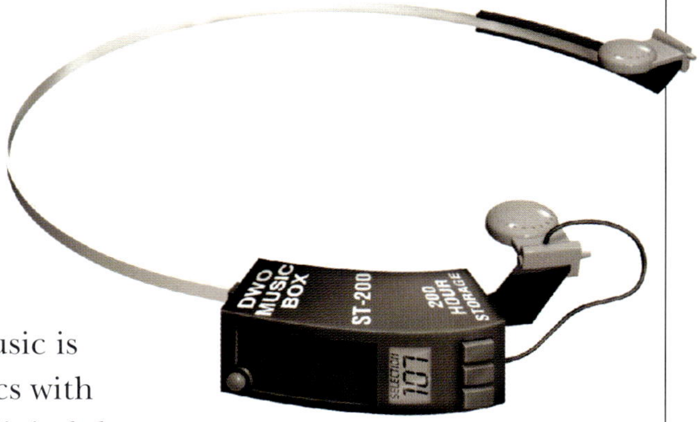

People will have to be convinced of the reliability of writable non-mechanical storage before they start using them to replace hard disks, though; no one wants a small spark to wipe out all their data.

These same advances could radically change how music is distributed. Instead of having individual tapes or discs with music on them, music could be distributed as pure digital data. To buy a new recording, you might bring your data unit to a store where they would copy it from their computer to your storage. You might even be able to download it across the computer network. As density of storage increases, you may be able to keep an entire music library in a small cube, easily transported wherever you want to go, and free of the jarring problems of CDs or jamming problems of tapes.

The Information Superhighway

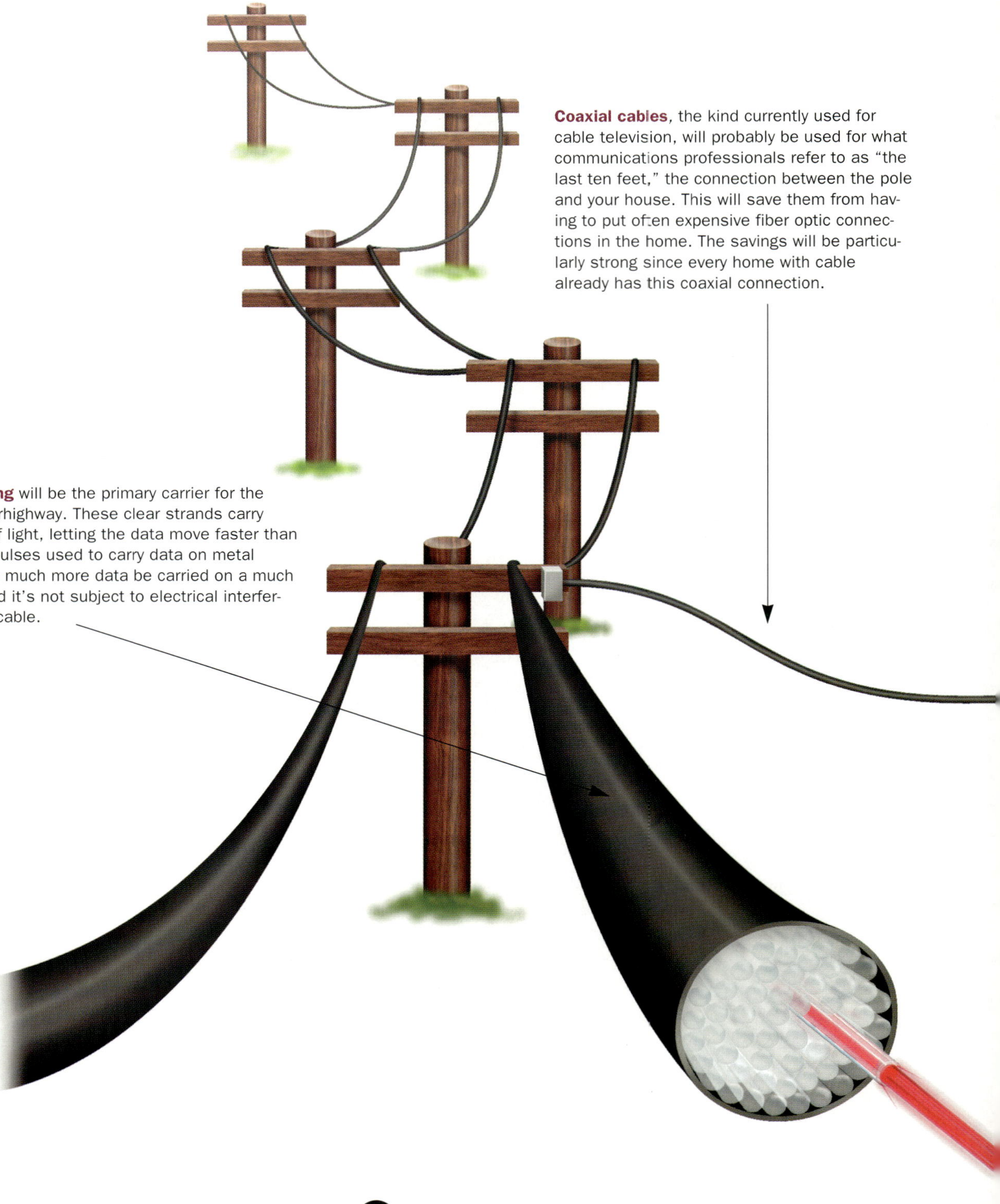

Coaxial cables, the kind currently used for cable television, will probably be used for what communications professionals refer to as "the last ten feet," the connection between the pole and your house. This will save them from having to put often expensive fiber optic connections in the home. The savings will be particularly strong since every home with cable already has this coaxial connection.

Fiber optic cabling will be the primary carrier for the information superhighway. These clear strands carry data as pulses of light, letting the data move faster than the electrical impulses used to carry data on metal wires. It also lets much more data be carried on a much thinner cable, and it's not subject to electrical interference, like metal cable.

The United States is already wired together in two ways. Almost every household is connected to the telephone system, which uses a mix of wire, fiber optic cable, and microwave and satellite relays to monophonic (non-stereo) medium-quality sound in two directions. About half of the households are hooked up to cable television, which uses coaxial cable and satellite transmission to carry dozens of channels of uncompressed standard resolution video and stereo sound, but generally only in a single direction with no interactivity.

Now the nation's getting wired again with the **information superhighway**. The goal is to connect every home with two-way, high-speed data communications, allowing you to establish interactive data, sound, and/or video communications with distant places. This is multimedia communication and remote computing combined into one tidy package.

With the drive for cable companies to get into the telephone business and for telephone companies to get into the cable TV business, the United States' two wiring systems were already headed toward being combined into a single system. The information superhighway will likely link both of them, using the same local cabling setup for data, telephone, and cable TV where possible.

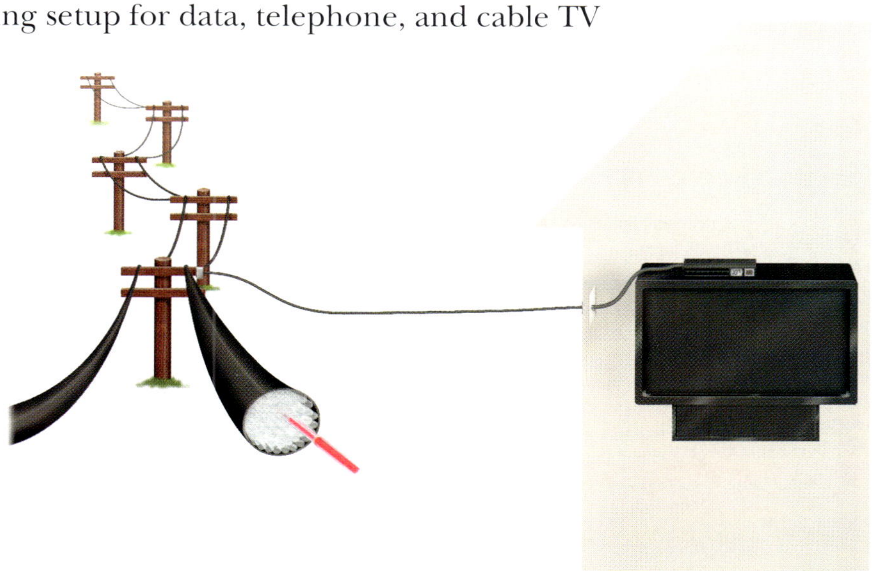

Television

Not everybody has a desktop PC in their home. For most people, the central device for accessing this vast data network will be the TV set. With an intelligent cable box that serves as a computer, the TV will act as a computer monitor, and the remote control will replace the keyboard. Everyone will have this multimedia system.

Many of the applications that people are anticipating are just improved access to TV shows. While many people don't understand computers, almost everyone understands TV, so it's the item being publicized right now. The main superTV feature is **video-on-demand**, the ability to watch what you want, when you want it. Instead of having to wait for the broadcast time of a given program, you will be able to call up a menu system on the screen and ask for a specific TV show or movie. That specific show will be sent directly to your cable box, in compressed form, in quick bursts of data. (Current versions of this feature limit your choices to a hundred or so movies, but it should expand to cover a much wider selection of content.)

Even though standard set-time broadcast material still will be available, ultimately most people will be choosing what to view and when. This could decimate the power of the networks, with any production company able to get material on-line for ordering. All the head-to-head battles for rating points would be gone, since there would no longer be the concept of two interesting programs competing in the same time slot. If you watch two hours of TV a night, it won't be trying to choose the best thing that happens to be on at each of four half hours, it will be choosing the best two hours from all the TV and movies that you haven't seen yet, whether it be a classic *Dick Van Dyke Show* episode or the just released episode of *Deep Space Bunnies: The Next Few Generations.*

Selecting movies is only a limited form of interactivity, and many more interactive things will be available. You'll be able to play games on your TV that will interact with other players all over the country. You'll be able to shop via your computer—not this "we offer you what you want, when you want it, and you've got to call us" shopping that QVC and Home Shopping Network currently offer, but being able to page through video catalogues and order, all just using your remote control. The combination of multimedia and data communications makes many things possible.

Various cable boxes designed for bi-directional communication are already in use in some test markets. It's becoming clear that some standard elements will be needed in the long term. MPEG decoding circuitry will be built-in, allowing all video to be sent compressed and thus permitting ten times as many channels of standard cable television to be put in the same space. Hundreds of megabytes, perhaps even gigabytes, of storage will hold software, data, and shows that will be downloaded to the box. It also will connect to computers and other data devices, making it the link point between your home and all the computers and services connected to the information superhighway.

Many multimedia technologies will be an inherent part of the new **high definition television** (**HDTV**, for short) standard. New wider, higher resolution screens will use compressed digital video instead of the traditional uncompressed analog signal to create a sharper picture with better color reproduction. The sets also will be clearer to read for computer applications.

Virtual Reality

There are many people who would refuse to accept **virtual reality** as its own medium. After all, virtual reality is composed of information carried by other media, including on-the-fly animation and audio. Then again, video is just a series of still pictures shown very fast with some audio thrown in, but nobody argues with calling that a medium.

Virtual reality is a goal. The aim is to create a computer-generated world that you can interact with as if it were real. That sounds nice, but what does it really mean?

In reality, the levels of simulation of reality achieved by things labeled "virtual reality" vary widely. At the simplest level, it can be simply a game where you are looking through the viewpoint of the player you are controlling (as with *Doom*, or *The 7th Guest*, or many car race games and flight simulators) as opposed to an overhead or distant view (as with *Pac-Man* or *Space Invaders*).

Other virtual reality, however, goes much further. Much effort has gone into developing systems that can detect your movement in various ways, as well as systems that can make you feel like you're in an artificial environment (a **virtual space**).

Perhaps the device most associated with virtual reality is the **head mounted display** (**HMD**). This is a helmet that covers much of your head, including your ears and your eyes.

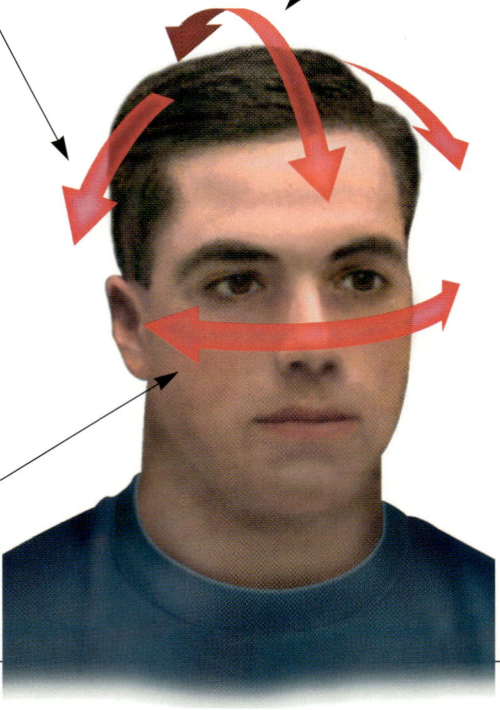

The helmet can detect how far you are tilting your head back and forth...

...or leaning side to side...

...or turning your head, and thus can tell the computer where you are looking.

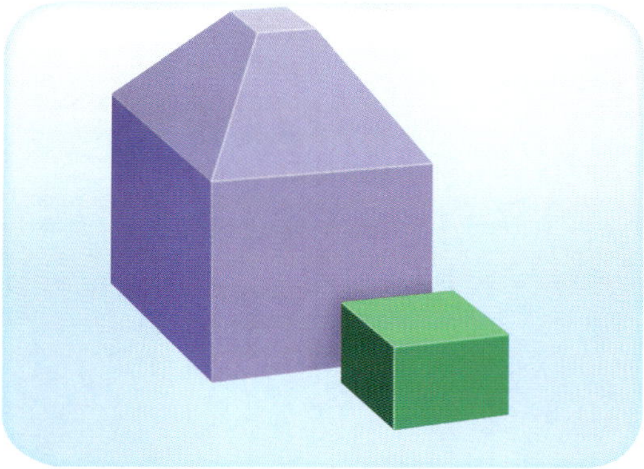

The helmet has two **liquid crystal display** monitors (similar to those used on laptop computers), one for the left eye...

...and one which will show a slightly different image for the right eye.

Your mind interprets these two images as part of a single, three-dimensional reality. As you move your head, the computer will constantly recalculate the image so that you are seeing whatever you would now be facing in virtual space.

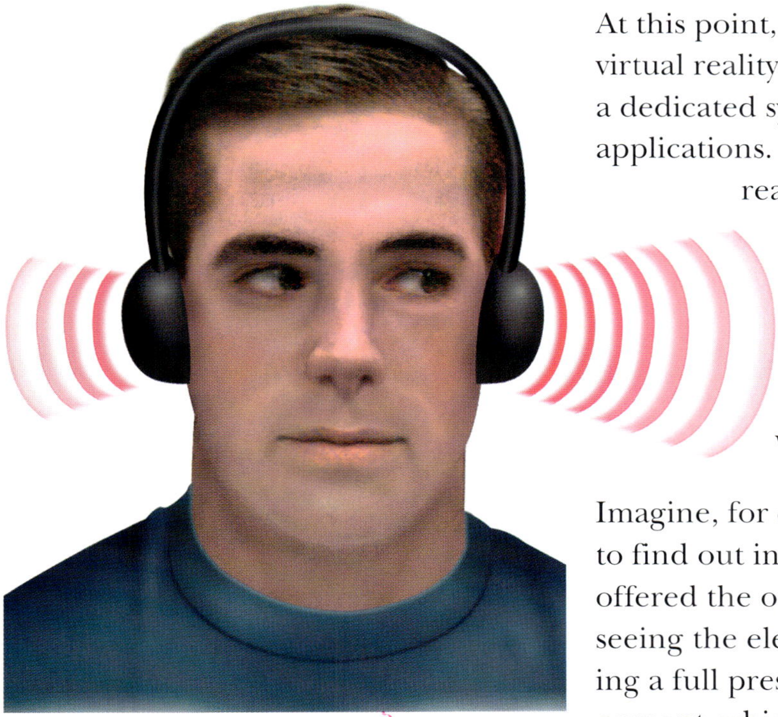

Built-in stereo sound headphones are used to create a similar, audio illusion. If something is supposed to be off to your left, it will sound louder in your left ear. As you turn your head to face it, the sound will become even in both ears.

At this point, due to both costs and creative inspiration, virtual reality is generally used as its own medium on a dedicated system, and not mixed into multimedia applications. The military is a prime consumer of virtual reality systems, using them for both simulation and advanced fighter control. Expensive virtual reality games have been finding a place at high-end arcades and in technology museums. However, as time goes on, costs will likely go down and inspiration will increase.

Imagine, for example, using a multimedia encyclopedia to find out information about the atom, and being offered the opportunity to walk around through an atom, seeing the electrons fly about from various angles. Or seeing a full presentation on a new proposed building development, which includes not only the text of the environmental impact statement and images of the architect's drawings, but also being able to simulate a walk around the buildings. Or a computerized driver's education course, which mixes stored lectures, videos, and quizzes with an accurate driving simulator.

What a Multimedia News Service Might Look Like

So everybody's talking about **digital video** and the **information superhighway**, but it all keeps coming back to video-on-demand, and it sounds like all it will do is save you an occasional trip to the video store. That's perhaps the easiest thing to understand, but it's really a technology that can change your everyday life. Let's just consider one aspect: news.

If you're like most people, you get your news from television. You probably watch an hour of TV to get maybe 20 minutes of the news that you really care about. Or perhaps you read the paper for more in-depth coverage, but by the time it hits your doormat, it's hours old. It's easier to skip over the stories you don't care about, but who knows how many stories you do care about that aren't in there?

And no matter which news source you're using, if you have further questions or want more background information than the source provides, you are out of luck.

But with cable box multimedia and the information superhighway, you could be getting just the news you want—as you want it. This isn't the definite shape of the future, but something that technology would support. Whether it (or something similar) becomes available relies more on a series of business decisions about what will be profitable than on any question of what is possible. The technology is really already here, waiting to be applied.

The first decision you have to make is what kind of news style you prefer. You do this now when you decide to get your information from the dry, conservative MacNeil/Lehrer News Hour, or the more traditional CBS News, or the Christian-oriented 700 Club, or the youth-oriented viewpoint of MTV News. You may prefer to eschew the news anchor altogether, in favor of a text presentation of all the non-video information. It's up to you. Different providers will compete to give you a different slant on the news, trying to grab a market that the others aren't.

This could be the end of the supposed objectivity of the news media. Just as a two-newspaper town will generally have a conservative paper and a more liberal one, you will have a range of viewpoints and special interest news delivery, each choosing the wording they think best reflects the greater truth that may lie beyond the facts.

Your Own News Profile

Now you've selected the style and spin you want to see on the news. Next, you get to choose exactly which news you'll see. There are thousands of news stories everyday. Along with everything you see on TV, and all you see in the papers, there are bits of local news all over the world. There is also specialty news—news about computers, medicine, baseball card collecting, or any of hundreds of other special interests that now have their own newsletters.

The major part of your news profile, which would be stored at some central location, is your list of news interests. You may want to hear only the most important news out of Congress, and nothing about hockey, but every little news tidbit about stock car racing is important to you, and you'd like to hear something about the royal family about once a week. By giving the central computer your list of interests, it will know what news to send out to you.

The profile would be available through your cable box remote control. Using a simple menu system, you can set your level of interest on every topic about the news, which the system will use to decide what news item to bring to your attention.

By breaking the possible news items into a wide variety of topics and subtopics, the system should be able to pinpoint precisely what interests you. With thousands of news items everyday, this kind of accuracy is needed, or else you'd never get through the day's headlines. In a world glutted with information, you need a good filter. You couldn't read all the news if you wanted to (if you could read it all, you wouldn't want to).

Your level of interest would have to be indicated in multiple ways that could apply to each article. Of course, you'll always be able to go back and adjust these settings later, if you find you are getting too many news items, or missing things of importance. Menus will make it very easy to set up for common interests like major league baseball, but setting up for a specific high school baseball team five states away would be more difficult.

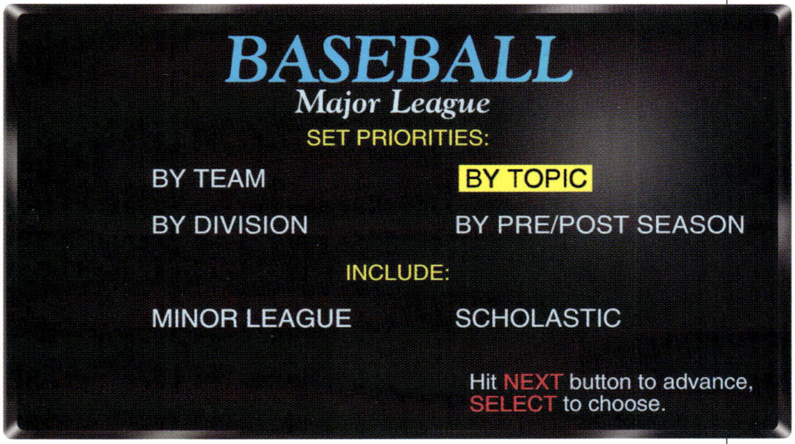

Each setting will be a weighing factor. When considering whether to present you with a news item about a trade between the Phillies and the Yankees, for example, the system would consider your level of interest in trades, and your level of interest in both the Phillies and the Yankees. It also will weigh the importance of the story—it will much more likely bring up an announced trade of two major players than the rumor of a trade under consideration that would swap a couple of traditional bench warmers.

Selecting Stories

Once the system is set up, you can check your news whenever you want. Twenty-four hours a day a newscast will be available with all the stories you want. You can check the news every few hours and get just the latest stories and updates. Or maybe you don't check in for a few days—you won't miss any news. The stories aren't being sent to you until you check for the news, so those days' worth of news would still be waiting for you.

When you check your news, a menu of headlines will be waiting for you. As with a newspaper, you can just skip over the ones you don't want to read to the ones you do.

Of course, instead of reading the big story, you get a full television presentation produced by the news service that you selected, just like you currently do on TV.

From *Best of MediaClips 2.0*, © 1991-1994 Aris Multimedia Entertainment, Inc. Photograph by NASA.

Once you've seen all you've wanted to of this story, you can fast forward to the next one!

Or maybe not. You might get stuck on an ad. After all, somebody has to pay for this thing. This would actually be a wonderful place for advertisers, because they can select whether to send you an ad based not only on what news source you chose, but also on what interests you highlighted. A seed company could afford to advertise by having their commercials sent only to those who selected *gardening* as one of their interests.

The system would lock you out from fast forwarding the commercials. After all, if you could skip the commercials, everyone would. Then nobody would buy any of the products advertised, the companies would close down, the economy would collapse, and civilization as we know it would come to a grinding halt.

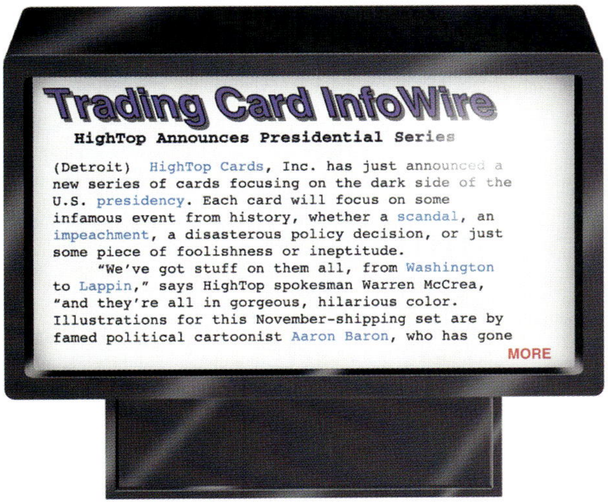

With thousands of stories, no news service could produce a full video segment for all of them. Many of the specialty stories would probably be farmed out to specialty news providers. Many of the stories aimed at smaller audiences would be done audio-only or even text-only, as both are much cheaper to produce than a video segment.

Getting More In-Depth

So you've found a story that interests you, but you want more information. There are aspects of it you don't understand or you are curious about. That's great, because the news system is just a front end for the most amazing reference source you can imagine.

Text stories would all have hypertext capabilities, and stories on video would have a menu of related topics that could pop up by remote control. These features would lead you to information on these topics. Some would be text-only, including not only standard dictionary and encyclopedia topics, but things like medical guides, price guides, movie guides, the congressional record, and of course the text from every news item since the inception of this system and every article from major newspapers for the years before that.

It'll all be multimedia—mere text won't cut it! You'll have access to hundreds of thousands of pictures and thousands of hours of audio and video, just like the current multimedia reference systems only many times larger. Research that would be impossible at a large library will become possible and with unbeatable speed and privacy.

Connecting your computer to your cable box will give you more powerful information search tools, and allow you to capture the information for further use. Connect a printer directly to your cable box, and it will be able to print out all the text and still image information.

This is a likely direction for the multimedia revolution. The dividing lines between different media are getting blurred. The line between computing and all other forms of communication is getting erased entirely.

But the real future of multimedia computing has not yet been written (or turned into a picture, video, sampled sound, or any other presentation, for that matter). Multimedia of the future will be whatever you and everyone else choose to make of it—and the possibilities are amazing!

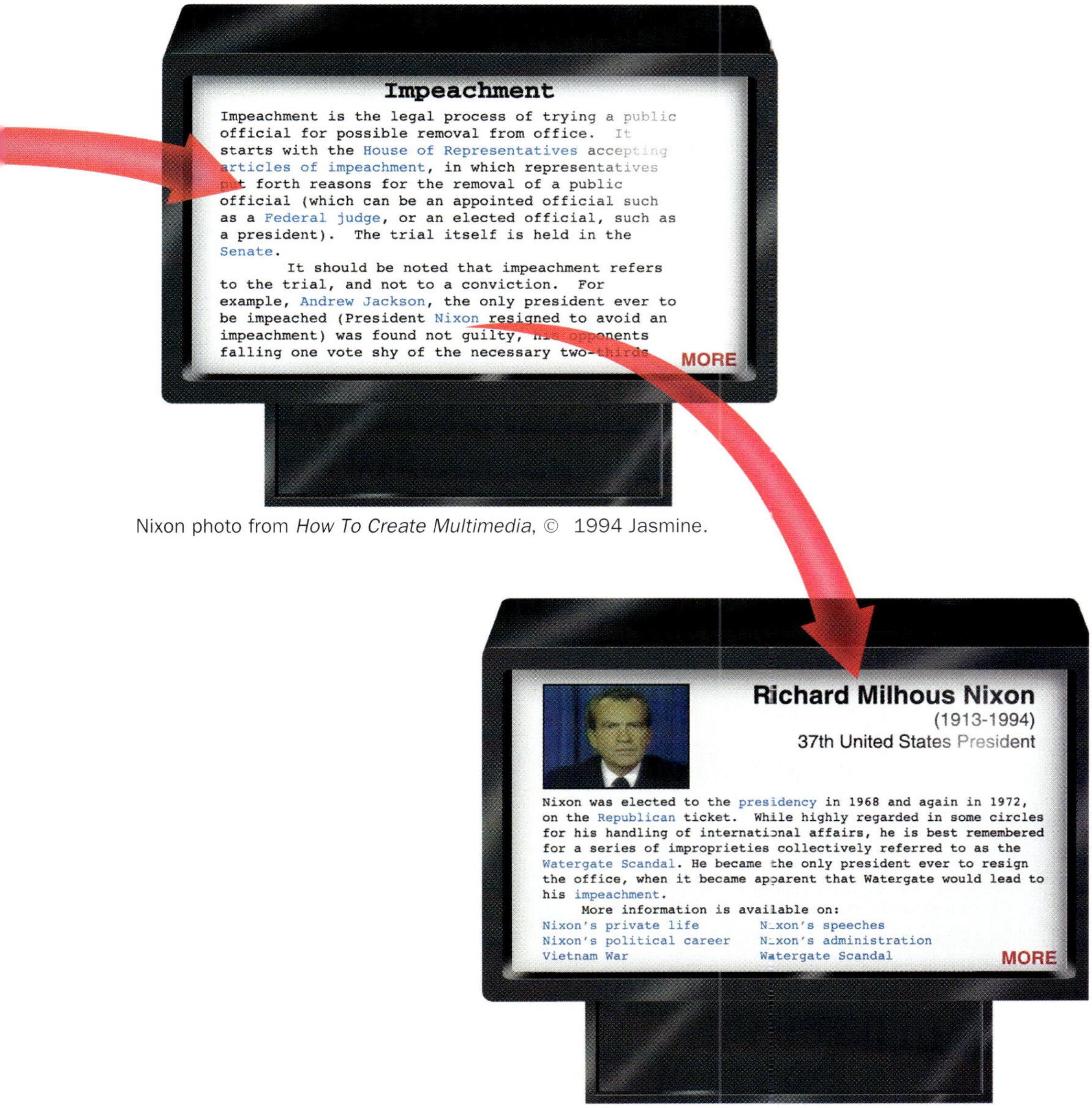

Nixon photo from *How To Create Multimedia*, © 1994 Jasmine.

CAH-RAH-VAH-GEE-OH

Art Gallery

Michelangelo Merisi da CARAVAGGIO

ARTISTS' LIVES

1571 - 1610
Italy

Portrait of Caravaggio
Ottavio Leoni
Biblioteca Marcelliana
Florence

▸ Boy bitten by a Lizard
CARAVAGGIO
painted 1598-1600

▸ The Supper at Emmaus, CARAVAGGIO
1601

▸ Salome...
CARAVAGG...
painted 1...

Caravaggio is often seen as the archetypal artist-rebel whose tempestuous life (of only 37 years) matched the drama of his works. The immediacy of his mature paintings was achieved by the uncompromising representation of people and objects from life, intense and theatrical lighting which heightens the dramatic content, and strong foreshortenings.

Help | Options... | Go Back

History Painting

A 'history painting' is one which has a serious narrative, or includes exemplars of actions which are intended to have didactic overtones. In this sense the word history relates to the Italian istoria, meaning narrative or story (and not the accurate or documentary description of actual events).

History paintings are often large in scale. Their subjects can be taken from the Bible, from mythology or other forms of secular literature, from historical events; or they can be allegories. Noble themes are seen as being particularly worthy of depiction.

History painting was viewed as the most important of the genres from about the 16th century, and the climax of an academic painter's training. It was the equivalent of Epic or Tragedy in literature.

Art Gallery

...elshazzar's Feast

PAINTINGS

A Theatrical Composition

▸ Juno discovering Jupiter with Io
LASTMAN (NG)

▸ Supper at Emmaus
CARAVAGGIO (NG)

Belshazzar's Feast is a dramatic ***history painting**. Its style is based on that of Rembrandt's teacher ▸ **Lastman.**

Lastman had studied the work of the influential Italian ▸ **Caravaggio** during his stay in Rome. The theatrical composition of *Belshazzar's Feast* with its crowded picture space, emphatic gestures and theatrical lighting derives from Caravaggio.

Belshazzar's Feast as it survives is slightly more dramatic than originally intended.

At some point the painting was cut and placed at a slight angle on the reclining canvas, giving it a diagonal tilt, which increases the dramatic effect.

Help | Options... | Go Back | 4 of 4 pages on Belshazzar's Feast
6 of 25 paintings by REMBRANDT | Next Page | See Also | Contents

The LUTE represents the love of music. The lute was the chief courtly instrument at this time. There was a large repertoire of music and songs for the lute.

One of the lute strings is broken. Death abruptly stops life as a breaking string stops a song.

Art Gallery

PAINT...

Glossary

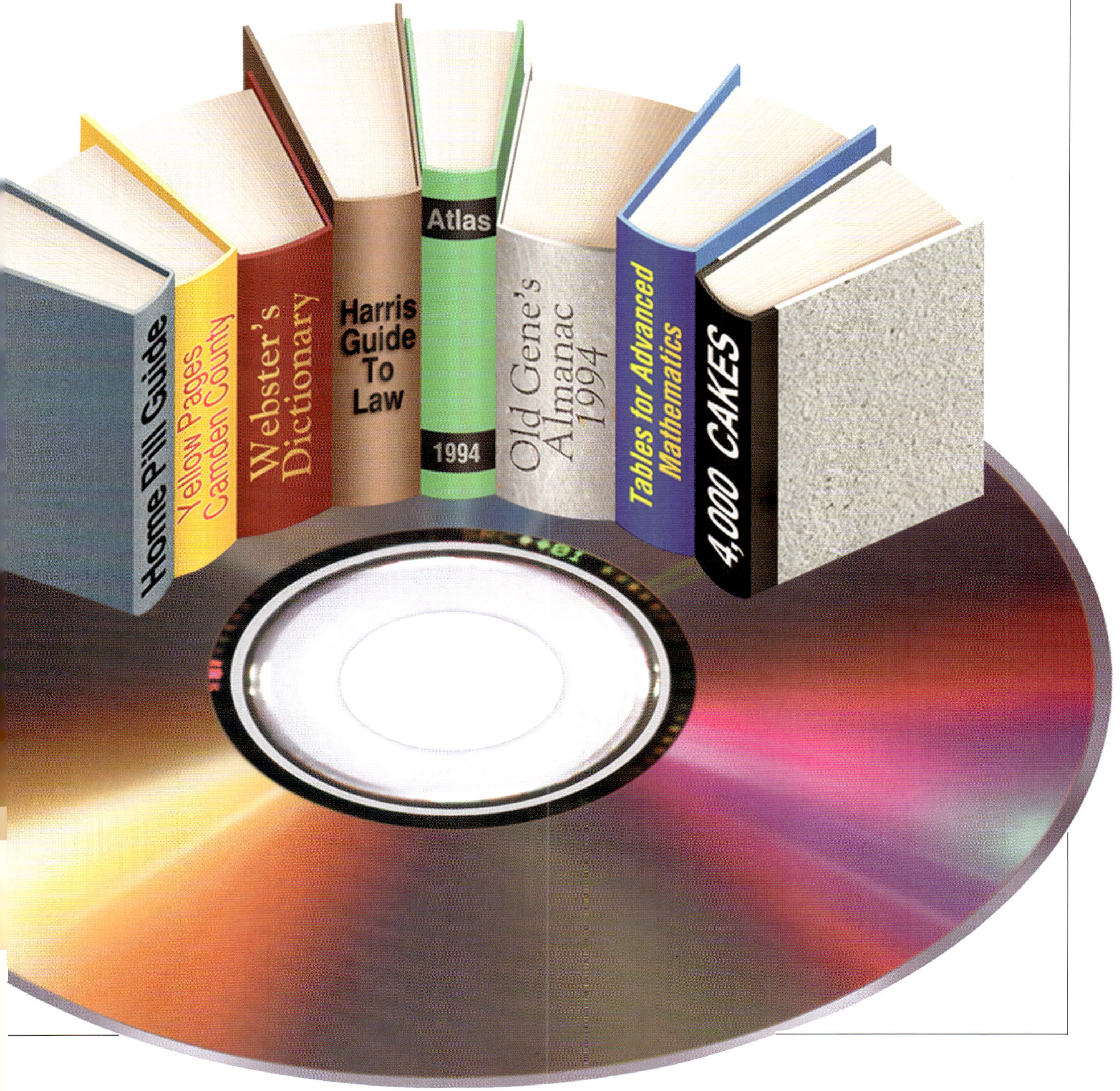
Home Pill Guide
Yellow Pages Camden County
Webster's Dictionary
Harris Guide To Law
Atlas
1994
Old Gene's Almanac 1994
Tables for Advanced Mathematics
4,000 CAKES

Glossary

16-bit sound Computer processed sound that uses 16 bits of information to describe each sampled interval, allowing it to be one of 65,536 different values. See p. 24.

3DO interactive multiplayer A standard design for multimedia consoles, created by The 3DO Company. See pp. 34-35.

3-D modeling Creating computer images and animations by describing a three dimensional object or set of objects to the computer, and having the computer recreate those objects from a desired viewpoint on- screen. See p. 90.

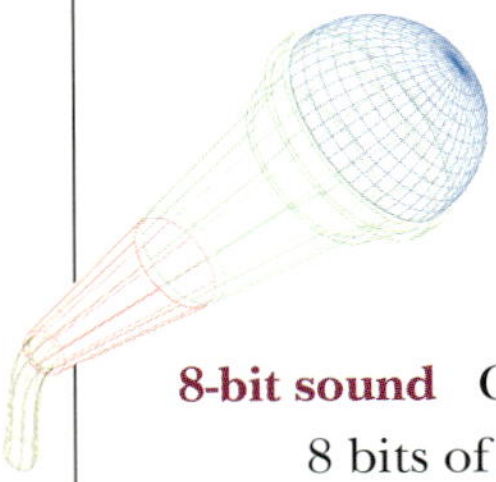

8-bit sound Computer processed sound that uses 8 bits of information to describe the wave position of each sampled interval, allowing it to be one of 256 different values. See p. 24.

A

access time The amount of time that it takes for a compact disk or other data retrieval system to locate and become prepared to read a specific piece of data. See p. 27.

analog video Video stored or transmitted in a form where the description of color and intensity of each displayed point is not limited to a fixed set of values, but is rather infinitely variable. See p. 97.

animation Simulated motion. See pp. 102-107.

authoring package A software package that allows you to combine your individual pictures, videos, sounds, or other files into a single, complete project. See pp. 114-119.

B

B-frames The most common type of frames in an MPEG-compressed video, which are described by how they vary from the two closest I-frames or P-frames. See p. 101.

blue laser CD-ROM drives A coming technology that will use a higher wavelength laser to read CDs, and thus will be able to handle CDs with more data in the same space. See p. 146.

button An on-screen area that is linked to a command or option by selecting that area with the pointer. See p. 41.

C

CD *See compact disc.*

card-based storyboard A series of cards, each of which describes one scene or decision point of a project, that reference each other, so that together they describe the entire project. See p. 113.

CD-32 A multimedia console produced by Commodore, more advanced than CDTV. See p. 34.

CD-I A multimedia console produced by Phillips. See p. 34.

CD-R Short for *Compact Disc-Recordable*: A compact disc that can have information written onto it by a CD-writer. See p. 138.

CD-ROM Short for *Compact Disc-Read-Only Memory*: A compact disc that is used to store computer data. See p. 26.

CD-ROM controller An internal board for personal computers that acts as an interface to a CD-ROM drive, interpreting commands and controlling the flow of information. See p. 24.

CDTV A multimedia console produced by Commodore. See p. 34.

CD-WO Short for *Compact Disc-Write Once*. Another name for CD-R. See p. 138.

CD-WORM Short for *Compact Disc-Write Once, Read Mostly*. Another name for CD-R. See p. 138.

CD-writer A device that can store information on CD-R discs. See p. 139.

chart type storyboard A chart that describes the scenes and decision points of a project. See pp. 112-113.

clip art disk A disk-based collection of images designed for those who need images to add to their project. See p. 86.

coaxial cables The type of cables used for most cable television connections, consisting of one or more conductors surrounded by a metal shielding layer. See p. 148.

codecs Short for *compression/decompression*. Algorithms used to decrease the amount of data necessary to describe a video sequence, and to recreate the video from the reduced data. See p. 100.

collision detection The ability to detect when two screen sprites overlap. See p. 105.

compact disc A data storage medium that holds data as a series of dents and flat areas on a reflective disc, which is itself enclosed in a layer of clear plastic. See p. 26.

computer program A series of instructions that describe to the computer how to perform a given function. See p. 118.

context-sensitive help A system where the computer decides which user assistance information is displayed based on what action the user is currently performing. See p. 133.

D

DAT Short for *Digital Audio Tape*. A tape format used for both audio recordings and computer data storage. See p. 139.

digital camera A camera that captures pictures as digital images for computer use. See p. 87.

digital video Video in which each frame is depicted as a gridwork of precise colors taken from a limited set, as opposed to analog video where the color values are infinitely variable. See p. 154.

digitizing Computer processing and storage of sound or pictures that describes the item as a series of numbers. See pp. 76-77.

E

elevator bar Another name for *scroll bar*. See p. 40.

F

fades Techniques for smoothly changing from a displayed image to a blank screen. See p. 114.

fiber optic cabling
A form of non-metalic cabling that carries information as pulses of light. See p.148.

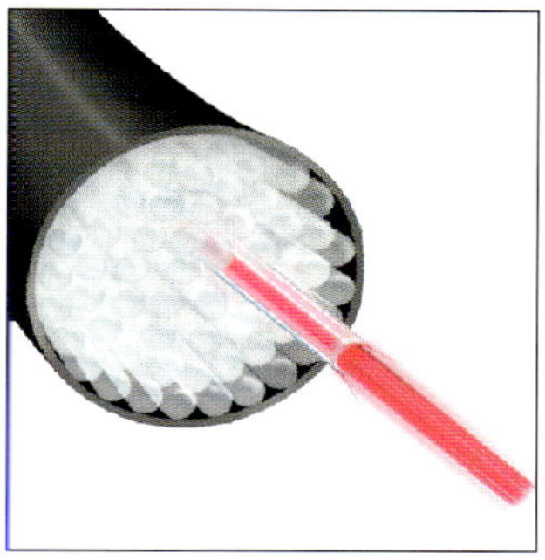

fractals Mathematically described curves that can

effectively mimic a wide range of natural phenomena. See p. 100.

frame A single image from a video image stream. See p. 100.

frame grabber A device that captures single frames from an incoming video image stream and converts them into a digitized form for computer use. See p. 87.

freeware Computer software that you can copy and use for free. See p. 115.

G

game port A connector on the computer that allows you to connect joysticks and other specialty devices. See p. 24.

Genesis A popular home video game console, manufactured by Sega. See p. 32.

graphical user interface A system of using items such as icons, windows, pointers, and mice to allow the user to control a computer's operations. See p. 41.

GUI Short for *graphical user interface.* See p. 41.

H

HDTV Short for *High Definition Television.* See p. 151.

head mounted display A helmet with built-in video screens and position detectors, used in virtual reality. See p. 152.

high definition television Any of a number of emerging standards for television with a sharper image. See p. 151.

HMD Short for *Head Mounted Display*. See p. 152.

hypermedia A system that allows you to get further information on an item from a screen of information, simply by selecting or indicating that item. See pp. 12-13.

hypertext A system that allows you to get further information on a single word or phrase from a screen of text simply by selecting or indicating that word or phrase. See p. 12.

I

icon A small picture or diagram used to represent a single command, option, piece of information, or file. See p. 40.

I-frames Individual frames in an MPEG-compressed video, which are each fully described as a complete JPEG-compressed image. See p. 100.

image file A single file that contains all of the data and structure information that is to be transferred onto a CD-ROM. See p. 136.

information superhighway The planned high-bandwidth data network that will provide access across the USA. See pp. 148-149.

interactive multimedia Multimedia projects or presentations that require or can accept some form of user involvement. See pp. 14-15.

ISO 9660 A standard approved by the International Standards Organization for the structure of data and directories on CD-ROM. ISO 9660 CD-ROMs can be used by computers that use different operating systems. See p. 137.

J

jewel boxes The standard cases used to hold CDs. See p. 141.

joypad A control device commonly used on home video games and multimedia consoles, in which the direction of movement is indicated by placing your finger on a selected portion of a circular or cross-shaped button. See p. 42.

JPEG A standard format for storage and compression of digitized pictures, defined by the Joint Photographic Experts Group. See p. 93.

K

kHz Short for *kilohertz*. See p. 83.

kilohertz A measurement of electrical or wave cycle speed. One kilohertz is equal to one thousand cycles per second. See p. 83.

L

land A flat area on the reflective surface of a compact disc. See p. 26.

liquid crystal display An information display made up of small segments of liquid crystal. Each segment is clear except when a small electrical charge is run through it, at which point it turns black. Often abbreviated LCD. See p. 153.

local bus video A display system in the personal computer in which a video display adapter is connected to the local bus on the system board, which is much faster than the system bus. See p. 25.

M

master A glass version of a CD that is used to create the stampers. See pp. 140-141.

media The plural of *medium*. See p. 8.

medium Any single form of communication, such as text, sound, or pictures. See p. 8.

MIDI Short for *Musical Instrument Digital Interface*. See pp. 80-81.

millisecond A thousandth of a second. See p. 27.

mixing The combining of multiple sound recordings into a single recording. See p. 79.

motion JPEG A codecthat treats each frame of video as a separate JPEG-compressed image. See p. 100.

mouse A hand-held computer interface device that is run across a pad or blank space on a table or other flat surface. The computer detects the motion of the mouse and translates that into movement of an on-screen pointer. See p. 43.

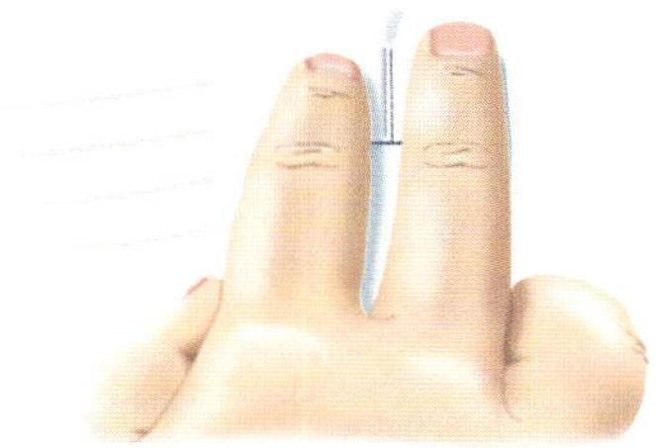

MPC Short for *Multimedia Personal Computer*. A standard for the performance levels of various elements of a computer, designed to assure that a given computer is sufficiently equipped to handle a given piece of software. See pp. 28-29.

MPC2 Short for *Multimedia Personal Computer Two*, a higher standard for computer performance than MPC. See pp. 28-29.

MPEG A high-quality codec defined by the Motion Picture Experts Group. See p. 100.

multimedia The use of more than one medium in a presentation or program. See pp. 6-11.

multimedia authoring package *See authoring package.*

multimedia computing Computer software that uses multiple media to convey information to the user. See pp. 6-11.

multimedia console A complete hardware unit designed to run special multimedia software without the full cost or capabilities of a personal computer. See pp. 34-35.

multimedia upgrade package A prepackaged set of materials (generally including a CD-ROM drive, a sound card, a microphone, and software) that is designed to enhance a personal computer so that it can use multimedia software. See p. 22.

multisession A compact disc format that handles information that was added to the disc at different times. See p. 138.

Musical Instrument Digital Interface A standard for communications between computers and musical instruments (including many sounds cards). See pp. 80-81.

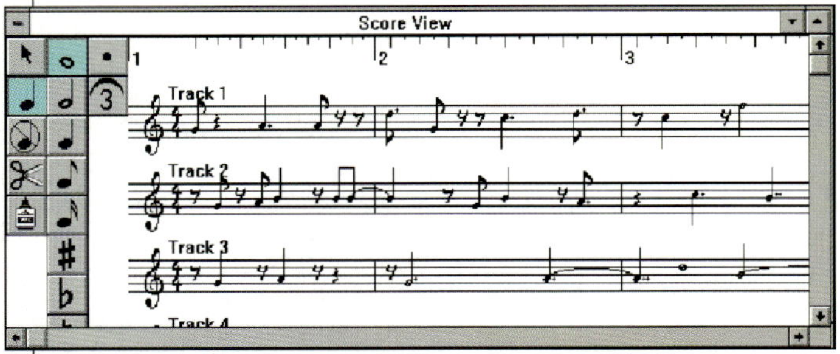

N

non-mechanical media Any form of data storage that does not require moving or spinning parts. See p. 147.

O

observer The viewer of a presentation. See p. 14.

P

paint program A program that lets you design or alter computer images that consist of grids of pixels. See pp. 88-89.

palette The set of colors available for use on a computer display. See p. 88.

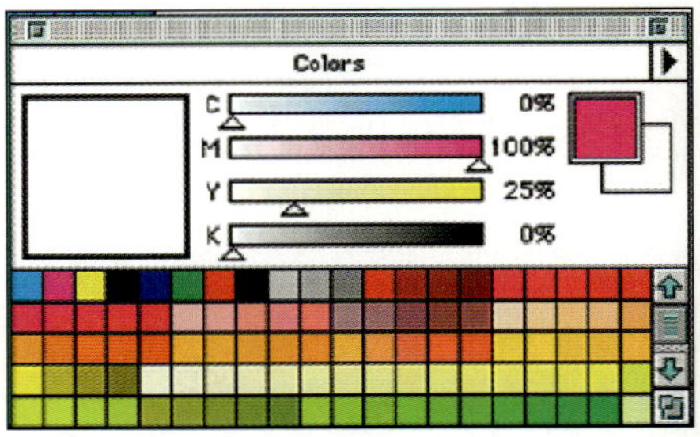

passive multimedia Multimedia presentations that do not require any substantive interaction with the viewer. See pp. 14-17.

p-frames Individual frames in MPEG video that are described by describing the difference between the image to be displayed and the image displayed on a single previous frame. See p. 101.

pit A dented area on the reflective surface of a compact disc. See p. 26.

pixel An individual rectangle of color that is part of the grid of rectangles that make up the computer display. See p. 25.

pointer A user-controlled on-screen picture used to indicate selected positions on the screen. See p. 40.

polycarbonate A clear plastic that is used as a protective coating on CDs. See p. 141.

pop-up menu A menu that, when requested, appears wherever the pointer is on-screen. See p. 41.

primitives Simple shapes used to construct objects for 3-D modeling. See p. 90.

programming language A set of defined commands and syntax that can be used to create a computer program. See p. 118.

programming library A set of predefined routines designed to perform specific functions that you can include in a computer program. See p. 118.

pull-down menu A command menu that the user pulls down from a menu bar. See p. 40.

R

RAM Short for *Random-Access Memory*. See p. 146.

random-access memory Data storage chips that the processor can access directly and can change the information stored within. See p. 146.

ray tracing A method of creating a 3-D modeled image in which the computer traces the path of each beam of light viewed as it reflects and refracts off of the modeled objects. See p.90.

Read-Only Memory Any form of computer data storage designed so that the data is not altered by standard computer use. See p. 32.

REAL 3DO A multimedia console produced by Panasonic that meets the 3DO standard. See p. 34.

real estate Computer jargon for the space that files take up on a disk. See p. 146.

ROM Short for *Read-Only Memory*. See p. 32.

royalty Money paid for the use of intellectual property, such as a copyrighted picture or song. See p. 86.

S

sample editor Software used to alter and combine digital sound samples. See p. 78.

sampling The process of converting a sound into digital data. See p. 77.

scanner A device that takes an image from a piece of paper or photograph, and turns it into a digitized form for computer use. See pp. 86-87.

screen depth The number of bits used to describe the color of each screen pixel. See p. 99.

scroll bar An on-screen device used to select which area of a picture or text item is displayed when that item is too large to be displayed in the area provided for it. A *slider* within the bar represents the current position of the displayed segment within the whole picture, and the user can move that slider using his pointer to view other segments of the item. See p. 40.

SCSI Short for *Small Computer System Interface*. A standard for the connection between the computer and input and output devices such as scanners, hard disks, and CD-writers. See p. 139.

Sega CD A CD-ROM subsystem that attaches to a Genesis home video game console. See p. 33.

sequencer Software used to create, capture, or edit songs in the MIDI format. See pp. 80-81.

shareware Computer software that you can initially copy for free, and then pay for only if you find it will be of use to you. See p. 115.

slider The moving rectangle within a scroll bar that is used to represent the position of the current segment being viewed within the item as a whole. See p. 40.

slide show software Software designed to create and display multimedia projects with little or no user interaction. See p. 114.

SNES Short for *Super Nintendo Entertainment System.* See pp. 32-33.

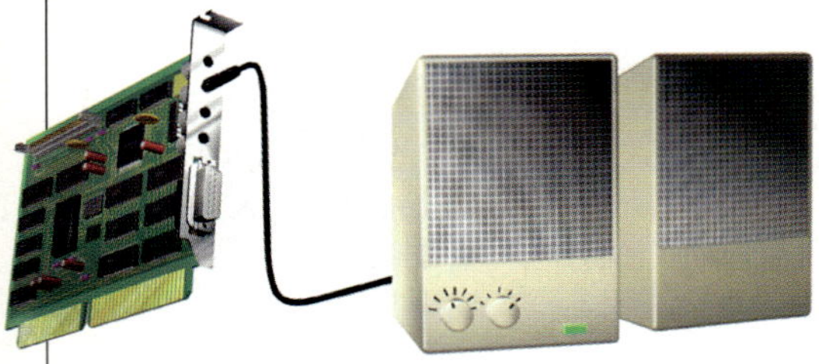

sound card An internal board for personal computers that can process sounds and music. See p. 24.

sprite An on-screen object that the computer can place and move independent of the background and other objects. See p. 105.

stamper A reverse image of a CD, which is used in a pressing machine to create the CDs themselves. See pp. 140-141.

storyboard A diagram or other organized plan that describes the scenes of a presentation and the possible paths through those scenes. See pp. 112-113.

Super Nintendo Entertainment System A popular home video game console. See pp. 32-33.

symmetrical codec Any codec that takes the same amount of time to decompress a frame of video as it took to compress it. See p. 100.

syntax The grammar of a computer language. See p. 118.

synthesizing Using mathematical formulas to describe the shape of the sound wave for computer-generated sounds. See pp. 76-77.

T

texture mapping Designating a design or texture for a 3-D modeled object. See p. 91.

touch screen A special computer monitor that is able to detect when a user touches the screen, as well as what part of the screen was touched. See p. 44.)

trackball A computer interface device that consists of a plastic ball contained mostly within a plastic box. The user slides his hand across the exposed top of the ball, and the computer translates the motion of the ball into the motion and position of the on-screen pointer. See p. 43.

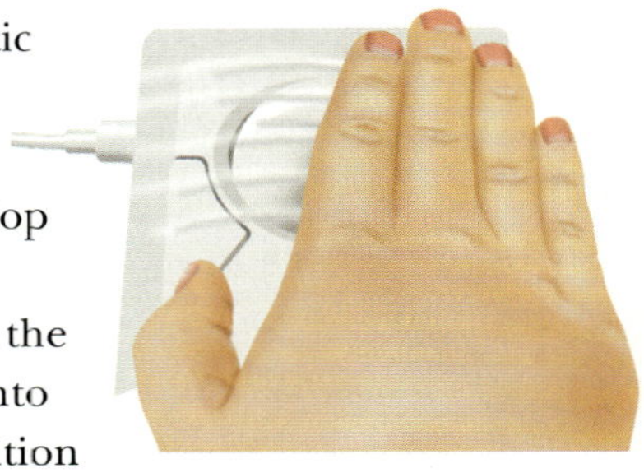

transitions Techniques for smoothly changing from displaying one image to displaying another. See p. 114.

TWAIN-compatible A term used to describe software and devices that follow the TWAIN, a standard for communications between computers and devices that creates digitized pictures, such as scanners and digital cameras. This way, any TWAIN-compatible piece of software can get images from any TWAIN-compatible image capturing device. See p. 87.

V

VCR controls A set of on-screen program controls designed to imitate the look and function of video cassette recorder controls. See p. 41.

VESA A standard for communication of graphics information over the local bus, set by the Video Electronics Standards Association. See p. 25.

video A series of images stored or transmitted in electronic form. See pp. 94-95.

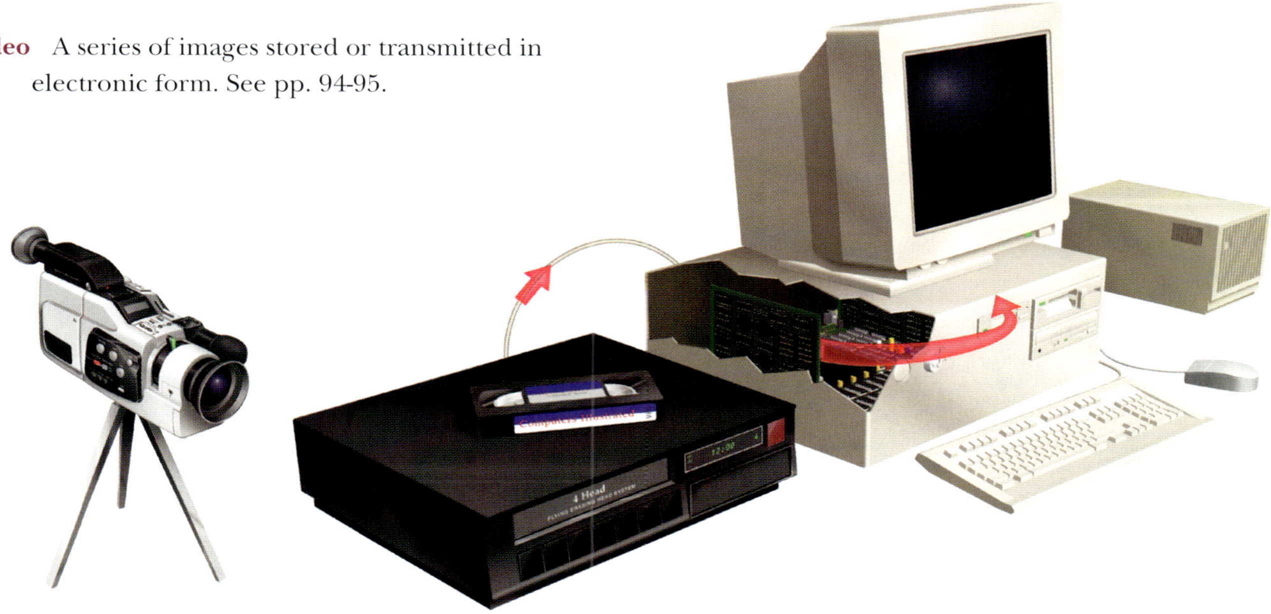

video on demand A feature of advanced cable TV systems that allows you to request that a given program be sent specifically to your TV when you request it. See p. 150.

virtual reality Computer programs and interfaces that attempt to create the feeling that the user is interacting with a real world rather than with a computer. See pp. 152-153.

virtual space A simulated world that a virtual reality system places a user in. See p. 152.

voice recognition The ability of a computer to recognize certain spoken words as commands or input. See p. 45.

W

WAVE A standard file format for digitized sound. See p. 79.

Wavetables A set of sampled sounds stored on a sound card that are used when the computer plays MIDI music. See p. 24.

wireframe An outline of a three dimensional object used in 3-D modeling. See p. 90.

Index

D

E

F

G

H

I

J

K-L

M

T

U-V

W-Z

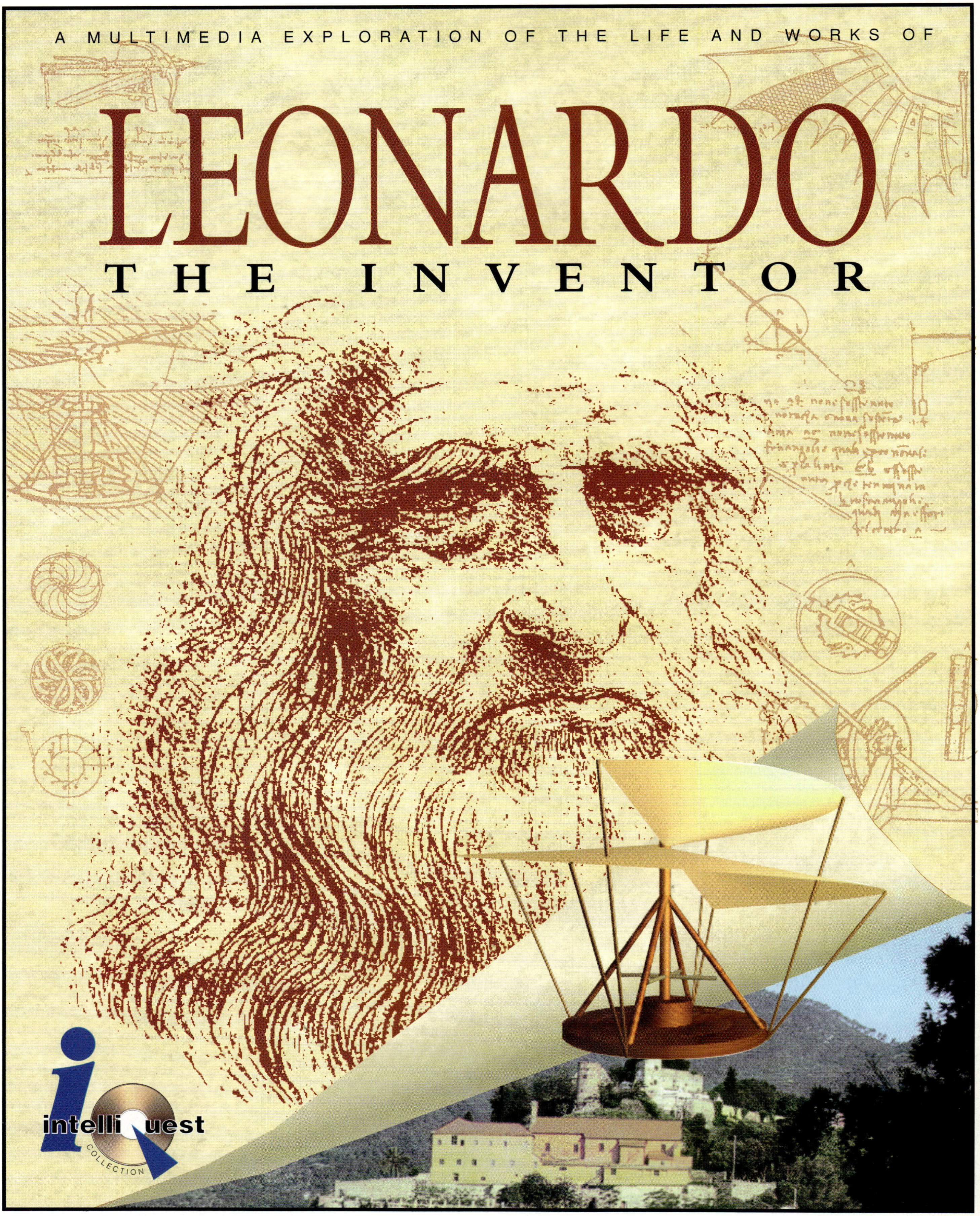
A MULTIMEDIA EXPLORATION OF THE LIFE AND WORKS OF
LEONARDO
THE INVENTOR
intelliquest
COLLECTION

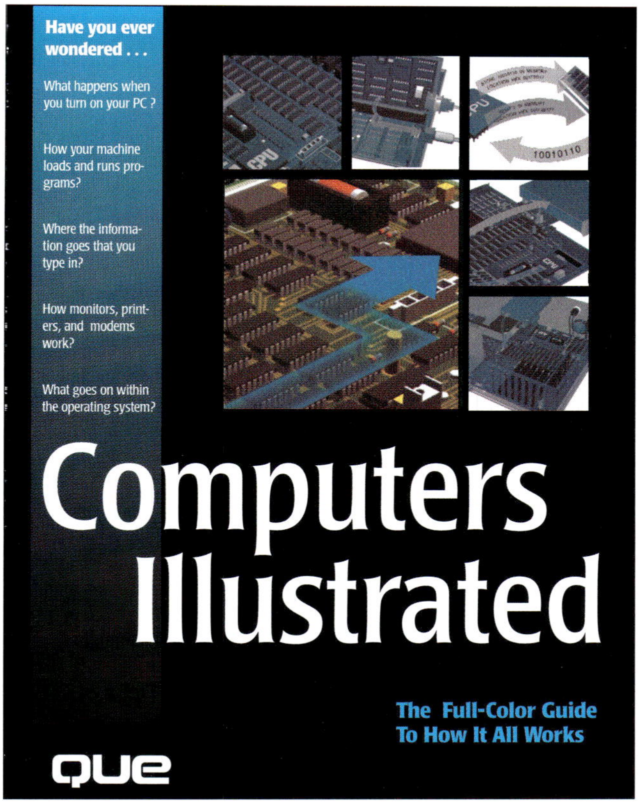

Computers Illustrated shows you in full color:

- What happens when you turn on your PC
- How your machine loads and runs programs
- Where the information that you type in goes
- How monitors, printers, and modems work
- What goes on within the operating system

Upgrading Your PC Illustrated shows you in full color:

- How to upgrade a computer's processor and memory
- What's needed to install a disk drive, modem, or sound card
- How to add a mouse, printer, game port, or video system
- How DOS, Windows, OS/2, and Mac programming differ
- What loops, clauses, and instructions are